# RSF: The Russell Sage Foundation Journal of the Social Sciences

*Biosocial Pathways of Well-Being Across the Life Course*

**VOLUME 4, NUMBER 4, APRIL 2018**

**RSF: The Russell Sage Foundation Journal of the Social Sciences**    ISSN 2377-8261

## The Russell Sage Foundation

The Russell Sage Foundation, one of the oldest of America's general purpose foundations, was established in 1907 by Mrs. Margaret Olivia Sage for "the improvement of social and living conditions in the United States." The foundation seeks to fulfill this mandate by fostering the development and dissemination of knowledge about the country's political, social, and economic problems. While the foundation endeavors to assure the accuracy and objectivity of each book it publishes, the conclusions and interpretations in Russell Sage Foundation publications are those of the authors and not of the foundation, its trustees, or its staff. Publication by Russell Sage, therefore, does not imply foundation endorsement.

## Board of Trustees

Claude M. Steele, *Chair*
Larry M. Bartels
Karen S. Cook
Sheldon H. Danziger
Kathryn Edin
Michael Jones-Correa
Lawrence F. Katz
David Laibson
Nicholas Lemann
Sara S. McLanahan
Martha Minow
Peter R. Orszag
Mario Luis Small
Shelley E. Taylor
Hirokazu Yoshikawa

## Mission Statement

*RSF: The Russell Sage Foundation Journal of the Social Sciences* is a peer-reviewed, open-access journal of original empirical research articles by both established and emerging scholars. It is designed to promote cross-disciplinary collaborations on timely issues of interest to academics, policymakers, and the public at large. Each issue is thematic in nature and focuses on a specific research question or area of interest. The introduction to each issue will include an accessible, broad, and synthetic overview of the research question under consideration and the current thinking from the various social sciences.

## RSF Journal Editorial Board

Elizabeth O. Ananat, Duke University
Karen S. Cook, Stanford University
Sheldon H. Danziger, Russell Sage Foundation
Mesmin Destin, Northwestern University
Janet C. Gornick, The CUNY Graduate Center
Jennifer Hochschild, Harvard University
Mary E. Pattillo, Northwestern University
Becky Pettit, University of Texas at Austin
James Sidanius, Harvard University
Miguel S. Urquiola, Columbia University
Mary C. Waters, Harvard University

Copyright © 2018 by Russell Sage Foundation. All rights reserved. Printed in the United States of America. No part of this publication may be reproduced, stored in a retrieval system, or transmitted in any form or by any means, electronic, mechanical, photocopying, recording, or otherwise, without the prior written permission of the publisher. Reproduction by the United States Government in whole or in part is permitted for any purpose.

Opinions expressed in this journal are not necessarily those of the editors, editorial board, trustees, or the Russell Sage Foundation.

We invite scholars to submit proposals for potential issues through the *RSF* application portal: https://rsfjournal.onlineapplicationportal.com/. Submissions should be addressed to Suzanne Nichols, Director of Publications.

To view the complete text and additional features online please go to **www.rsfjournal.org**.

## Open Access Policy

*RSF: The Russell Sage Foundation Journal of the Social Sciences* is an open access journal. It is published under a Creative Commons Attribution-NonCommercial-No Derivs 3.0 Unported License

## Russell Sage Foundation
112 East 64th Street
New York, NY 10065

**ISSN (print):**     2377-8253
**ISSN (electronic):**  2377-8261
**ISBN:**        978-0-87154-744-6

## The Ford Foundation

The Ford Foundation is an independent, nonprofit grant-making organization that makes more than $500 million in grants around the world every year. Through the generous bequests of Henry and Edsel Ford, the foundation grew from its establishment in 1936 to become one of the largest philanthropies in history. Across eight decades, the Ford Foundation has invested in innovative ideas, visionary individuals, and frontline institutions advancing human dignity around the world. Today, the foundation is focusing its efforts on challenging inequality in all its forms. With headquarters in New York, the foundation has ten regional offices across Africa, Asia, and Latin America.

Darren Walker, *President*
Kofi Appenteng, *Chair, Board of Trustees*

RSF: *The Russell Sage Foundation Journal of the Social Sciences*
VOLUME 4, NUMBER 4,
APRIL 2018

# Biosocial Pathways of Well-Being Across the Life Course

ISSUE EDITORS
Thomas W. McDade, Northwestern University
Kathleen Mullan Harris, University of North Carolina at Chapel Hill

## CONTENTS

### Part I. Introduction

The Biosocial Approach to Human Development, Behavior, and Health Across the Life Course  2
*Kathleen Mullan Harris and Thomas W. McDade*

### Part II. Disadvantage, Discrimination, and Health

Neighborhood Disadvantage and Telomere Length: Results from the Fragile Families Study  28
*Douglas S. Massey, Brandon Wagner, Louis Donnelly, Sara McLanahan, Jeanne Brooks-Gunn, Irwin Garfinkel, Colter Mitchell, and Daniel A. Notterman*

Perceived Discrimination and Adolescent Sleep in a Community Sample  43
*Bridget J. Goosby, Jacob E. Cheadle, Whitney Strong-Bak, Taylor C. Roth, and Timothy D. Nelson*

The Great Recession and Immune Function  62
*Elizabeth McClure, Lydia Feinstein, Sara Ferrando-Martínez, Manuel Leal, Sandro Galea, and Allison E. Aiello*

### Part III. Developmental and Intergenerational Processes

A Biopsychosocial Approach to Examine Mexican American Adolescents' Academic Achievement and Substance Use  84
*Yang Qu, Adriana Galván, Andrew J. Fuligni, and Eva H. Telzer*

Gender Differences in Biological Function in Young Adulthood: An Intragenerational Perspective  98
*Margot I. Jackson and Susan E. Short*

### Part IV. Genes and Environments over the Life Course

The Sociogenomics of Polygenic Scores of Reproductive Behavior and Their Relationship to Other Fertility Traits  122
*Melinda C. Mills, Nicola Barban, and Felix C. Tropf*

Geographic Clustering of Polygenic Scores at Different Stages of the Life Course  137
*Benjamin W. Domingue, David H. Rehkopf, Dalton Conley, and Jason D. Boardman*

# PART I
# Introduction

# The Biosocial Approach to Human Development, Behavior, and Health Across the Life Course

KATHLEEN MULLAN HARRIS AND THOMAS W. MCDADE

Social, cultural, economic, and biological factors are widely recognized as critical determinants of well-being across the life course. Yet an integrative understanding of the multilevel biosocial pathways linking society, biology, health, and socioeconomic attainment remains elusive. The objective of this issue is to showcase research that integrates theory, data, and methods from the social and biological sciences to advance our understanding of social and biological processes that contribute to, or derive from, social stratification across the life course. In this introduction, we describe the state of current research and discuss both the motivation for and relevant concepts underlying a biosocial perspective. We review the themes and research contributions in this issue, and chart a course forward for understanding biosocial pathways of well-being across the life course.

## BRINGING TOGETHER THE BIOLOGICAL AND THE SOCIAL

The term *biosocial* is widely used in the social sciences, but rarely defined. Perhaps its meaning is self-evident. And though the term has appeared in the scientific literature for more than fifty years, approaches and applications in biosocial research have shifted qualitatively over the past fifteen years.[1] In this section, we discuss these developments and the synergies afforded by integrating perspectives from the social and biological sciences.

We define *biosocial* as a broad concept referencing the dynamic, bidirectional interactions between biological phenomena and social relationships and contexts, which constitute processes of human development over the life course. It is difficult, if not impossible, to represent the complexities of these biosocial dynamics in two dimensions, but we attempt to

---

**Kathleen Mullan Harris** is James E. Haar Distinguished Professor of Sociology and faculty fellow of the Carolina Population Center at the University of North Carolina at Chapel Hill. She is also a member of the National Academy of Sciences and director of the National Longitudinal Study of Adolescent to Adult Health (Add Health). **Thomas W. McDade** is Carlos Montezuma Professor of Anthropology and faculty fellow of the Institute for Policy Research at Northwestern University. He is also a senior fellow in the Child and Brain Development Program of the Canadian Institute for Advanced Research.

© 2018 Russell Sage Foundation. Harris, Kathleen Mullan, and Thomas W. McDade. 2018. "The Biosocial Approach to Human Development, Behavior, and Health Across the Life Course." *RSF: The Russell Sage Foundation Journal of the Social Sciences* 4(4): 2–26. DOI: 10.7758/RSF.2018.4.4.01. Direct correspondence to: Kathleen Mullan Harris at kathie_harris@unc.edu, University of North Carolina, 206 W. Franklin St., Chapel Hill, NC 27516; and Thomas W. McDade at t-mcdade@northwestern.edu, Northwestern University, 1810 Hinman Ave., Evanston, IL 60208.

Open Access Policy: *RSF: The Russell Sage Foundation Journal of the Social Sciences* is an open access journal. This article is published under a Creative Commons Attribution-NonCommercial-NoDerivs 3.0 Unported License.

1. In 1969, both the *Journal of Biosocial Science* and *Social Biology* began publishing. In 2008, *Social Biology* was renamed to *Biodemography and Social Biology*, the journal of the Society for Biodemography and Social Biology.

**Figure 1.** Conceptual Model of Biosocial Dynamics Across the Life Course

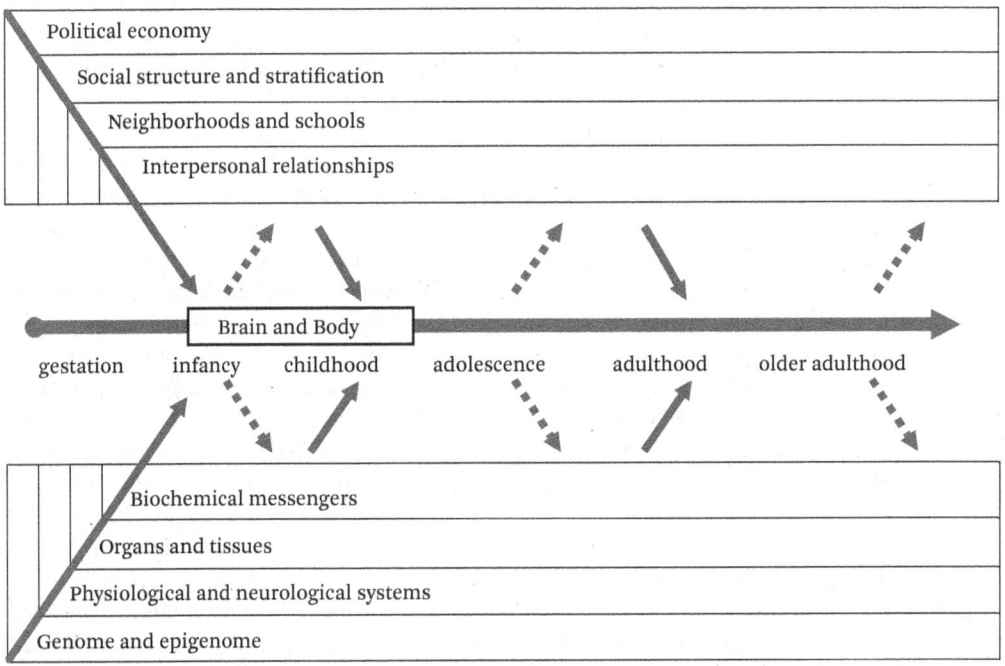

*Source:* Authors' compilation.

do so in figure 1, which builds on prior efforts to highlight the multilevel domains and pathways of particular importance in biosocial approaches to health and social inequality (Kuh and Ben-Shlomo 2004; Glass and McAtee 2006). The top boxes represent the set of nested and interacting social contexts "outside" the body that affect the developing brain and body of an individual throughout all stages of the life course. Similarly, the bottom boxes represent the nested and interacting levels of biological organization "inside" the brain and body that respond to, and shape, social worlds. What constitutes *biological* can be characterized as processes and structures within an individual that contribute to the growth, reproduction, and maintenance of the soma from conception to death. Biology is typically organized across multiple levels, including the genome, molecular interactions (such as gene expression, hormone production); integrated physiological and neurological systems (such as the cardiovascular system; the sympathetic adrenal medullary axis); organs and other tissues; and cells and cellular processes.

Social phenomena are similarly complex and multidimensional, and are illustrated by the relationships and interactions among individuals living in groups and within social contexts (families, neighborhoods, schools) who share the norms, institutions, and hierarchies that structure them. The social realm can also include aspects of the physical environment of relevance to biology (such as exposure to environmental contaminants, public space for recreation) that are structured by social relations and hierarchies.

A biosocial perspective, therefore, draws on models and methods from the biological, medical, behavioral, and social sciences. It conceptualizes the biological and the social as mutually constituting forces, and blurs boundaries between phenomena inside the body and outside of the body. It implies that attempts to understand one without the other are incomplete. It is a transdisciplinary approach to understanding human development, behavior, and health, developed and applied by scholars that often have disciplinary backgrounds in anthropology, psychology, epidemiology, sociology, economics, public health, genomics, medicine, and demography.

Ongoing calls for a more integrative, multimethod, multilevel interdisciplinary approach to research on human development, health, and social inequality underscore the importance and potential contribution of a biosocial perspective (Halfon and Hochstein 2002; Harris 2010; Weinstein, Vaupel, and Wachter 2007). The recent expansion of methodological options for collecting biological samples in nonclinical settings has facilitated this effort, and innovative biological measures are increasingly being incorporated into social science research designs and data collection efforts. A new generation of biosocial research is poised to bridge the gap between community- and clinic-based approaches to understanding the dynamic interplay of biology and social context across the life course.

## Integrating Biology into the Social and Behavioral Sciences

Why should social and behavioral scientists care about biology? Although we recognize that most, if not all, social and economic outcomes have some biological component, social scientists—with a few notable exceptions—have generally not considered biological processes with specificity or depth. This position does not always derive from theoretical or epistemological stances, and is often due to gaps in data, constraints of training and motivational structures that are set within disciplinary frameworks, and logistical challenges associated with collecting biological measures in nonclinical settings. Many of these gaps are narrowing.

Putting the *bio* in *biosocial* has the potential to make important contributions to the social and behavioral sciences for several reasons. First, humans are biological creatures, embedded in families, social networks, communities, and cultures. Context matters to human biology, and engagement with biological concepts and measures reflects this reality. This is especially clear in the case of human health, where the importance of social determinants is well established and widely known (Adler et al. 1994; Glass and McAtee 2006; Link and Phelan 1995), and where social impacts on underlying physiological processes are apparent and increasingly elaborated (Uchino, Cacioppo, and Kiecolt-Glaser 1996; Yang et al. 2016). Attention to biology has the potential to illuminate mechanisms through which socioeconomic, demographic, and psychosocial factors shape human development and health within the context of everyday life.

The importance of context to human biology is evident across multiple time dimensions (Lasker 1969). In the short term, homeostasis and allostasis—processes of adaptation to changes in current or anticipated environments (McEwen 1998; Sterling and Ayer 1988)—facilitate physiological or behavioral responses to the shifting demands and opportunities of local environments. For example, a perceived danger or social threat increases the production of cortisol, a hormone that plays a central role in mobilizing the body's response to stress. When the threat is removed, cortisol production returns to baseline (Gruenewald et al. 2004). But repeat, or chronic, exposure to adverse environmental conditions can reset regulatory set points, resulting in "wear and tear" on key physiological systems (Seeman et al. 2001). Lower socioeconomic status—a source of chronic stress—is associated with high cortisol in the evening and with a flatter rhythm of production across the day relative to the normative pattern of declining cortisol production over the day to low levels in the evening (Cohen, Schwartz, et al. 2006; DeSantis et al. 2007). Longer term effects of environments on biological systems emerge from critical or sensitive periods of development, when exposures can have disproportionate, enduring effects on biological structure and function. Continuing with the example of cortisol, individuals born with a lower birth weight have elevated cortisol in adulthood (Phillips et al. 2000), pointing toward a biological mechanism through which lower socioeconomic status (a strong predictor of lower birth weight) may affect health within and across generations.

By getting "under the skin," biological measures provide direct, objective information on pathophysiological processes that contribute to the emergence of disease, before clinically diagnosable disease is evident. For example, relative levels of blood pressure—a robust indicator of future risk of cardiovascular disease—tend to track from childhood into adulthood (Berenson et al. 1995; Li et al. 2004).

Although measuring blood pressure in childhood or young adulthood will reveal few clinical cases of hypertension, it will identify individuals most at risk for the future development of cardiovascular disease and early death (Nguyen et al. 2011). Biological measures therefore enhance our understanding of how social environments influence pre-disease pathways and provide opportunities for intervention prior to the emergence of clinical disease.

Attention to biology can also identify which aspects of social and physical environments are most detrimental to health and socioeconomic well-being, as well as point toward resiliency and protective factors that buffer groups of individuals from the effects of adverse environments. The concept of *embodiment* has been invoked repeatedly in the social sciences to underscore the social and political nature of the human body and its responsiveness to social and cultural context (Gravlee 2009; Krieger 2005; Scheper-Hughes and Lock 1987; Seligman 2014). The body tells stories—literally and figuratively—and biological measures offer opportunities to access information that reflects the quality of social environments. Recent work on "skin deep resilience" provides a case in point: among African Americans from low socioeconomic status (SES) backgrounds, measures of self-control predict better psychosocial outcomes, such as lower depression or lower likelihood of substance use, but worse physical health outcomes, as revealed by several biological measures (Brody et al. 2013; Miller et al. 2015). Biological measurement may therefore add an important dimension to our understanding of health; that is, self-report, psychosocial, and biological measures may tell different stories. They may be particularly useful in settings where accurate self-reports are especially difficult to obtain, such as in research with children, or across international settings where linguistic or cultural factors may contribute to variation in perception, experience, or reporting (Hahn 1995; Kleinman 1986).

Social factors affect biological process and health outcomes, but the reverse is also true. For example, lower birth weight—a biological variable reflecting the quality of the prenatal environment, which is in turn shaped by genetic, developmental, and social factors—has adverse effects on cognitive development and adult educational attainment (Conley and Bennett 2000; Figlio et al. 2014). Education level is also a partial function of inherited genotype, and common genetic factors can account for some of the well-established association between education and health (Boardman, Domingue, and Daw 2015; Okbay et al. 2016). Biological processes, therefore, influence individual life course trajectories, shape social and educational attainments, and inform selection into social and physical environments that can feed back onto biological processes. When scholars do not consider how biological mechanisms shape developmental outcomes, or interact with social environments to influence social stratification across the life course, models may be incomplete or misspecified, parameter estimates of environmental effects overstated, and results biased.

A biosocial perspective is also important for translating social science research into policy. As noted, biological measures can reveal the quality of social conditions, and in some cases may motivate action to improve conditions to prevent disease rather than treat individuals already on the path toward disease. For example, lead screening in children can be used to inform housing policy, where initiatives aimed at reducing lead exposure can prevent the development of costly cognitive and behavioral disorders. Consistent evidence on the importance of social relationships for biological processes affecting health suggests that routine health screenings should include questions about the quantity and quality of individuals' social connections, and physicians should be encouraged to ask their patients about their relationships as part of their annual wellness check-ups (Yang et al. 2016).

Biological measures can also add important dimensions to the evaluation of social policies. For example, the Moving to Opportunity demonstration project was initiated in 1994 to investigate the impact of residential contexts on educational attainments, income, and overall well-being. Families in public housing were randomized into an experimental condition that subsidized their move into a low-poverty neighborhood; controls were not offered new assistance. The intervention had limited effects on education and income—the outcomes of primary interest when the study was designed—but large impacts on health: assignment to the low-poverty group resulted in a 13 percent to 19 percent reduction in obesity and 22 percent reduction in diabetes relative to the control group (Ludwig et al. 2011). A biosocial approach to policy evaluation can identify the biological processes and pre-disease pathways that are affected by contextual factors like neighborhood poverty, and point toward social programs that improve health. Given the high costs of health care, this kind of information may add an important, but often overlooked, component to cost-benefit analyses of social policies.

**The Importance of "Socializing" Biology**
The biosocial approach occupies an important and expanding space in the social and behavioral sciences, where the emphasis has been on integrating biological concepts and methods into research designed to address questions of interest to social and behavioral scientists (Harris 2010; Weinstein et al. 2007). Less appreciated is the opportunity we have to colonize the biological sciences—as well as public discourse regarding the determinants of health—to have an impact on how we conceptualize and study human biology.

For the most part, research in the biological sciences privileges explanations "inside the body," and is speeding down a reductionist road that elaborates cellular and molecular processes while ignoring contextual influences outside the body (Lewontin and Levins 2007). As just one example, the sequencing of the human genome, accomplished in 2003, was celebrated as providing "the first glimpse at our own instruction book," and "the possibility of achieving all we ever hoped for in medicine."[2] Clinical medicine also privileges reduction, seeking to isolate single, proximate factors as causes of disease and as targets for treatment. Pathogens cause infection. Tumors cause cancer (Ahn et al. 2006).

In contrast, for more than a hundred years, social scientists have documented the impact of contextual factors on human development, physiology, and health. For example, in the early 1900s, the anthropologist Franz Boas showed that cranial form—at the time interpreted as a fixed, inherited marker of racial identity—was in fact malleable, and that it changed within a single generation of immigrants to the United States in response to environmental influences (Boas 1912). For more than forty years, social scientists and social epidemiologists have reported that interpersonal relationships affect health, and that social isolation is a risk factor for early death that is comparable in magnitude to established risk factors such as smoking, obesity, and lack of physical activity (House, Landis, and Umberson 1988). More recently, social isolation has been associated with physiological dysregulation in all stages of human development, pointing toward biological mechanisms through which social relationships affect health (Yang et al. 2016). Socioeconomic status—of keen interest to many social scientists—is consistently associated with multiple measures of physiological function, morbidity, and mortality (Adler et al. 1994; Yang et al. 2017; Wolfe, Evans and Seeman 2012).

Human biology is a social biology and it is probably up to social scientists to make this point. Biosocial research, conducted in diverse, community-based settings, encourages an epistemological shift that reframes human biology, development, and health as complexly determined by multiple forces inside and outside the body. It engages issues and processes of interest to biological scientists, but foregrounds social and contextual factors as potentially important contributors to variation in human physiological function and health (Stinson, Bogin, and O'Rourke 2012). This should be familiar ground for developmental and social-behavioral scientists who have long emphasized the complex interplay of genes, biology, and society across the life course (Engel 1978; Glass and McAtee 2006; Gottlieb 1991; Shanahan and Boardman 2009). With an increasingly sophisticated toolkit for integrating biological measures into community-based, social science research, the

---

2. "What They Said: Genome in Quotes," BBC News Science/Nature, June 26, 2000, http://news.bbc.co.uk/2/hi/science/nature/807126.stm (accessed October 4, 2017).

time is right for a new generation of biosocial scholarship that enriches both the biological and the social sciences and helps build stronger links between them.

**Methodological Developments**

Historically, community- and population-based research in the social sciences has relied on vital records or self-reported, survey-based measures of health and disease. Information can be readily collected from large representative samples across a wide range of settings, but insight into biological processes is limited. In contrast, biomedical research employs in-depth biological measures collected in controlled clinical or laboratory settings, but typically relies on smaller, select groups of participants who are invited to participate based on preexisting criteria. Generalizability and external validity are limited, and social factors are generally not considered, beyond standard measures of socioeconomic status or self-reported health behaviors.

Methodological options for collecting and generating biological data have expanded greatly over the past fifteen years, allowing us to bridge this gap (Weinstein et al. 2007). Low-cost, field-friendly options for collecting blood, saliva, or urine in the home or local community allow investigators to gain access to physiological information from large numbers of participants in naturalistic settings (Adam and Kumari 2009; McDade, Williams, and Snodgrass 2007). Developments in assay technology have facilitated the measurement of proteins, gene transcripts, epigenetic marks, and DNA sequences with higher resolution in smaller quantities of sample, at lower costs (Dedeurwaerder et al. 2011; McDade et al. 2016). Portable devices and low-cost monitors facilitate assessment of sleep, physical function and activity, blood pressure, and body size and composition (Lindau and McDade 2007; Marino et al. 2013).

These methodological innovations have encouraged wide-scale integration of objective biological measures into social science surveys. For example, dried blood spots—drops of whole blood collected from a simple finger stick—have been collected from more than thirty-five thousand participants in the United States in studies such as the National Longitudinal Study of Adolescent to Adult Health (Add Health), the Health and Retirement Study, the National Social Life, Health, and Aging Project, and Moving to Opportunity. International studies, including the Cebu Longitudinal Health and Nutrition Survey, the Mexican Family Life Survey, and the Study on Global AGEing and Adult Health are collecting tens of thousands more. In another example, Add Health developed its own kit for the collection of buccal cell DNA in 1996 to test for the zygosity of sampled twin pairs. Ten years later, commercial kits for saliva DNA collection (such as Oragene) are routinely used by multiple studies to collect thousands of DNA samples both in the home setting and through the mail via self-collection.

The integration of objective measures of biological function and health has advanced the biosocial perspective by directly contributing to our understanding of how social, economic, and community factors shape human biology and health, and vice versa. These methods also address the goal of socializing biology. By taking our methods into the community, where participants are living their daily lives, we greatly expand the range of environmental variation that can be evaluated in relation to biological phenomena. Contextual factors are therefore brought into relief as potentially important determinants of human physiological function and health in ways not possible with lab- or clinic-based research designs. Last, these methods serve as a catalyst for productive collaboration among social, life, and biomedical scientists. The growing availability of social and biological data in large, representative samples, and the emphasis on interdisciplinary scholarship, has laid fertile ground for the integration of complementary expertise to generate novel insights into the ways in which social and biological processes interact in pathways of human development.

## THE IMPORTANCE OF THE LIFE COURSE

Human development has social and biological determinants and intergenerational linkages beginning in utero and continuing throughout all stages of the human life span (Hertzman and Boyce 2010). Despite a consensus that early life conditions and childhood experiences matter for subsequent social and biological development in adolescence, early adulthood, mid-adulthood and old age, most social and biomedical research does not capture the ways in which developmental processes are linked and interrelated across phases of human life, nor does it capture the dynamic interactions of social and biological forces that underlie development across time and space. Part of this research gap is due to a lack of longitudinal, multilevel life course data and intergenerational study designs, and part to disciplinary approaches designed to identify disciplinary-specific determinants of social, behavioral, or health outcomes at a point in time.

A life course perspective is essential in biosocial research because outcomes at any point reflect the product of prior interactions between social and biological forces that occur across human development (Shanahan, Hofer, and Shanahan 2003). Life phases and social roles are often intimately tied to biological events or trajectories (George 2009). For example, a woman's first birth marks her transition into parenthood just as menopause defines the end of the reproductive phase of her life. Although a woman can biologically become a mother when she reaches puberty in adolescence, most young people in the United States delay parenthood until well after puberty to continue social and emotional maturation and invest in human capital and career development before becoming a parent. Thus, social and biological forces jointly shape transitions between roles and patterns of continuity and discontinuity that extend across the phases of life. Biosocial approaches, therefore, require the researcher to dynamically assess both biological and social features of the developing person and their changing social context through time and across generations to achieve a full understanding of the determinants of social and physical well-being.

### Biosocial Processes Across the Life Course
Within social and behavioral sciences, research on aging has been at the forefront of biosocial approaches. Because aging integrates forces inside the body and outside the body to shape function and health in older adulthood (figure 1), aging research has led the field in study designs incorporating inputs across social and biological levels of analysis. Understandably, this line of research focuses on phenomena such as disability, illness and disease, and longevity and mortality. The biosocial approach in aging research, however, has not been well-informed by a life course perspective.

For a long time, aging research used self-reported health and behavioral information and cross-sectional designs to study, for example, the age distribution of the prevalence of illness and chronic disease (see, for example, National Center for Health Statistics 2016; Ward, Schiller and Goodman 2014), activities of daily living and instrumental activities of daily living designed to assess whether older adults can independently care for themselves (Freedman and Spillman 2014), and family and social relationships among the elderly (Waite and Das 2010). Demographic studies also use cross-sectional data but dynamic life table methodology to document onset and years of disability and chronic illness and to estimate mortality risks and life expectancy based on point-in-time rates of these respective events (Crimmins, Zhang, and Saito 2016). Perhaps the most influential contribution of aging research with implications for the biosocial paradigm is long-standing evidence of large and persistent social gradients in health and mortality (Adler et al. 1994; Wolfe, Evans, and Seeman 2012; Marmot and Wilkinson 2005). Still, this research remains primarily cross-sectional, documenting how SES is associated with aging-related outcomes at a given point.

With the advent of nationally representative longitudinal aging studies in the 1990s, such as the Health and Retirement Study (HRS) and the National Social Life, Health and Aging Project (NSHAP), and longitudinal community-based aging studies, such as Framingham, Atherosclerosis Risk in Communities Study (ARIC) and Reasons for Geographic and Racial Differences in Stroke (REGARDS), a life course design could now be applied to understand how previous social, behavioral, and environmental conditions were related to health and disease outcomes among older adults. In addition, as new survey field methods for measuring objective health outcomes were incorporated into many of these ongoing longitudinal aging studies, the ability to understand biological mechanisms and markers of health and disease further enhanced longitudinal life course data for biosocial research. However, the life phase examined in these studies is still limited to older adults because observations begin when individuals are forty-five (ARIC) or fifty (HRS) or fifty-five (NSHAP), thus missing earlier life stages that certainly bear on aging processes that arguably begin at birth. The social gradient in health and mortality, for example, can now be studied by examining how SES trajectories beginning at age fifty influence the onset of disease or death.

From a life course perspective, this research design has four major limitations. First, SES does not change much beyond age fifty because the components of socioeconomic status—education, occupation, income and wealth—are typically developed earlier in the life course during adolescence, early, and mid-adulthood and vary little in old age. Second, the early and midlife biological precursors to disease onset and death are not observed in these studies. Relatedly, the lack of biological data from earlier ages precludes opportunities to consider how early life course health and biological processes shape SES attainments in adulthood. Fourth, studies that begin observation at older ages miss those who have died, typically the more disadvantaged individuals who have been more exposed to earlier life trauma and illnesses and have fewer resources for health care, thus biasing the SES-health relationship. One solution to this lack of prior life course information that bears directly on older age social and physical well-being is to collect retrospective information about status earlier in life, enabling a modified life course perspective for biosocial research. Here aging studies have focused on retrospective reports of SES and health conditions at birth and during early childhood.

Along these lines, research on the developmental origins of health and disease (DOHaD) has exploded, following early biomedical research by Barker documenting significant links between birth weight and later cardiovascular disease risk within cohorts (Barker 1997, 1998, 2006). The life course approach has had a major impact on epidemiologic research on the determinants of adult disease risk, with a particular emphasis on cardiovascular diseases and the physiological processes through which they are influenced by early life nutritional environments (Gluckman et al. 2008; Wadhwa et al. 2009, Smith and Ryckman 2015; Kuh and Ben-Shlomo 2004). Numerous studies have linked uterine, birth, and childhood exposures to adult physical health and disease (Bengtsson and Broström 2009; Cameron and Demerath 2002; Crimmins and Finch 2006; Smith and Ryckman 2015). Demographic and social research on the "long arm of childhood" has also demonstrated the value of a life course perspective when early life circumstances are both directly and indirectly associated with health outcomes that emerge decades later in adulthood (Blackwell, Hayward, and Crimmins 2001; Case and Paxson 2010; Elo and Preston 1992; Hayward and Gorman 2004; Preston, Hill, and Drevenstedt 1998).

Most of this research, however, links early life conditions with physiological processes or chronic disease outcomes in later adulthood with cross-sectional research designs, paying limited attention to what happens in between—during the majority of the early life course from later childhood to adulthood. From a biosocial perspective, this means we are missing a lot, especially the social processes and contexts that structure, mediate, and moderate biology over the life course.

Adolescence and the transition to adulthood, for example, are life stages when young people first begin to choose their environments, health behaviors, habits, and future lifestyles (Harris 2010). These life course choices shape or alter social and biological pathways originating in childhood and moving into adulthood. Investments in human capital begin in early childhood, but intensify and become more self-directed during adolescence and the transition to adulthood. Profound and protracted physical, biological, and neurological changes linked to puberty occur throughout adolescence and early adulthood. Hormonal changes prompt a literal remodeling of cortical and limbic circuits in the brain that were previously organized in the perinatal period and that, in combination with adolescent social experiences and contexts, affect general cognition, decision making, and behavior into adulthood (Sisk and Zehr 2005). Behavioral changes and exploration in diet, exercise, sleep patterns, substance use, sexual activity, and aggression during adolescence and young adulthood further shape social and biological pathways into adulthood (Hubert et al. 1987). DOHaD research, and other life course perspectives, ideally should include the contributions of these critical developmental stages to illuminate health and well-being pathways into adulthood.

Although neurological development and change slows down as young people settle into adulthood, these demographically dense years bring new stresses to daily life as young adults juggle the multiple interrelated life domains of relationships, schooling, work, and family. Stress processes are perhaps the most commonly considered biological mechanisms through which the social environment gets under the skin to affect health and development in biosocial models, as described earlier in the case of the stress hormone cortisol (Gruenewald et al. 2004; McEwen and Lasley 2002). Middle adulthood may usher in greater life course stability and security in socioeconomic status, work, and family, but only for certain subgroups of the population. Middle adulthood has become more dynamic and demanding in contemporary U.S. society—high divorce and repartnering rates, greater dependency from both the child and parent generations, and uncertain work schedules, low wages, and a lack of employment benefits for those with low education or few job skills. Relative to other life stages, middle-aged adults are highly embedded in social relationships with aging parents, children, the parents of children's friends, neighbors, work colleagues and within community institutions. These relationships are important social mechanisms that can buffer (through social support) or exacerbate (through strain and conflict) the daily stresses of middle adulthood (Yang, Schorpp, and Harris 2014; Yang et al. 2016).

All life course stages have unique social and biological forces that determine life-long human development and that operate independently and jointly to influence physical and social well-being in that life stage and beyond. Biosocial research cannot examine social and biological forces in all life stages in one project or with one dataset, but should contribute knowledge about how social and biological phenomena operate in distinct life stages and are linked to health and social inequities in subsequent stages across the life course. Although we have made some progress documenting the association between early life conditions and late life health and disease outcomes (such as lower birth weight and increased cardiovascular disease risk), we need to move beyond cross-sectional designs to uncover the underlying life course processes that explain these associations. Both the intergenerational precursors that lead to these conditions and the subsequent intragenerational life course pathways such conditions initiate are yet to be explored. However, a small but growing literature links these kinds of early life health factors to later social attainments, but more research on health and biology as underlying factors in social stratification processes is needed.

## Biosocial Study Designs of Health and Social Inequality Across the Life Course

Here we describe two general life course orientations for understanding how biological phenomena are related to social and economic status and opportunities in direct, indirect, and reciprocal ways. One orientation examines how social stratification processes across the life course are related to subsequent health outcomes in different life stages. This orientation stems primarily from the large literature on the social gradients of health discussed (or more commonly, the social determinants of health), but with a life course perspective. Social stratification is both an inter- and intragenerational process. At birth, we enter a social hierarchy tied to parental SES that determines access to material and social resources for both physical and social development. The developing individual then faces constraints and opportunities in each life stage that determine social and economic status across time. Inter- and intragenerational social stratification processes have both direct and indirect effects on health across the life course. Understanding the social and biological mechanisms for how social stratification processes get under the skin to influence health is at the heart of this conceptual orientation of biosocial research.

Ideally, social stratification is measured longitudinally, as a life course process, conceived as social exposures that can be positive (supportive parenting behaviors, college education) or negative (childhood poverty, neighborhood disadvantage). Exposure to both beneficial and adverse experiences over the life course will vary for each individual and constitute a unique social stratification trajectory. Biological outcomes are conceived of as the consequence of exposure in social stratification trajectories and can be measured at a point in time in a particular life stage or over time as biological and developmental change. Importantly, social stratification trajectories represent social processes that enable the biosocial researcher to explore fundamental life course mechanisms involving the timing, duration, and intensity of beneficial or adverse social exposures that occur in different and across phases of life and that affect health and development in subsequent life stages. The ability to measure the timing, duration, and intensity of social exposures across the life course allows for testing life course models for how social experiences that occur outside the body are linked to biological mechanisms inside the body that affect health and well-being.

The stress response framework is the most prominent biosocial paradigm to explicate how trajectories of social structural inequalities are associated with greater exposure to stress and its biological and health-related manifestations (Pearlin 1989; Aneshensel 1992; McEwen 1998; McEwen and Lasley 2002). When social exposures are intense, or the magnitude of structural disadvantage is high (depth of poverty, multiple disadvantages of poor neighborhoods), stress response is chronic and biological dysregulation is greater, resulting in poor health and developmental outcomes. The life stage timing of social exposures, however, may differ for both the biological mechanisms and subsequent health outcomes associated with stress exposure. Figure 2 provides an illustration of various life course models that describe how exposure to social disadvantage in particular developmental periods may operate to increase health risk in subsequent life stages.

The top model illustrates *sensitive period* timing effects in which exposures during sensitive periods of development have stronger effects on health outcomes than they would at other life stages (Hayward and Gorman 2004; Gluckman et al. 2008; Cohen, Janicki-Deverts et al. 2010). Sensitive period effects operate through a *biological embedding* mechanism whereby social exposures during sensitive windows of development have the potential to induce structural and functional changes to the developing individual through biological programming that cannot be reversed regardless of intervening experience. Thus, the dark shadowed line represents a direct effect of exposure in the earlier stage of development with no indirect effects and no direct effects of subsequent social disadvantage on later life health. This life course model posits that the effect of the sensitive period exposure is typically latent in that its impact on health outcomes may not appear until later life stages, often decades later.

Duration effects of social stratification processes can be explored through the accumulation life course model (middle model of figure 2), which emphasizes the role of persistent advantage or disadvantage over time—both in specific life stages and over life stages—on health and development. The effects of multiple exposures over the life course are both additive and interactive and combine in synergistic ways to influence biological mechanisms and, in turn, health and development outcomes. Cumulative effects can either be multiple exposures to a recurrent stressor (such as chronic poverty) or a series of exposures to different social environments or life experiences. For example, poverty experienced only during childhood is not as detrimental as poverty during childhood, adolescence, and the transition to adulthood on subsequent adult health.

A third life course model that might explain how social stratification processes are related to health outcomes is the pathway model, which tracks how social exposures in one life stage influence the probability of related social exposures in subsequent stages. Also known as the *chains of risk* model, it emphasizes pathway

**Figure 2.** Life Course Models of Social Disadvantage Trajectories and Health

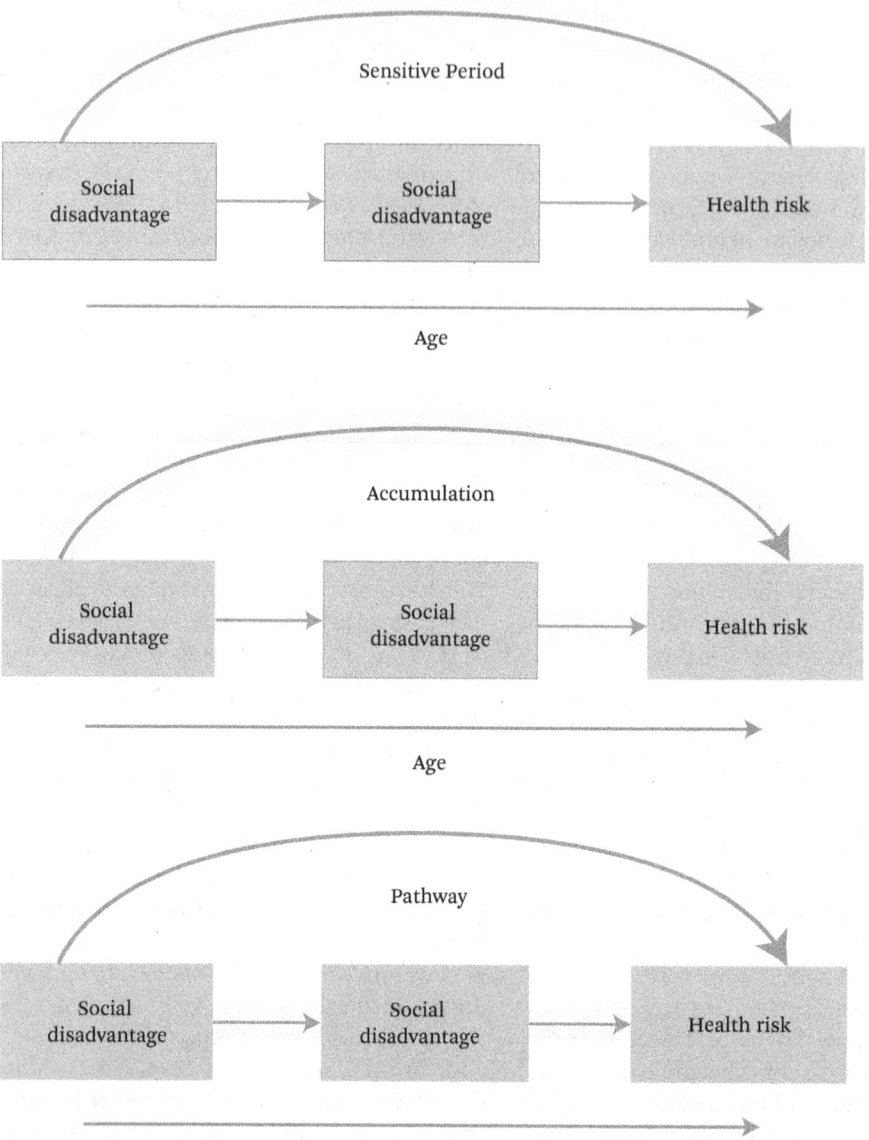

*Source:* Authors' compilation.

effects whereby early experiences set in motion a chain of events that put individuals on paths differentiated by types and levels of stress exposures to social and biological factors (Marmot et al. 2001; Pudrovska and Anikputa 2014). This model elaborates on the ways in which inter- and intragenerational social stratification pathways are linked across the life course. For example, the connection between early life conditions and adult health and disease may be explained by the SES pathway where early life SES determines adult SES, which in turn, is a more proximate and important predictor of adult health and disease (Yang et al. 2017).

A second orientation for understanding biosocial pathways in well-being across the life course is consideration of the role of biology or health in social stratification processes (Palloni 2006). In this orientation, biological mechanisms and health trajectories are important

**Figure 3.** Role of Health in Social Stratification Processes

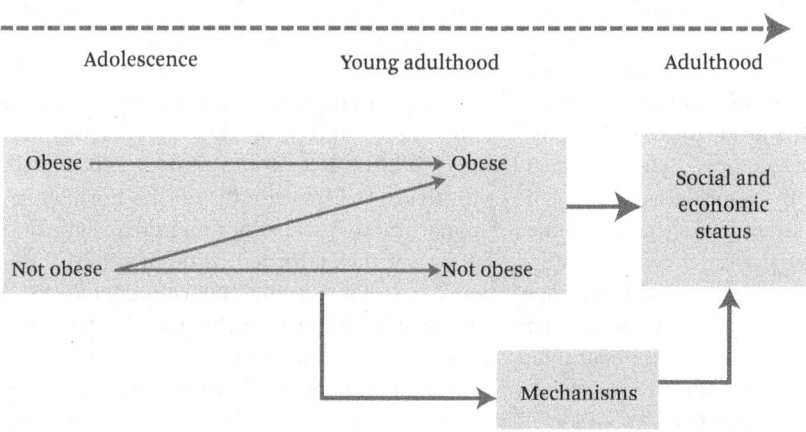

*Source:* Authors' compilation.

contributors to subsequent socioeconomic outcomes and attainment. For example, economic research has focused on how childhood health influences human capital and labor force outcomes in adulthood, including educational attainment, labor force participation, income, and occupation (Case, Lubotsky, and Paxson 2002; Currie and Stabile 2003; Currie and Moretti 2007; Case, Fertig, and Paxson 2005; Almond and Currie 2011). Figure 3 illustrates the case of how early life course health can influence later socioeconomic status. In particular, life course trajectories of obesity during adolescence and into young adulthood contribute to social stratification outcomes in adulthood. Research findings indicate that those who become obese in early adolescence and remain obese for a longer period of time have lower levels of education, marriage, wages, household income, employment, assets, and subjective social status (Cawley 2004; Han, Norton, and Stearns 2009; Harris and Lee 2011; Glass, Haas, and Reither 2010). These life course effects of obesity operate through such mechanisms as low self-esteem, social isolation, societal views of attractiveness and lost work days, illustrating the biosocial connections. Similar effects are found for chronic health conditions and diabetes during adolescence and young adulthood, which truncate educational trajectories and reduce the stability of work (Fletcher and Richards 2012).

In this orientation, life course models will illuminate the often missing, underlying role of biology in social stratification processes. Understanding whether, when, and how biological processes matter for social and economic outcomes across the life course will help identify when biomedical interventions might be most effective for reducing social inequality. These models are not mutually exclusive and in reality coexist (see Hallqvist et al. 2004). Most important, they provide a framework for biosocial research made possible by longitudinal data and study designs that enable researchers to identify the social and biological processes that operate in pathways of well-being across the life span. The life course perspective articulates the longitudinal and multidimensional of social and biological forces that operate in all life stages and underlie human development across time, emphasizing the need to conceptualize social conditions and biological mechanisms as dynamic constructs that unfold across time, beginning in early life and continuing into young adulthood, midlife, and old age.

## SOCIAL GENOMICS

Consensus is now widespread that social, behavioral, and health outcomes are a function of both nature and nurture, and are best understood in a life course context. Even in the age of genome mapping, research on the impact of genetic variance alone has limited explanatory power, and is often of less interest to social and behavioral scientists given that individual DNA sequence is fixed and not subject to intervention. Instead, social and behavioral scientists have been drawn to understanding gene-environment interplay, or how environmental and genetic factors interact over time to affect social, behavioral, and health outcomes, along the lines of figure 1. Because such outcomes represent the cumulative history of a person's social experiences as they combine with genetic makeup, gene-environment interplay reflects life course processes. Although appreciation is widespread that the links between genes and behavioral outcomes, for example, are conditioned by the social environment, consideration of the dynamic features, of social environments and life experiences as processes occurring across the life course is not. To date, most studies of gene-environment interplay are cross-sectional or use longitudinal data without explicit modeling of life course features, including pathways, transitions, trajectories, durations, or timing (Conley 2016; Shanahan and Boardman 2009).

Nevertheless, substantial social science research examines gene-environment interplay focusing on two general approaches: gene-environment interactions (GxE) and gene-environment correlations (rGE). GxE research has captured social science attention by elaborating on processes by which the effect of genetic factors on a social or biological outcome is conditioned by environmental factors and vice versa (Boardman, Daw, and Freese 2013; Hutter et al. 2013). Provocative findings have been published, for example, showing that genetic effects on children's cognition are dampened in low SES environments, genetic propensities for adolescent substance use are enhanced or suppressed according to the prevalence of substance use in the adolescents' schools, stressful life events increase the risk of depression depending on one's genetic profile for processing neurotransmitters, and adolescents are more genetically similar to their friends in more highly structured and segregated environments (Boardman, Domingue, and Fletcher 2012; Caspi et al. 2003; Rowe, Jacobson, and Van den Oord 1999; Daw et al. 2013). Although such findings highlight the important role of the social environment in genetic processes, especially from a policy perspective, GxE research has come under significant criticism for a poor record of replication, lack of statistical power for GxE associations, and the endogenous nature of most measures of E (Boardman, Daw, and Freese 2013; Conley 2016; Freese and Shostak 2009; Charney and English 2012; North and Martin 2008). Still, promising GxE research is on the horizon using natural or quasi-experimental designs and larger samples afforded through genetic consortia (see, for example, Boardman et al. 2012; Okbay et al. 2016; Schmitz and Conley 2016, 2017; Rietveld et al. 2013).

Research exploring gene-environment correlations is especially valuable to social and behavioral sciences because it confronts the worrisome endogeneity problem of estimated environmental effects being due to unobserved heterogeneity (genetic factors) associated with the selection of one's environment. Gene-environment correlation (rGE) refers to processes by which genetic factors are associated with features of the environments in which individuals live their lives (friendships, peer groups, romantic relationships, schools, neighborhoods, work environments, and so on). Sorting out and controlling for genetic variance in selection of these environments enables social and behavioral scientists to isolate the causal impacts of social environments on social, behavioral, and health outcomes. In sum, perhaps the main impact of the evidence on gene-environment interplay has been to dispel notions of the nature-nurture dichotomy and build consensus on the need for integrative models of genetic and social factors to better understand human development and health. But two general weaknesses remain: the G (genotype) is still fixed and therefore unresponsive to social change; and the dynamics of life course changes and their biological interactions with changing social environments and experiences over time have not been exploited in either GxE or rGE research.

Human social genomics, on the other hand, is an emerging field of research that examines why and how external social conditions affect the activity of the genome (Slavich and Cole 2013; Boyce and Kobor 2015). Social genomics includes the study of gene expression (transcriptome) and epigenetics (epigenome). It emerges from the scientific understanding that while the gene sequences we inherit from our parents are fixed, the expression of these genes is shaped by forces "outside" the body. The focus of social genomics is inherently biosocial as it seeks to uncover how social experiences can alter gene expression and thereby affect physiological function and social and behavioral outcomes (Cole 2014; Hertzman 2012). Indeed, human social genomics research is demonstrating that certain genes can be "turned on" or "turned off" by different social-environmental conditions, and in some cases these social exposures can affect the activity of hundreds of genes in a coordinated manner.

This line of research provides new opportunities for understanding how social and genetic factors interact to shape complex biological and social pathways of well-being. Indeed, it has the potential to reframe our understanding of the genome as a dynamic substrate that incorporates information from the environment over developmental time, rather than the prevailing view of the genome as static sequences of DNA that are fixed at conception. Current social genomics research has examined, for example, how social processes, such as social status, social supports or isolation, social capital, early life adversity, exposure to toxicants and microbes, and health behaviors, alter the expression of hundreds of human genes (such as suppression of antiviral and antibody-related genes and stimulation of pro-inflammatory genes) to affect human development and health over many years (see, for example, Cole 2013, 2014; Murphy et al. 2012; Miller et al. 2009; Fry et al. 2012; McDade et al. 2017).

The term *epigenetics*—first used by Waddington in the 1940s (Jablonka and Lamb 2002)—literally means above or on top of genetics, and refers to chemical modifications to DNA and its packaging that change the accessibility of gene regions to transcription factors, and thereby affect the level of transcription. These modifications alter the physical structure of DNA in ways that are relatively stable and conserved with cell replication. Therefore, epigenetics represents a biological mechanism through which the body "remembers" prior environmental exposures to shape gene expression—a key reason why epigenetics has captured the attention of many social scientists. Methylation of DNA has been the major focus of human research, and involves the binding of methyl groups to cytosine residues in CpG dinucleotides (Bird 2002). At a point in an individual's life course, analysis of DNA methylation may reveal how and which genes have been modified in response to the cumulative life course environmental, behavioral, and biological trajectories of that individual. Thus, epigenetics specifies a life course biosocial process that entails the dynamic interactions and feedback loops of social and genetic phenomena both inter- and intragenerationally over the life course (Boyce and Kobor 2015). For example, epigenetic patterns have been shown to be altered by a range of environmental conditions such as diet, tobacco smoking, exercise, and exposure to chemicals (Christensen et al. 2009; Grönniger et al. 2010; Langevin et al. 2011). More broadly, measures of socioeconomic and psychosocial adversity in childhood have been linked to patterns of DNA methylation later in life (Essex et al. 2013; Needham et al. 2015). Epigenetic patterns have also been shown to affect physical traits and appearance, behavior, and health outcomes (IHEC 2013). Thus, environmental variation may routinely change epigenetic patterns, and those epigenetic patterns may in turn influence developmental outcomes over time.

One of the more provocative—but also controversial—findings for social scientists is that environmentally triggered behavior or biological change might be transmitted across generations through epigenetic mechanisms and without the involvement of DNA sequence (Jablonka and Lamb 2015; Thayer and Kuzawa 2011). Fascinating early evidence on the inheritance of epigenetic marks comes from research done on mice. Human evidence is much more difficult to establish. Studies of humans whose ancestors survived through periods of starvation in Sweden and the Netherlands suggest that the effects of famine on epigenetics and development can pass through at least three generations (Heijmans et al. 2008; Tobi et al. 2009). Nutrient deprivation in a recent ancestor seems to prime the body for diabetes and cardiovascular problems, a biological response that may have evolved to mitigate the effects of future famines. The findings on intergenerational epigenetic inheritance could have far-reaching significance. Much social science research documents how parental characteristics, such as lifestyle, behaviors, and living habits, influence children's well-being. Epigenetic processes may provide biological mechanisms through which lifestyles and behaviors are stored and transmitted to children and their children's children, who do not have any direct environmental exposure to these lifestyles or behaviors.

Social genomics is an exciting area for future biosocial research that emphasizes the instrumental role of the social environment in altering how genes are expressed to affect behavior, biology, and social and health outcomes. The more we understand how the social environment regulates genes that affect health and social stratification processes, the more potential we have for intervening on those environmental exposures to reduce health and social inequalities. The molecular models of social genomics do require new methodological skills and technical capacities for working with these data, over and above the application of standard social science methods used in GxE and rGE analysis. Interdisciplinary training, however, is already coming online to equip social scientists with these skills through summer boot camps and graduate training programs around the country. The potential for understanding these social and biological phenomena has captured the attention of the scholarly and public worlds alike. The ability of social genomics to fill diverse gaps in our understanding of human development and health and to provide scientific explanations of the mechanisms underlying our lived experiences makes it a compelling avenue for future biosocial research.

## ISSUE THEMES AND CHAPTERS

Contributors to the volume represent a wide range of disciplines, and their work advances the biosocial perspective on human development, behavior, and health across the life course. The issue is loosely organized around three themes.

### Disadvantage, Discrimination, and Health

The impact of social adversity on human welfare is of long-standing concern to social scientists. A biosocial perspective addresses questions regarding the health impacts of adversity, and the biological mechanisms through which social environments "get under the skin" to impact human development and health. This aspect of biosocial research has been greatly advanced by recent methodological developments that have facilitated the collection of objective biological data in nonclinical, community- and population-based settings. All three articles in this section showcase the value of these kinds of measures for advancing our understanding of how social adversity affects health.

Douglas Massey and his colleagues build on a long tradition of scholarship on neighborhood effects, with a particular emphasis on residential segregation and concentrated poverty. The majority of this work has been sociological, including some links to health but paying little attention to biology. Massey and his colleagues introduce a biosocial framework for linking spatially concentrated disadvantage at the geographic level with an individual-level biological measure of cellular aging (telomere length) to reveal mechanisms through which social structure contributes to race-based differences in morbidity and mortality in the United States. Aside from contributing to the literature on neighborhood effects, the article demonstrates how collaborative, interdisciplinary teams can leverage novel insights from molecular biology to cast new light on long-standing social science questions.

The article by Bridget Goosby and her colleagues also investigates the health impact of social disadvantage, but at the individual, micro-social level of analysis. Their focus on perceived discrimination draws on a well-established line of biosocial research that attends to the appraisal of stress as a key part of the causal pathway linking social adversity with physical health. Sleep quality and quantity are the key outcomes in their study, based on recent clinical and epidemiological research demonstrating the importance of sleep for a wide range of physical and mental health outcomes. Like Massey and colleagues, the article showcases the value of borrowing from biological and health sciences to illuminate issues of interest to social scientists. This point is underscored by the counterintuitive nature of their results. Global ratings of discrimination are negatively associated with sleep quantity and quality, as one might expect, but participants slept better the night following a day when they reported a discriminatory encounter. This finding reveals the potential of biological or health-related measures to provide novel insights into psychosocial dynamics that might otherwise be obscured. It also highlights the value of measuring these dynamics at multiple levels of analysis.

The article by Elizabeth McClure and her colleagues provides an excellent example of how a biosocial approach can be used to "socialize" biology. The ratio of signal-joint to beta T-cell receptor excision circles (sj/beta-TREC ratio) is used by immunologists to measure the function of the thymus, an organ that produces cells (T lymphocytes) that are essential for immunity. In their study in Detroit following the Great Recession, they show that neighborhood-level measures of home foreclosure and abandonment predict lower levels of thymic function among residents. Furthermore, reduced social cohesion—a product of home foreclosure and abandonment—predicts lower thymic function. With a clearly articulated conceptual model that informs their study design and analytic strategy, McClure and her colleagues move from the macro- (Great Recession) to the mezzo- (neighborhood characteristics) to the micro- (thymic function) levels of analysis to demonstrate how human biology is a social biology.

## Developmental and Intergenerational Processes

The two articles in this section use a biosocial approach to assess the biological and social features of the developing person and their changing social contexts through time and space to provide new insights into the determinants of social and physical well-being. The articles examine outcomes in specific life stages as a function of earlier life course exposures and interactions between social and biological forces that occur across human development.

Yang Qu and his colleagues use a biopsychosocial approach to understand adolescent development among a growing U.S. ethnic minority group—Mexican American youth. They identify adolescence as a dynamic life stage in which neural changes in both brain function and brain structure are likely associated with individual differences in academic and psychological adjustment. They also argue that the environment becomes especially salient during adolescence for Mexican American youth when ethnic parents attempt to socialize children about their cultural values and heritage, and at the same time, adolescents yearn to spend more time with peers and fit into adolescent social life and activities. The longitudinal research in this article examines the independent and interactive effects of adolescents' brain development and their family and peer environment in determining educational achievement and substance use. By integrating imaging data with rich social variables on cultural socialization and peer deviance, Qu and his colleagues find important independent contributions of biological and psychosocial factors in youth's achievement and adjustment.

The Margot Jackson and Susan Short article uses a life course intragenerational design to examine both gender differences in physical health in young adulthood and the ways in which adolescent development and social environments might explain those differences. Documenting gender differences in objective biological markers of health (inflammation and immunosuppression) during young adulthood is a contribution to the health disparities literature given most research on sex differences focuses on older aged populations. Jackson and Short report strong differentials in inflammation and immune function that disadvantage women in these biological systems. They explore a wealth of childhood, adolescent, and early adulthood circumstances—including demographic, family socioeconomic, health behavior, and young adult family formation and socioeconomic attainment—as potential explanatory factors underlying the sex differences. Identifying gender disparities early in the adult life course is critical to curbing their growth throughout adulthood by designing interventions to improve female health and reduce the disparities before chronic disease and long-term physical damage occurs.

## Genes and Environments over the Life Course

Interest in gene-environment interplay has captured the imagination of biosocial researchers, who isolate the role of genes in relation to environmental influence and focus on the ways in which genes and environments operate together in social stratification processes across the life course. The advent of new sources of molecular genetic data, especially genome-wide data, and statistical tools for analyzing massive amounts of individual-level genome-wide data linked to survey and biomarker information in large studies has opened exciting new research opportunities for understanding gene-environment interplay in biosocial models of attainment and behavior. Two articles in this issue take advantage of an analytic approach that combines the genetic associations with specific phenotypes (that is, behavioral, attainment, and health outcomes) across the entire genome using polygenic scores (PGS) based on genome-wide association studies (GWAS). A PGS is a linear combination of the effects of genetic variants present in the entire genome specific to a phenotype that can be interpreted as a single quantitative measure of genetic predisposition for that phenotype.

The article by Melinda Mills and her colleagues builds on their recently published meta-GWAS study on human reproductive behavior (Barban et al. 2016) by examining the predictive power of two PGS discovered in that study for age at first birth and number of children ever born in four independent extant data sources. Despite extensive research on the role of genetics in such outcomes as obesity, substance use, and education, little attention has been directed to fertility behavior, perhaps because age at first birth and number of children ever born are complex outcomes related to biological fecundity, behavioral choice, and socio-environmental factors. Consistent with most of the research on genetic influence using molecular data, Mills and her colleagues find relatively low levels of predictive power for the PGSs based on the entire genome, revealing the more predominant role of social-environmental and behavioral factors in determining age at first birth and number of children ever born. Rather than speculating on how much environmental and behavioral estimates are overstated by their confounding with genetic effects, social scientists use these models to control for this genetic confounding while estimating the importance of social and behavioral factors of fertility behavior. Moreover, age at first birth and number of children ever born are well-established markers of social stratification, illustrated by the voluminous literature on teenage childbearing and family size (reviews in Furstenberg 2003; Powell et al. 2016; Sweeney and Raley 2014; Wilcox and Lerman 2014). Indeed, Mills and her coauthors show that the PGSs are also correlated with other fertility traits, such as childlessness, and are independent of the effects of education.

Benjamin Domingue and his colleagues focus on the role of genes in environmental selection processes, or gene-environment correlation. They examine geographic clustering of PGSs for multiple phenotypes related to anthropometry, education, and physical and mental health by state of residence at different points in the life course to explore the extent to which state-level genetic composition explains state-level clustering of various phenotypes and how these relationships change over age. Domingue and his coauthors expertly discuss the important motivation behind examining gene-environment correlations, the mechanisms through which gene-environment correlations may operate, and test for the penetrance of PGSs (association of genotype and phenotype) at both the individual and ecological (that is, state) levels. For most of the phenotypes they examine, the authors find that the ecological correlations are much larger than the individual correlations, suggesting the environmental context of the state may moderate the genotype-phenotype associations. In particular, they identify two phenotypes, depression and educational attainment, for which the genetic context of a state is especially salient.

## CONCLUSIONS

The articles in this issue advance our understanding of the biosocial pathways of well-being across the life course, and their complex associations with social stratification. They build on a solid foundation of biosocial research in the social sciences, and they showcase the value of blurring the boundaries between phenomena outside the body and inside the body. In some cases, they use novel methods to cast new light on old questions. In others, novel methods reframe the questions and open new lines of inquiry. In all cases, the integration of biological information with measures of social environments and behavior across the life course is generating unique insights and unprecedented opportunities for discovery. In many ways, this issue can be seen as marking the "coming of age" of a new generation of biosocial scholarship, and the future looks bright for those of us who are invested in illuminating the complex pathways linking society, biology, and health across the life course.

## REFERENCES

Adam, Emma K., and Meena Kumari. 2009. "Assessing Salivary Cortisol in Large-Scale, Epidemiological Research." *Psychoneuroendocrinology* 34(10): 1423–36. DOI: 10.1016/j.psyneuen.2009.06.011.

Adler, Nancy E., Thomas Boyce, Margaret A. Chesney, Sheldon Cohen, Susan Folkman, Robert L. Kahn, and S. Leonard Syme. 1994. "Socioeconomic Status and Health: The Challenge of the Gradient." *American Psychologist* 49(1): 15–24.

Ahn, Andrew C., Muneesh Tewari, Chi-Sang Poon, and Russell S. Phillips. 2006. "The Limits of Reductionism in Medicine: Could Systems Biology Offer an Alternative?" *PLoS Medicine* 3(6): e208. DOI: 10.1371/journal.pmed.0030208.

Almond, Douglas, and Janet Currie. 2011. "Killing Me Softly: The Fetal Origins Hypothesis." *Journal of Economic Perspectives* 25(3): 153–72. DOI: 10.1257/jep.25.3.153.

Aneshensel, Carol S. 1992. "Social Stress: Theory and Research." *Annual Review of Sociology* 18(1): 15–38. DOI: 10.1146/annurev.soc.18.1.15.

Barban, Nicola, Rick Jensen, Ronald de Vlaming, Ahmad Vaez, et al. 2016. "Genome-Wide Analysis Identifies 12 Loci Influencing Human Reproductive Behavior." *Nature Genetics* 48(12): 1462–72. DOI: 10.1038/ng.3698.

Barker, David J. P. 1997. "Maternal Nutrition, Fetal Nutrition, and Disease in Later Life." *Nutrition* 13(9): 807–13. DOI: 10.1016/s0899-9007(97)00193-7.

———. 1998. *Mothers, Babies and Health in Later Life*, 2nd ed. Edinburgh: Churchill Livingstone.

———. 2006. "Adult Consequences of Fetal Growth Restriction." *Clinical Obstetrics and Gynecology* 49(2): 270–83. DOI: 10.1097/00003081-200606000-00009.

Bengtsson, Tommy, and Göran Broström. 2009. "Do Conditions in Early Life Affect Old-Age Mortality Directly and Indirectly? Evidence from 19th-Century Rural Sweden." *Social Science and Medicine* 68(9): 1583–90. DOI: 10.1016/j.socscimed.2009.02.020.

Berenson, Gerald S., Wendy A. Wattigney, Weihang Bao, Sathanur R. Srinivasan, and Bhandaru Radhakrishnamurthy. 1995. Rationale to Study the Early Natural History of Heart Disease: The Bogalusa Heart Study. *The American Journal of the Medical Sciences* 310(S1): S22–28.

Bird, Adrian. 2002. "DNA Methylation Patterns and Epigenetic Memory." *Genes and Development* 16(1): 6–21. DOI: 10.1101/gad.947102.

Blackwell, Debra L., Mark D. Hayward, and Eileen M. Crimmins. 2001. "Does Childhood Health Affect Chronic Morbidity in Later Life?" *Social Science and Medicine* 52(8): 1269–84. DOI: 10.1016/s0277-9536(00)00230-6.

Boardman, Jason D., Jonathan Daw, and Jeremy Freese. 2013. "Defining the Environment in Gene-Environment Research: Lessons from Social Epidemiology." *American Journal of Public Health* 103(S1): S64–72. DOI: 10.2105/ajph.2013.301355.

Boardman, Jason D., Benjamin W. Domingue, and Jonathan Daw. 2015. "What Can Genes Tell Us About the Relationship Between Education and Health?" *Social Science and Medicine* 127 (February): 171–80. DOI: 10.1016/j.socscimed.2014.08.001.

Boardman, Jason D., Benjamin W. Domingue, and Jason M. Fletcher. 2012. "How Social and Genetic Factors Predict Friendship Networks." *Proceedings of the National Academy of Sciences* 109(43): 17377–81. DOI: 10.1073/pnas.1208975109.

Boardman, Jason D., Michael E. Roettger, Benjamin W. Domingue, Matthew B. McQueen, Brett C. Haberstick, and Kathleen M. Harris. 2012. "Gene-Environment Interactions Related to Body Mass: School Policies and Social Context as Environmental Moderators." *Journal of Theoretical Politics* 24(3): 370–388. DOI: 10.1177/0951629812 437751.

Boas, Franz. 1912. "Changes in the Bodily Form of Descendants of Immigrants." *American Anthropologist* 14(3): 530–62. DOI: 10.1525/aa.1912.14 .3.02a00080.

Boyce, W. Thomas, and Michael S. Kobor. 2015. "Development and the Epigenome: The 'Synapse' of Gene–Environment Interplay." *Developmental Science* 18(1): 1–23.

Brody, Gene H., Tianyi Yu, Edith Chen, Gregory E. Miller, Steven M. Kogan, and Steven R. H. Beach. 2013. "Is Resilience Only Skin Deep? Rural African Americans' Socioeconomic Status–Related Risk and Competence in Preadolescence and Psychological Adjustment and Allostatic Load at Age 19." *Psychological Science* 24(7): 1285–93. DOI: 10.117/0956797612471954.

Cameron, Noe, and Ellen W. Demerath. 2002. "Critical Periods in Human Growth and Their Relationship to Diseases of Aging." *American Journal of Physical Anthropology* 119(S35): 159–84. DOI: 10.1002/ajpa.10183.

Case, Anne, Angela Fertig, and Christina Paxson. 2005. "The Lasting Impact of Childhood Health and Circumstance." *Journal of Health Economics* 24(2): 365–89. DOI: 10.1016/j.jhealeco.2004.09 .008.

Case, Anne, Darren Lubotsky, and Christina Paxson. 2002. "Economic Status and Health in Childhood: The Origins of the Gradient." *American Economic Review* 92(5): 1308–34. DOI: 10.1257/000282802762024520.

Case, Anne, and Christina Paxson. 2010. "Causes and Consequences of Early-Life Health." *Demography* 47(Suppl 1): S65–85.

Caspi, Avshalom, Karen Sugden, Terrie E. Moffitt, Alan Taylor, et al. 2003. "Influence of Life Stress on Depression: Moderation by a Polymorphism in the 5-HTT Gene." *Science* 301(5631): 386–89. DOI: 10.1126/science.1083968.

Cawley, John 2004. "The Impact of Obesity on Wages." *The Journal of Human Resources* 39(2): 451–74.

Charney, Evan, and William English. 2012. "Candidate Genes and Political Behavior." *American Political Science Review* 106(1): 1–34. DOI: 10.1017 /s0003055411000554.

Christensen, Brock C., E. Andres Houseman, Carmen J. Marsit, Shichun Zheng, et al. 2009. "Aging and Environmental Exposures Alter Tissue-Specific DNA Methylation Dependent upon CpG Island Context." *PLoS Genetics* 5(8): e1000602. DOI: 10.1371/journal.pgen.1000602.

Cohen, Sheldon, Denise Janicki-Deverts, Edith Chen, and Karen A. Matthews. 2010. "Childhood Socioeconomic Status and Adult Health." *Annals of the New York Academy of Science* 1186 (February): 37–55.

Cohen, Sheldon, Joseph E. Schwartz, Elissa Epel, Clemens Kirschbaum, Steve Sidney, and Teresa Seeman. 2006. "Socioeconomic Status, Race, and Diurnal Cortisol Decline in the Coronary Artery Risk Development in Young Adults (CARDIA) Study." *Psychosomatic Medicine* 68(1): 41–50. DOI: 10.1097/01.psy.0000195967.51768.ea.

Cole, Steven W. 2013. "Social Regulation of Human Gene Expression: Mechanisms and Implications for Public Health." *American Journal of Public Health* 103(S1): S84-S92. DOI: 10.2105/ajph .2012.301183.

———. 2014. "Human Social Genomics." *PLoS Genetics* 10(8): e1004601. DOI: 10.1371/journal.pgen .1004601.

Conley, Dalton 2016. "Socio-Genomic Research Using Genome-Wide Molecular Data." *Annual Review of Sociology* 42(1): 275–99. DOI: 10.1146/ annurev-soc-081715-074316.

Conley, Dalton, and Neil G. Bennett. 2000. "Is Biology Destiny? Birth Weight and Life Chances." *American Sociological Review* 65(3): 458–67. DOI: 10.2307/2657467.

Crimmins, Eileen M., and Caleb E. Finch. 2006. "Infection, Inflammation, Height, and Longevity." *Proceedings of the National Academy of Sciences* 103(2): 498–503. DOI: 10.1073/pnas.0501470103.

Crimmins, Eileen M., Yuan Zhang, and Yasuhiko. Saito. 2016. "Trends over 4 Decades in Disability-Free Life Expectancy in the United States." *American Journal of Public Health* 106(7): 1287–93. DOI: 10.2105/ajph.2016.303120.

Currie, J., and E. Moretti. 2007. "Biology as Destiny? Short- and Long-Run Determinants of Intergenerational Transmission of Birth Weight." *Journal of Labor Economics* 25(2): 231–64. DOI: 10.1086 /511377.

Currie, Janet, and Mark Stabile. 2003. "Socioeconomic Status and Child Health: Why Is the Relationship Stronger for Older Children?" *American Economic Review* 93(5): 1813–23. DOI: 10.1257/000282803322655563.

Daw, Jonathan, Michael Shanahan, Kathleen M. Harris, Andrew Smolen, Brett Haberstick, and Jason D. Boardman. 2013. "Genetic Sensitivity to Peer Behaviors: 5HTTLPR, Smoking, and Alcohol Consumption." *Journal of Health and Social Behavior* 54(1): 92–108. DOI: 10.1177/0022146512468591.

Dedeurwaerder, Sarah, Matthieu Defrance, Emilie Calonne, Hélène Denis, Christos Sotiriou, and François Fuks. 2011. "Evaluation of the Infinium Methylation 450K Technology." *Epigenomics* 3(6): 771–84. DOI: 10.2217/Epi.11.105.

DeSantis, Amy S., Emma K. Adam, Leah D. Doane, Susan Mineka, Richard E. Zinbarg, and Michelle G. Craske. 2007. "Racial/Ethnic Differences in Cortisol Diurnal Rhythms in a Community Sample of Adolescents." *Journal of Adolescent Health* 41(1): 3–13. DOI: 10.1016/j.jadohealth.2007.03.006.

Domingue, Benjamin W., David H. Rehkopf, Dalton Conley, and Jason D. Boardman. 2018. "Geographic Clustering of Polygenic Scores at Different Stages of the Life Course." *RSF: The Russell Sage Foundation Journal of the Social Sciences* 4(4): 137–49. DOI: 10.7758/RSF.2018.4.4.08.

Elo, Irma T., and Samuel H. Preston. 1992. "Effects of Early-Life Conditions on Adult Mortality: A Review." *Population Index* 58(2): 186–212. DOI: 10.2307/3644718.

Engel, George L. 1978. "The Biopsychosocial Model and the Education of Health Professionals." *Annals of the New York Academy of Sciences* 310 (June): 169–87.

Essex, Marilyn J., W. Thomas Boyce, Clyde Hertzman, Lucia L. Lam, Jeffrey M. Armstrong, Sarah M. Neumann, and Michael S. Kobor. 2013. "Epigenetic Vestiges of Early Developmental Adversity: Childhood Stress Exposure and DNA Methylation in Adolescence." *Child Development* 84(1): 58–75. DOI: 10.1111/j.1467-8624.2011.01641.x.

Figlio, David, Jonathan Guryan, Krzysztof Karbownik, and Jeffrey Roth. 2014. "The Effects of Poor Neonatal Health on Children's Cognitive Development." *American Economic Review* 104(12): 3921–3955.

Fletcher, Jason M., and Michael R. Richards. 2012. "Diabetes's 'Health Shock' to Schooling and Earning: Increased Dropout Rates and Lower Wages and Employment in Young Adults." *Health Affairs* 31(1): 27–34. DOI: 10.1377/hlthaff.2011.0862.

Freedman, Vicki A., and Brenda C. Spillman. 2014. "Disability and Care Needs Among Older Americans." *Milbank Quarterly* 92(3): 509–41. DOI: 10.1111/1468-0009.12076.

Freese, Jeremy, and Sara Shostak. 2009. "Genetics and Social Inquiry." *Annual Review of Sociology* 35(1): 107–28. DOI: 10.1146/annurev-soc-070308-120040.

Fry, Rebecca C., Julia E. Rager, Haibo Zhou, Baiming Zou, June W. Brickey, Jenny Ting, Davids B. Peden, and Neil E. Alexis. 2012. "Individuals with Increased Inflammatory Response to Ozone Demonstrate Muted Signaling of Immune Cell Trafficking Pathways." *Respiratory Research* 13(1): 89. DOI: 10.1186/1465-9921-13-89.

Furstenberg, Frank F. 2003. "Teenage Childbearing as a Public Issue and Private Concern." *Annual Review of Sociology* 29(1): 23–39. DOI: 10.1146/annurev.soc.29.010202.100205.

George, Linda K. 2009. "Conceptualizing and Measuring Trajectories." In *The Craft of Life Course Research*, edited by Glenn H. Elder Jr. and Janet Z. Giele. New York: Guilford Press.

Glass, Christy, Steven Haas, and Eric N. Reither. 2010. "The Skinny on Success: Adolescent Body Mass, Gender and Occupational Attainment." *Social Forces* 88(4): 1777–806.

Glass, Thomas A., and Matthew J. McAtee. 2006. "Behavioral Science at the Crossroads in Public Health: Extending Horizons, Envisioning the Future." *Social Science and Medicine* 62(7): 1650–71. DOI: 10.1016/j.soescimed.2005.08.044.

Gluckman, Peter D., Mark A. Hanson, Cyrus Cooper, and Kent L. Thornburg. 2008. "Effect of In Utero and Early-Life Conditions on Adult Health and Disease." *New England Journal of Medicine* 359(1): 61–73. DOI: 10.1056/nejmra0708473.

Goosby, Bridget J., Jacob E. Cheadle, Whitney Strong-Bak, Taylor C. Roth, and Timothy D. Nelson. 2018. "Perceived Discrimination and Adolescent Sleep in a Community Sample." *RSF: The Russell Sage Foundation Journal of the Social Sciences* 4(4): 43–61. DOI: 10.7758/RSF.2018.4.4.03.

Gottleib, Gilbert. 1991. "Experiential Canalization of Behavioral Development: Theory." *Developmental Psychology* 27(1): 4–13.

Gravlee, Clarence C. 2009. "How Race Becomes Biology: Embodiment of Social Inequality." *American Journal of Physical Anthropology* 139(1): 47–57. DOI: 10.1002/Ajpa.20983.

Grönniger, Elke, Barbara Weber, Oliver Heil, Nils Peters, Franz Stäb, Horst Wenck, Bernhard Korn, Marc Winnefeld, and Frank Lyko. 2010. "Aging and Chronic Sun Exposure Cause Distinct Epigenetic Changes in Human Skin." *PLoS Genetics* 6(5): e1000971. DOI: 10.1371/journal.pgen.1000971.

Gruenewald, Tara L., Margaret E. Kemeny, Najib Aziz, and John L. Fahey. 2004. "Acute Threat to the Social Self: Shame, Social Self-Esteem, and Cortisol Activity." *Psychosomatic Medicine* 66(6): 915–24.

Hahn, Rovert A. 1995. *Sickness and Healing: An Anthropological Perspective*. New Haven, Conn.: Yale University Press.

Halfon, Neal, and Miles Hochstein. 2002. "Life Course Health Development: An Integrated Framework for Developing Health, Policy, and Research." *Milbank Q* 80(3): 433–79.

Hallqvist, Johan, John Lynch, Mel Bartley, Thierry Lang, and David Blane. 2004. "Can We Disentangle Life Course Processes of Accumulation, Critical Period and Social Mobility? An Analysis of Disadvantaged Socio-economic Positions and Myocardial Infarction in the Stockholm Heart Epidemiology Program." *Social Science and Medicine* 58(8): 1555–62. DOI: 10.1016/s0277-9536(03)00344-7.

Han, Euna, Edward C. Norton, and Sally C. Stearns. 2009. "Weight and Wages: Fat Versus Lean Paychecks." *Health Economics* 18(5): 535–48.

Harris, Kathleen M. 2010. "An Integrative Approach to Health." *Demography* 47(1): 1–22.

Harris, Kathleen M., and Hedwig Lee. 2011. "Social and Economic Consequences of Obesity During the Transition to Adulthood." Paper presented at the Annual Meetings of the Popualtion Association of America, Washington, D.C. (March 31–April 2, 2011).

Hayward, Mark D., and Bridget K. Gorman. 2004. "The Long Arm of Childhood: The Influence of Early-Life Social Conditions on Men's Mortality." *Demography* 41(1): 87–107. DOI: 10.1353/dem.2004.0005.

Heijmans, Bastiaan. T., Elmar W. Tobi, Aryeh D. Stein, Hein Putter, Gerard J. Blauw, Ezra S. Susser, P. Eline Slagboom, and L. H. Lumey. 2008. "Persistent Epigenetic Differences Associated with Prenatal Exposure to Famine in Humans." *Proceedings of the National Academy of Sciences* 105(44): 17046–49. DOI: 10.1073/pnas.0806560105.

Hertzman, Clyde. 2012. "Putting the Concept of Biological Embedding in Historical Perspective." *Proceedings of the National Academy of Sciences* 109(Supplement 2): 17160–67.

Hertzman, Clyde, and Tom Boyce. 2010. "How Experience Gets Under the Skin to Create Gradients in Developmental Health." *Annual Review of Public Health* 31: 329–47. DOI: 10.1146/annurev.publhealth.012809.103538.

House, James S., Karl R. Landis, and Debra Umberson. 1988. "Social Relations and Health." *Science* 241(4865): 540–45.

Hubert, H. B., E. D. Eaker, R. J. Garrison, and William P. Castelli. 1987. "Life-Style Correlates of Risk Factor Change in Young Adults: An Eight-Year Study of Coronary Heart Disease Risk Factors in the Framingham Offspring." *American Journal of Epidemiology* 125(5): 812–31. DOI: 10.1093/oxfordjournals.aje.a114598.

Hutter, Carolyn M., Leah E. Mechanic, Nilanjan Chatterjee, Peter Kraft, et al. 2013. "Gene-Environment Interactions in Cancer Epidemiology: A National Cancer Institute Think Tank Report." *Genetic Epidemiology* 37(7): 643–57. DOI: 10.1002/gepi.21756.

International Human Epigenome Consortium (IHEC). 2013. "Goals, Structure, Policies and Guidelines." Cambridge: IHEC.

Jablonka, Eva, and Marion J. Lamb. 2002. "The Changing Concept of Epigenetics." *From Epigenesis to Epigenetics: The Genome in Context* 981 (December): 82–96.

———. 2015. "The Inheritance of Acquired Epigenetic Variations." *International Journal of Epidemiology* 44(4): 1094–103. DOI: 10.1093/ije/dyv020.

Jackson, Margot I., and Susan E. Short. 2018. "Gender Differences in Biological Function in Young Adulthood: An Intragenerational Perspective." *RSF: The Russell Sage Foundation Journal of the Social Sciences* 4(4): 98–119. DOI: 10.7758/RSF.2018.4.4.06.

Kleinman, Arthur. 1986. *Social Origins of Distress and Disease*. New Haven, Conn.: Yale University Press.

Krieger, Nancy 2005. "Embodiment: A Conceptual Glossary for Epidemiology." *J Epidemiol Community Health* 59(5): 350–55. DOI: 10.1136/jech.2004.024562.

Kuh, Diana, and Yoav Ben-Shlomo. 2004. "A Life Course Approach to Chronic Disease Epidemiology." In *A Life Course Approach to Chronic Disease Epidemiology*, 2nd ed., ed. Yoav Ben-Shlomo. Oxford: Oxford University Press.

Langevin, Scott M., E. Andresa Houseman, Brock C. Christensen, John K. Wiencke, Heather H. Nelson, Margaret R. Karagas, Carmen J. Marsit, and Karl T. Kelsey. 2011. "The Influence of Aging, Environmental Exposures and Local Sequence Features on the Variation of DNA Methylation in Blood." *Epigenetics* 6(7): 908–19. DOI: 10.4161/epi.6.7.16431.

Lasker, Gabriel W. 1969. "Human Biological Adaptability: The Ecological Approach in Physical Anthropology." *Science* 166(3912): 1480–86.

Lewontin, Richard C., and Richard Levins. 2007. *Biology Under the Influence: Dialectical Essays on Ecology, Agriculture, and Health*. New York: Monthly Review Press.

Li, Shengxu, Wei Chen, Sathanur R. Srinivasan, and Gerald S Berenson. 2004. "Childhood Blood Pressure as a Predictor of Arterial Stiffness in Young Adults." *Hypertension* 43(3): 541–46.

Lindau, Stacy T., and Thomas W. McDade. 2007. "Minimally Invasive and Innovative Methods for Biomeasure Collection in Population-Based Research." In *Biosocial Surveys*, edited by Maxine Weinstein, James W. Vaupel, and Kenneth W. Wachter. Washington, D.C.: National Academies Press.

Link, Bruce G., and Jo Phelan. 1995. "Social Conditions as Fundamental Causes of Disease." *Journal of Health and Social Behavior*, Extra Issue: Forty Years of Medical Sociology: The State of the Art and Directions for the Future: 80–94.

Ludwig, Jens, Lisa Sanbonmatsu, Lisa Gennetian, Emma Adam, Greg J. Duncan, Lawrence F. Katz, and Thomas W. McDade. 2011. "Neighborhoods, Obesity, and Diabetes—A Randomized Social Experiment." *New England Journal of Medicine* 365(16): 1509–19.

Marino, Miguel, Yi Li, Michael N. Rueschman, John Winkelman, J. M. Ellenbogen, Jo M. Solet, Hilary Dulin, Lisa F. Berkman, and Orfeu M. Buxton. 2013. "Measuring Sleep: Accuracy, Sensitivity, and Specificity of Wrist Actigraphy Compared to Polysomnography." *Sleep* 36(11): 1747–55.

Marmot, Michael, Martin Shipley, Eric Brunner, and Harry Hemingway. 2001. "Relative Contribution of Early Life and Adult Socioeconomic Factors to Adult Morbidity in the Whitehall II Study." *Journal of Epidemiology and Community Health* 55(5): 301–07.

Marmot, Michael, and Richard G. Wilkinson. 2005. *Social Determinants of Health*, 2nd ed. Oxford: Oxford University Press.

Massey, Douglas S., Brandon Wagner, Louis Donnelly, Sara McLanahan, Jeanne Brooks-Gunn, Irwin Garfinkel, Colter Mitchell, and Daniel A. Notterman. 2018. "Neighborhood Disadvantage and Telomere Length: Results from the Fragile Families Study." *RSF: The Russell Sage Foundation Journal of the Social Sciences* 4(4): 28–42. DOI: 10.7758/RSF.2018.4.4.02.

McClure, Elizabeth, Lydia Feinstein, Sara Ferrando-Martínez, Manuel Leal, Sandro Galea, and Allison E. Aiello. 2018. "The Great Recession and Immune Function." *RSF: The Russell Sage Foundation Journal of the Social Sciences* 4(4): 62–81. DOI: 10.7758/RSF.2018.4.4.04.

McDade, Thomas W., Kharah M. Ross, Ruby L. Fried, Jesusa M. Arevalo, Jeffrey Ma, Gregory E. Miller, and Steve W. Cole. 2016. "Genome-Wide Profiling of RNA from Dried Blood Spots: Convergence with Bioinformatic Results Derived from Whole Venous Blood and Peripheral Blood Mononuclear Cells." *Biodemography and Social Biology* 62(2): 182–97. DOI: 10.1080/19485565.2016.1185600.

McDade, Thomas W., Calen Ryan, Meaghan Jones, Julia L. MacIsaac, Alexander M. Morin, Jess M. Meyer, Judith B. Borja, Gregory E. Miller, Michael S. Kobor, and Christopher W. Kuzawa. 2017. "Social and Physical Environments Early in Development Predict DNA Methylation of Inflammatory Genes in Young Adulthood." *Proceedings of the National Academy of Sciences* 114(29): 7611–16.

McDade, Thomas W., Sharon Williams, and J. Josh Snodgrass. 2007. "What a Drop Can Do: Dried Blood Spots as a Minimally Invasive Method for Integrating Biomarkers into Population-Based Research." *Demography* 44(4): 899–925.

McEwen, Bruce S. 1998. "Stress, Adaptation and Disease: Allostasis and Allostatic Load." *Annals of the New York Academy of Sciences* 840 (May): 33–44.

McEwen, Bruce S., and Elizabeth N. Lasley. 2002. *The End of Stress as We Know It*. New York: Dana Press.

Miller, Gregory E., Edith Chen, Alexandra K. Fok, Hope Walker, Alvin Lim, Erin F. Nicholls, and Michael S. Kobor. 2009. "Low Early-Life Social Class Leaves a Biological Residue Manifested by Decreased Glucocorticoid and Increased Proinflammatory Signaling." *Proceedings of the National Academy of Sciences* 106(34): 14716–21. DOI: 10.1073/pnas.0902971106.

Miller, Gregory E., Tianyi Yu, Edith Chen, and Gene H. Brody. 2015. "Self-Control Forecasts Better Psychosocial Outcomes but Faster Epigenetic Aging in Low-SES Youth." *Proceedings of the National Academy of Sciences* 112(33): 10325–30.

Mills, Melinda C., Nicola Barban, and Felix C. Tropf. 2018. "The Sociogenomics of Polygenic Scores of Reproductive Behavior and Their Relationship to Other Fertility Traits." *RSF: The Russell Sage Foundation Journal of the Social Sciences* 4(4): 122–36. DOI: 10.7758/RSF.2018.4.4.07.

Murphy, Michael L. M., George M. Slavich, Nicolas Rohleder, and Gregory E. Miller. 2012. "Targeted Rejection Triggers Differential Pro- and Anti-inflammatory Gene Expression in Adolescents as a Function of Social Status." *Clinical Psychological Science* 1(1): 30–40. DOI: 10.1177/2167702612455743.

National Center for Health Statistics. 2016. *Health, United States. 2015: With Special Feature on Racial and Ethnic Health Disparities*. Hyattsville, Md.: U.S. Department of Health and Human Services.

Needham, Belinda L., Jennifer A. Smith, Wei Zhao, Xu Wang, Bhramar Mukherjee, Sharon L. Kardia, Teresa E. Seeman, Yongmei Liu, and Ana V. Diez Roux. 2015. "Life Course Socioeconomic Status and DNA Methylation in Genes Related to Stress Reactivity and Inflammation: The Multi-ethnic Study of Atherosclerosis." *Epigenetics* 10(10): 958–69. DOI: 10.1080/15592294.2015.1085139.

Nguyen, Quynh C., Joyce W. Tabor, Pamela P. Entzel, Yan Lau, Chirayath Suchindran, Jon M. Hussey, Carolyn T. Halpern, Kathleen M. Harris, and Eric A. Whitsel. 2011. "Discordance in National Estimates of Hypertension Among Young Adults." *Epidemiology* 22(4): 532–41. DOI: 10.1097/ede.0b013e31821c79d2.

North, Kari E., and Lisa J. Martin. 2008. "The Importance of Gene–Environment Interaction: Implications for Social Scientists." *Sociological Methods and Research* 37(2): 164–200. DOI: 10.1177/0049124108323538.

Okbay, Aysu, Jonathan P. Beauchamp, Mark A. Fontana, James J. Lee, et al. 2016. "Genome-Wide Association Study Identifies 74 Loci Associated with Educational Attainment." *Nature* 533(7604): 539–42.

Palloni, Alberto. 2006. "Reproducing Inequalities: Luck, Wallets, and the Enduring Effects of Childhood Health." *Demography* 43(4): 587–615. DOI: 10.1353/dem.2006.0036.

Pearlin, Leonard I. 1989. "The Sociological Study of Stress." *Journal of Health and Social Behavior* 30(3): 241. DOI: 10.2307/2136956.

Phillips, David I., Brian R. Walker, Rebecca M. Reynolds, Daniel E. Flanagan, Peter J. Wood, Clive Osmond, and Christopher B. Whorwood. 2000. "Low Birth Weight Predicts Elevated Plasma Cortisol Concentrations in Adults from 3 Populations." *Hypertension* 35(6): 1301–306.

Powell, Brian, Laura Hamilton, Bianca Manago, and Simon Cheng. 2016. "Implications of Changing Family Forms for Children." *Annual Review of Sociology* 42(1): 301–22. DOI: 10.1146/annurev-soc-081715-074444.

Preston, Samuel H., Mark E. Hill, and Greg L. Drevenstedt. 1998. "Childhood Conditions that Predict Survival to Advanced Ages Among African-Americans." *Social Science and Medicine* 47(9): 1231–46. DOI: 10.1016/s0277-9536(98)00180-4.

Pudrovska, Tetyana, and Benedicta Anikputa. 2014. "Early-Life Socioeconomic Status and Mortality in Later Life: An Integration of Four Life-Course Mechanisms." *Journals of Gerontology Series B: Psychological Sciences and Social Sciences* 69(3): 451–60.

Qu, Yang, Adriana Galván, Andrew J. Fuligni, and Eva H. Telzer. 2018. "A Biopsychosocial Approach to Examine Mexican American Adolescents' Academic Achievement and Substance Use." *RSF: The Russell Sage Foundation Journal of the Social Sciences* 4(4): 84–97. DOI: 10.7758/RSF.2018.4.4.05.

Rietveld, Cornelius, Sarah Medland, Jaime Derringer, Jian Yang, et al. 2013. "GWAS of 126,559 Individuals Identifies Genetic Variants Associated with Educational Attainment." *Science* 340(6139): 1467–71.

Rowe, David C., Kristen C. Jacobson, and Edwin J. Van den Oord. 1999. "Genetic and Environmental Influences on Vocabulary IQ: Parental Education Level as Moderator." *Child Development* 70(5): 1151–62. DOI: 10.1111/1467-8624.00084.

Scheper-Hughes, Nancy, and Margaret M. Lock.

1987. "The Mindful Body: A Prolegomenon to Future Work in Medical Anthropology." *Medical Anthropology Quarterly* 1(1): 6–41.

Schmitz, Lauren, and Dalton Conley. 2016. "The Long-Term Consequences of Vietnam-Era Conscription and Genotype on Smoking Behavior and Health." *Behavior Genetics* 46(1): 43–58. DOI: 10.1007/s10519-015-9739-1.

——. 2017. "Modeling Gene-Environment Interactions with Quasi-Natural Experiments." *Journal of Personality* 85(1): 10–21. DOI: 10.1111/jopy.12227.

Seeman, Teresa E., Bruce S. McEwen, John W. Rowe, and Burton H. Singer. 2001. "Allostatic Load as a Marker of Cumulative Biological Risk: MacArthur Studies of Successful Aging." *Proceedings of the National Academy of Sciences* 98(8): 4770–75.

Seligman, Rebecca 2014. *Possessing Spirits and Healing Selves: Embodiment and Transformation in an Afro-Brazilian Religion*. New York: Palgrave Macmillan.

Shanahan, Michael J., and Jason D. Boardman. 2009. "Genetics and Behavior in the Life Course: A Promising Frontier." In *The Craft of Life Course Research*, edited by Glenn H. Elder Jr., and Janet Z. Giele. New York: Guilford Press.

Shanahan, Michael J., Scott M. Hofer, and Lilly Shanahan. 2003. "Biological Models of Behavior and the Life Course." In *Handbook of Sociology and Social Research*, edited by Jeylan T. Mortimer and Michael J. Shanahan. New York: Springer Science.

Sisk, Cheryl L., and Julia L. Zehr. 2005. "Pubertal Hormones Organize the Adolescent Brain and Behavior." *Frontiers in Neuroendocrinology* 26(3–4): 163–74. DOI: 10.1016/j.yfrne.2005.10.003.

Slavich, George M., and Steven W. Cole. 2013. "The Emerging Field of Human Social Genomics." *Clinical Psychological Science* 1(3): 331–348. DOI: 10.1177/2167702613478594.

Smith, Caitlin J., and Kelli K. Ryckman. 2015. "Epigenetic and Developmental Influences on the Risk of Obesity, Diabetes, and Metabolic Syndrome." *Diabetes, Metabolic Syndrome and Obesity: Targets and Therapy* 8 (June): 295–302. DOI: 10.2147/DMSO.S61296.

Smith, James P. 2009. "Reconstructing Childhood Health Histories." *Demography* 46(2): 387–403. DOI: 10.1353/dem.0.0058.

Sterling, Peter, and Joseph Ayer. 1988. "Allostasis: A New Paradigm to Explain Arousal Pathology." In *Handbook of Life Stress, Cognition and Health*, edited by Shirley Fischer and James Reason. New York: John Wiley & Sons.

Stinson, Sara, Barry Bogin, and Dennis O'Rourke. 2012. *Human Biology: An Evolutionary and Biocultural Perspective*. New York: Wiley-Blackwell.

Sweeney, Megan M., and R. Kelly Raley. 2014. "Race, Ethnicity, and the Changing Context of Childbearing in the United States." *Annual Review of Sociology* 40(1): 539–58. DOI: 10.1146/annurev-soc-071913-043342.

Thayer, Zaneta M., and Christopher W. Kuzawa. 2011. "Biological Memories of Past Environments: Epigenetic Pathways to Health Disparities." *Epigenetics* 6(7): 798–803.

Tobi, Elmar W., L. H. Lumey, Rudolf P. Talens, Dennis Kremer, Hein Putter, Aryeh D. Stein, P. Eline Slagboom, and Bastiaan T. Heijmans. 2009. "DNA Methylation Differences After Exposure to Prenatal Famine Are Common and Timing- and Sex-Specific." *Human Molecular Genetics* 18(21): 4046–53. DOI: 10.1093/hmg/ddp353.

Uchino, Bert, John T. Cacioppo, and Janice K. Kiecolt-Glaser. 1996. "The Relationship Between Social Support and Physiological Processes: A Review with Emphasis on Underlying Mechanisms and Implications for Health." *Psychological Bulletin* 119(3): 488–531.

Wadhwa, Pathik. D., Claudia Buss, Sonja Entringer, and James M. Swanson. 2009. "Developmental Origins of Health and Disease: Brief History of the Approach and Current Focus on Epigenetic Mechanisms." *Seminars in Reproductive Medicine* 27(5): 358–68. PubMed: 19711246.

Waite, Linda, and Aniruddha Das. 2010. "Families, Social Life, and Well-Being at Older Ages." *Demography* 47 Suppl: S87–109. PMID:21302422.

Ward, Brian W., Jeannine S. Schiller, and Richard A. Goodman. 2014. "Multiple Chronic Conditions Among U.S. Adults: A 2012 Update." *Preventing Chronic Disease* 11. DOI: 10.5888/pcd11.130389.

Weinstein, Maxine, James W. Vaupel, and Kenneth W. Wachter, eds. 2007. *Biosocial Surveys*. Washington, D.C.: National Academies Press.

Wilcox, W. Bradford, and Robert I. Lerman. 2014. "For Richer, for Poorer: How Family Structures Economic Success in America." Washington, D.C.: American Enterprise Institute.

Wolfe, Barbara, William N. Evans, and Teresa E. Seeman. 2012. *The Biological Consequences of Socioeconomic Inequalities*. New York: Russell Sage Foundation.

Yang, Yang Claire, Courtnay Boen, Karen Gerken, Ting Li, Kristen Schorpp, and Kathleen M. Harris. 2016. "Social Relationships and Physiological Determinants of Longevity Across the Human Life Span." *Proceedings of the National Academy of Sciences* 113(3): 578–83. DOI: 10.1073/pnas.1511085112.

Yang, Yang Claire, Karen Gerken, Kristen Schorpp, Courtnay Boen, and Kathleen M. Harris. 2017. "Early Life Socioeconomic Status and Adult Physiological Functioning: A Life Course Examination of Biosocial Mechanisms." *Biodemography and Social Biology* 63(2): 87–103.

Yang, Yang Claire, Kristen Schorpp, and Kathleen M. Harris. 2014. "Social Support, Social Strain and Inflammation: Evidence from a National Longitudinal Study of U.S. Adults." *Social Science and Medicine* 107 (April): 124–35. DOI: 10.1016/j.socscimed.2014.02.013.

# PART II

# Disadvantage, Discrimination, and Health

# Neighborhood Disadvantage and Telomere Length: Results from the Fragile Families Study

DOUGLAS S. MASSEY, BRANDON WAGNER, LOUIS DONNELLY, SARA MCLANAHAN, JEANNE BROOKS-GUNN, IRWIN GARFINKEL, COLTER MITCHELL, AND DANIEL A. NOTTERMAN

*Telomeres are repetitive nucleotide sequences located at the ends of chromosomes that protect genetic material. We use data from the Fragile Families and Child Wellbeing Study to analyze the relationship between exposure to spatially concentrated disadvantage and telomere length for white and black mothers. We find that neighborhood disadvantage is associated with shorter telomere length for mothers of both races. This finding highlights a potential mechanism through which the unique spatially concentrated disadvantage faced by African Americans contributes to racial health disparities. We conclude that equalizing the health and socioeconomic status of black and white Americans will be very difficult without reducing levels of residential segregation in the United States.*

**Keywords:** telomere, segregation, neighborhood disadvantage, concentrated poverty

In his seminal book, *The Truly Disadvantaged*, William Julius Wilson (1987) notes the growing concentration of poverty within black inner city neighborhoods and hypothesized that long-term exposure to spatially concentrated disadvantage was central to the perpetuation of poverty among African Americans. Since that time, a large body of research has sought to establish the existence of "neighborhood effects" on individual social, economic, and health outcomes. Although analyses of multilevel survey data and nonexperimental results derived from static group comparisons generally produced results consistent with Wilson's hypothesis (see Rubinowitz and Rosenbaum 2000; Sampson, Morenoff, and Gannon-Rowley 2002; Massey and Clampet-Lundquist 2008), experimental findings from the Moving to Opportunity (MTO) Study were initially less supportive (Kling, Lieberman, and Katz 2007).

The MTO study randomly assigned poor residents of public housing projects in five metropolitan areas to experimental and control groups. Members of the former group were of-

**Douglas S. Massey** is professor of sociology and public affairs at Princeton University. **Brandon Wagner** is assistant professor of sociology at Texas Tech University. **Louis Donnelly** is a postdoctoral research associate at Princeton University. **Sara McLanahan** is professor of sociology and public affairs at Princeton University. **Jeanne Brooks-Gunn** is professor of child development and education at Columbia University. **Irwin Garfinkel** is professor of contemporary urban problems at Columbia University. **Colter Mitchell** is research assistant professor at the University of Michigan. **Daniel A. Notterman** is lecturer with the rank of professor in molecular biology at Princeton University.

© 2018 Russell Sage Foundation. Massey, Douglas S., Brandon Wagner, Louis Donnelly, Sara McLanahan, Jeanne Brooks-Gunn, Irwin Garfinkel, Colter Mitchell, and Daniel A. Notterman. 2018. "Neighborhood Disadvantage and Telomere Length: Results from the Fragile Families Study." *RSF: The Russell Sage Foundation Journal of the Social Sciences* 4(4): 28–42. DOI: 10.7758/RSF.2018.4.4.02. Direct correspondence to: Douglas S. Massey at dmassey@princeton.edu, Office of Population Research, Wallace Hall, Princeton University, Princeton, NJ 08544.

Open Access Policy: *RSF: The Russell Sage Foundation Journal of the Social Sciences* is an open access journal. This article is published under a Creative Commons Attribution-NonCommercial-NoDerivs 3.0 Unported License.

fered housing vouchers that required subjects to move into a low-poverty neighborhood and the latter received no offer of vouchers but continued to receive project-based assistance. Statistical comparisons of the two groups five to seven years after random assignment revealed that members of the experimental group did experience lower levels of neighborhood poverty and improved mental and physical health (Ludwig et al. 2011) but that the intervention offered "no convincing evidence of effects on educational performance; employment and earnings; or household income, food security, and self-sufficiency" (Orr et al. 2003, xv). These disappointing conclusions were generally sustained when the evaluation was repeated ten to fifteen years after random assignment (Sanbonmatsu et al. 2011).

More recently, however, the tide of evidence has begun to turn in favor of Wilson's "neighborhood effects" hypothesis. A quasi-experimental evaluation of a housing mobility project in New Jersey recently demonstrated that, when compared to members of a matched control group, adults who moved from a high- to low-poverty residential environment experienced significantly lower exposure to disorder and violence, a lower frequency of negative life events, better mental health, higher employment rates, more earned income, and lower rates of welfare receipt (Massey et al. 2013). At the same time, adults who moved also became more involved in their children's academic development, and the children themselves evinced a dramatic increase in hours spent studying while gaining greater access to a quiet study space, higher quality schools, and lower levels of disorder and violence within schools, all of which allowed them to maintain strong grades despite attending more demanding schools (and hence receiving a much better education).

Using data from the Panel Study of Income Dynamics, Jeffrey Wodtke, David Harding, and Felix Elwert followed children from age one to seventeen and find that long-term exposure to concentrated neighborhood disadvantage sharply reduced the likelihood of high school graduation (2011), especially for children from low-income families (2016). Drawing on the same data source, Jonathan Rothwell and Douglas Massey show that, after adjusting for regional differences in purchasing power, lifetime household income would have been $910,000 greater if people born into bottom-quartile of neighborhoods had instead been raised within a top-quartile neighborhood, indicating a powerful *neighborhood* income effect that was two-thirds of the *parental* income effect (2014).

Finally, a recent reanalysis of the MTO subjects drawing on tax and census data from 2012 finds that children whose families moved into a low-poverty neighborhood before the age of thirteen by their mid-twenties earned annual incomes that were nearly $3,500 greater than their counterparts in the control group (Chetty, Hendren, and Katz 2016). In addition, they displayed marriage rates that were two percentage points higher and attended college at rates that were 2.5 points greater. Children in the experimental group also attended higher quality colleges and universities.

At this point, a consensus seems to be emerging that neighborhoods do indeed matter across a variety of dimensions of human well-being (Massey 2013). Social scientists are consequently moving away from simple demonstrations of the existence of neighborhood effects and attempting to identify and model the specific mechanisms by which exposure to spatially concentrated disadvantage affects critical human outcomes (compare Sampson 2012; Sharkey 2013). In the current analysis, we focus on the relationship between neighborhood disadvantage and health, one of the earliest associations to emerge experimentally from the MTO study (Ludwig 2012). Rather than offering additional evidence simply to confirm the existence of such a relationship, however, we explore a potentially important pathway by which concentrated neighborhood disadvantage may get "under the skin" of people growing up and living in poor neighborhoods to create a potential biological precursor of elevated morbidity and mortality in later life.

## SOCIAL STRUCTURE, STRESS, AND HEALTH

We argue that one position within the social structure of society produces a high degree of exposure to spatially concentrated disadvantage. The social-structural position in question is defined by the intersection of high poverty and high residential segregation. The systematic residential segregation of any high-poverty group inevitably concentrates poverty spatially within neighborhoods inhabited by members of that group. Massey first identified this interaction using a simulation to show how rising rates of black poverty mechanically produced higher concentrations of black poverty as racial segregation increased, a relationship established empirically in subsequent research (Massey 1990; Massey and Eggers 1992; Massey and Fischer 2000). Although Massey's empirical confirmation of the segregation-poverty interaction was questioned on statistical grounds (Jargowsky 1997), the underlying mathematics of the interaction were later worked out and confirmed: "racial segregation and income segregation within race contribute importantly to poverty concentration, as Massey argued" (Quillian 2012, 354).

The group most subject to this interaction is African Americans, who in many metropolitan areas are simultaneously the poorest and most segregated minority group. These circumstances expose them to uniquely high concentrations of neighborhood disadvantage compared with other racial-ethnic groups (Massey and Rugh forthcoming). This fact is important because, as Robert Sampson points out, when it comes to urban ecology "things go together" (2012). Areas of spatially concentrated disadvantage also tend to be areas of high crime, elevated violence, excessive mortality, low collective efficacy, fragmented social ties, and limited capacity for collective action. It is hardly surprising, therefore, that neighborhood disadvantage has been identified as the critical nexus for the intergenerational transmission of poverty among African Americans (Sharkey 2013).

Previous work has found that neighborhood disadvantage is associated with biological markers linked to stress or health, including cortisol levels and C-protein reactivity (Rudolph et al. 2014; Hackman et al. 2012; Karb et al. 2012), blood pressure (Cathorall et al. 2015), DNA methylation (King et al. 2016), and summative measures such as allostatic load (Gustafsson et al. 2014; Finch et al. 2010). In this article, we conceptualize the attenuation of telomere length as a potential mechanism by which exposure to neighborhood disadvantage undermines health in later life. Telomeres are repetitive nucleotide sequences located at the ends of human chromosomes, which act as buffers to protect genetic material from deterioration and errant recombination during cell division (Blackburn 2006; Kipling 1995).

Telomeres naturally shorten in the course of human aging (Wilhide 2014). The normal process of shortening over time can be accelerated by exposure to environmental stressors, however (Sapolsky 2004). Despite some evidence of positive publication bias, meta-analyses provide support for the association between perceived stress and telomere length (Schutte and Malouf 2014; Mathur et al. 2016). These results support the conclusion of Elissa Epel and her colleagues that "stress . . . is significantly associated with higher oxidative stress, lower telomerase activity, and shorter telomere length" (2004, 17312).

We hypothesize that one critical source of environmental stress for African Americans is their elevated exposure to spatially concentrated disadvantage, thus yielding a potential biosocial pathway connecting their position in the U.S. social structure to health. Specifically, the combination of high poverty and high segregation uniquely expose African Americans to spatially concentrated disadvantage, yielding a prolonged exposure to stress, which functions over time to shorten telomeres of African Americans prematurely, with potential adverse health consequences later in life.

Admittedly, the nature of the relationship between shortened telomeres and poor health is not settled. Some scholars have argued that the poor prediction of mortality risk (Glei et al. 2016) and physical decline (Harris et al. 2016) by telomere length, particularly in the oldest-old (Yu et al. 2015; Martin-Ruiz et al. 2005), implies that telomere length is a "weak biomarker [of human aging] with poor predictive accuracy compared with many traditional covariates" (Sanders and Newman 2013). However, numerous other studies document associations between telomere length and a variety of subsequent health outcomes, including all-cause mortality risk, infectious disease mortality, coronary heart disease, stroke, myocardial infarction, diabetes, cancer incidence, and cancer mortality (Glei et al. 2016; see also Marioni et al. 2016; Fitzpatrick et al. 2011; Haycock et al. 2014; Goglin et al. 2016; D'Mello et al. 2014; Willeit, Willeit, and Mayr 2010).

Though the exact mechanisms that link telomere length to subsequent health is unclear, a recent review highlights a variety of potential mechanisms by which telomere length might influence health, concluding that "telomere attrition can lead to potentially maladaptive cellular changes, block cell division, and interfere with tissue replacement," and that "greater overall telomere attrition predicts mortality and age-related diseases" (Blackburn, Epel, and Lin 2015, 1193). Such a link between stressful social environments and compromised health has long been hypothesized, that persistent exposure to disadvantaged circumstances contributes to a process of human "weathering" in which disadvantaged populations age prematurely from high levels of stress and consequently experience poorer health as the life course proceeds (Geronimus 1992; see also DiPrete and Eirich 2006; Geronimus et al. 2006; Walsemann, Gee, and Geronimus 2009).

We argue here that a key source of stress for African Americans, beyond whatever instances of exclusion and discrimination they may experience while navigating U.S. society, is their long-term exposure to high spatial concentrations of disadvantage, which potentially contribute to weathering at the cellular level in the form of shortened telomeres (Epel et al. 2004; Sapolsky 2004). Because racial gaps in health and mortality typically are not eliminated by controlling for socioeconomic status and demographic factors, we argue that racial differences in exposure to concentrated disadvantage carry considerable potential to account more fully for black shortfalls in health (see Kitagawa and Hauser 1973; Geruso 2012).

One potential mechanism is the pathway hypothesized here, in which high levels of segregation and poverty interact to concentrate poverty within black neighborhoods, which in turn exposes African Americans to high concentrations of neighborhood disadvantage, which ultimately shortens black telomere lengths to foretell an elevated risk of health problems over the life course. The connection between segregation, poverty, and neighborhood disadvantage is well established (Quillian 2012) and evidence of a link between telomere length and poor health is rapidly accumulating (see Blackburn, Epel, and Lin 2015). Here we seek to demonstrate an association between concentrated neighborhood disadvantage and telomere length in a large nationally representative sample.

Prior work offers suggestive evidence of such a link. Katherine Theall and her colleagues, for example, gathered data from children in New Orleans and show that exposure to neighborhood disorder and poverty was associated with shorter telomeres (2013). Using a sample of adults from locations around the United States, Belinda Needham and her colleagues also find a strong negative relationship between telomere length and the quality of the neighborhood environment, as measured by aesthetics, safety, and social cohesion (2015). Likewise, Minjung Park and her colleagues used data from a longitudinal survey of Dutch adults to demonstrate that telomere length varied inversely with neighborhood quality, as measured by self-reported disorder, crime, and noise (2015).

Recently Arline Geronimus and her colleagues compiled a sample of respondents from three Detroit neighborhoods and find that respondents who were most satisfied with their neighborhood circumstances displayed significantly longer telomeres than others. Using data from the Fragile Families and Child Wellbeing Study, Colter Mitchell and his colleagues demonstrate that black boys who experienced disadvantaged home environments displayed significantly shorter telomeres by age nine than statistically similar boys who grew up in advantaged environments (2014). Likewise, Stacy Drury and her colleagues find that telomeres were significantly shorter among children who reported greater exposure to family violence and disruption (2014). Irdan Shalev and his colleagues discovered that children exposed to multiple sources of violence and mistreatment while growing up displayed significantly more telomere shrinkage between ages five and ten than other children (2013).

## DATA AND METHODS

Our data come from the Fragile Families and Child Wellbeing Study, which is based on a stratified, multistage, probability sample of children born in large U.S. cities between 1998 and 2000. Around three-quarters of the births were to unmarried mothers (hence yielding "fragile" families). Baseline interviews were conducted with mothers in the hospital soon after the child's birth, and fathers were interviewed in the hospital or by phone. Follow-up interviews were conducted with both parents when the child was one, three, five, and nine years old. About nine years after the birth of their child, 2,667 mothers provided saliva samples to enable biological assays of telomere length.

Telomere length was assessed using a quantitative real-time polymerase chain reaction (PCR) assay that yielded absolute measurements in numbers of kilobases. To guard against overly influential outlier cases, we eliminated respondents with telomere lengths below the 1st percentile or above the 99th percentile of the distribution and to facilitate analysis and we took the natural log of telomere length as our dependent variable in a simple linear model (see Mitchell et al. 2014). Most research on telomeres to date has relied on peripheral blood mononuclear cells from whole blood as a source of DNA. To consider the relationship between DNA from blood and that derived from saliva, Mitchell and colleagues asked sixteen healthy adult volunteers (ten females and six males) to contribute both blood and saliva samples (2014).

After discarding a single outlier (by four standard deviations) from one of the blood samples, they find that telomere length was greater in the saliva samples but nonetheless highly correlated with telomere length in the blood samples. This difference is not surprising since different cell types have different rates of division and thus different rates of telomere attrition. Because the saliva- and blood-based telomere lengths were highly correlated with one another, Mitchell and colleagues conclude there was no a priori reason to prefer one source over the other and proceeded with their analysis of telomere lengths derived from the Fragile Families data.

Our principal independent variable is an index of neighborhood disadvantage developed by Wodtke, Harding, and Elwert (2011). This measure is created from a principal component analysis of tract-level items that included rates of poverty, unemployment, female headedness, and welfare receipt, along with the percentages of persons age twenty-five and older who lacked a high school diploma, held a college degree, and occupied a managerial or professional occupation. We measured neighborhood disadvantage cumulatively from the first to the fifth wave of the survey using census tract records from the 2000 Census and the 2005–2009 American Community Survey (ACS), linking them to geocoded individual records for mothers and children. For the 2000 values and the few cases dating to 1998 or 1999, we used 2000 census estimates; for the 2007 and 2008 values, we used the ACS 2005–2009 estimates; and for years between, we interpolated.

To make sure that we were not capturing overall changes in tract values (stemming from nationwide events such as the Great Recession), we standardized all values within years across the national sample of census tracts. To incorporate the effects of moves between neighborhoods during the period of observation, we merged tract data from the census and the ACS; for individuals who changed tracts between waves, we set the midpoint between the two data collection dates as the year in which they moved. All models were estimated in Stata 14 and controlled as appropriate for indicators of demographic characteristics, educational attainment, living arrangements, and socioeconomic status.

Table 1 presents means for each independent variable by race-ethnicity for mothers at the time of the age-nine survey. The huge differential in exposure to cumulative neighborhood disadvantage between whites and blacks is immediately apparent in the first line of the table. Whereas the Wodtke index of neighborhood disadvantage stood at –0.252 for white mothers, the factor score for black mothers was 1.198. The mean age of mothers at the time of telomere collection was 33.4 years for blacks, and 36.4 years for whites, and the percentage foreign born was around 3 percent for whites and blacks. Black mothers displayed higher body mass indices (ratio of weight to height squared) than their white counterparts, with BMI Z-scores of 0.161 and –0.261 respectively. The average number of moves made before the child reached age nine differed slightly by race, with the number being 3.1 for blacks and 2.7 for whites.

As one might expect, education levels dif-

**Table 1.** Means of Variables in Analysis of Neighborhood Disadvantage and Telomere Length

| Variable | Total | Whites | Blacks |
|---|---|---|---|
| **Neighborhood disadvantage** | | | |
| Wodtke index | 0.760 | −0.252 | 1.198 |
| **Telomere length** | | | |
| Logged kilobases | 1.839 | 1.801 | 1.855 |
| **Mother's characteristics** | | | |
| Age at TL collection | 34.326 | 36.407 | 33.424 |
| Foreign born | 0.030 | 0.028 | 0.031 |
| Body mass (Z-score) | 0.034 | −0.261 | 0.161 |
| Moves during study | 2.997 | 2.679 | 3.136 |
| **Education at birth of child** | | | |
| Less than high school | 0.279 | 0.168 | 0.328 |
| High school | 0.329 | 0.249 | 0.363 |
| Some college | 0.271 | 0.281 | 0.266 |
| College or more | 0.121 | 0.302 | 0.043 |
| **Mother-father relationship at birth** | | | |
| Married | 0.238 | 0.509 | 0.120 |
| Cohabiting | 0.335 | 0.301 | 0.349 |
| Other | 0.427 | 0.189 | 0.531 |
| **Household SES at birth** | | | |
| Household poverty ratio | 2.431 | 4.060 | 1.726 |
| Household welfare | 0.379 | 0.213 | 0.450 |
| Number of cases | 1,661 | 502 | 1,159 |

*Source:* Authors' compilation of data from the Fragile Families and Child Wellbeing Survey.

fered by race. Whereas 33 percent of black respondents had less than a high school education, only 17 percent of white respondents did. Likewise, 30 percent of whites but only 4 percent of blacks were college graduates. A similar contrast was observed for the mothers' family situation at the time of the birth. Just 12 percent of black mothers were married and 35 percent were cohabiting, versus 50 percent and 31 percent of whites. In other words, nearly 80 percent of white mothers but only 47 percent of black mothers were married or cohabiting at the time of birth. As with mother's education, household income was greater for whites than for blacks. The income-to-poverty ratio was 4.1 for white and 1.7 for blacks. As one would expect given these income figures, the percentage on welfare for black mothers was double that of white mothers, with figures of 45 percent and 21 percent respectively.

## TELOMERES, SOCIOECONOMIC STATUS, AND NEIGHBORHOOD DISADVANTAGE

To set the stage for our multivariate analysis, we offer a simple description of intergroup differences in telomere length (TL), socioeconomic status, and neighborhood disadvantage. As table 1 shows, we observe clear differences in TL between whites and blacks. White mothers clearly stand out for their low values, averaging 1.801 kilobases to 1.855 for blacks, a statistically significant difference. To understand the distribution of telomere length, figure 1 plots mothers' telomere length (in logged kilobases) by race. Though they have a similar range of values, it is clear from this histogram that the distribution of telomere length is dis-

**Figure 1.** Density Distribution, Telomere Length

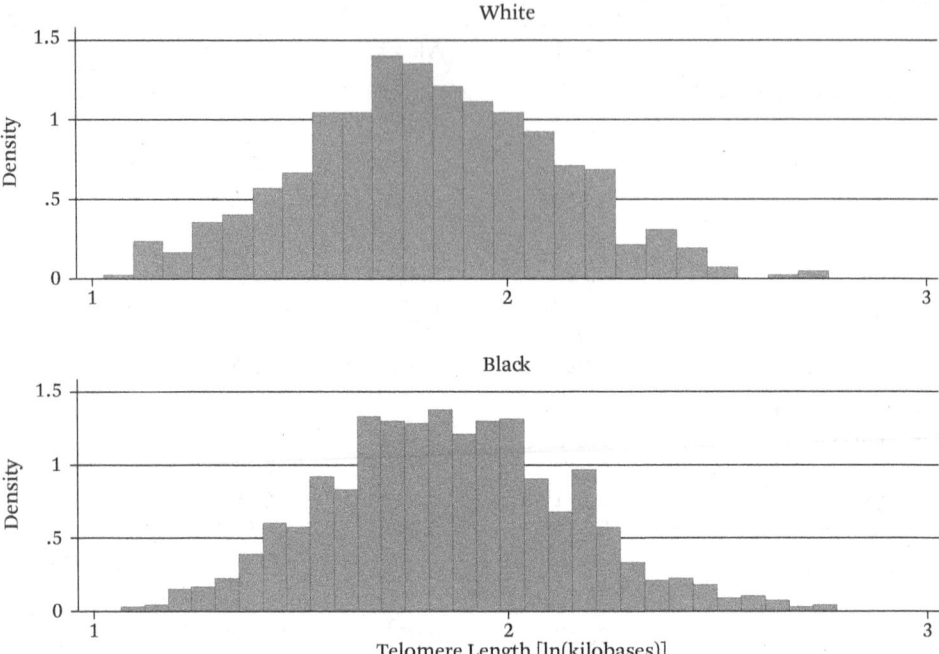

*Source:* Authors' compilation of data from the Fragile Families and Child Wellbeing Survey.

tributed more to the right for blacks relative to whites. It may seem surprising that black mothers have longer telomeres than white mothers given their greater exposure to disadvantage, but other researchers have noted similar black-white differentials over the life course (Needham et al. 2015; Brown et al. 2016; Hansen et al. 2016; Lynch et al. 2016; Drury et al. 2014; Hunt et al. 2008). Understanding the reasons for this racial differential in telomere length remains an important task for future research.

Whatever the baseline telomere length, what we are trying to test here is whether exposure to a stressor "speeds up" the rate at which telomeres attrite—that is, whether it affects the net difference between rates of telomere loss and synthesis. Thus we set aside any investigation of racial differences in baseline TL and focus simply on whether exposure to neighborhood disadvantage is indeed associated with shorter telomeres and whether the strength of this association differs between blacks and whites. Though the Fragile Families data limit us to a single measurement of telomere length and cannot sustain attributions of causality, observed point-in-time differences by neighborhood disadvantage nonetheless provide suggestive evidence of telomere attrition.

Besides neighborhood disadvantage, family deprivation might also influence telomere length and thus is important also to consider. Figure 2 calibrates the potential for intergroup differences in household income to shorten telomeres by showing the distribution of income-to-poverty ratios for respondents by race. In both cases, these ratios concentrate at values below 5.0; and as one might expect, values for blacks are skewed much more toward the low end of the scale and whites more toward the upper end. In addition, whereas black mothers display virtually no income-to-poverty ratios above 5.0, such values are frequent among white mothers. Thus, income differences are also likely to be associated with shorter TL and need to be controlled in statistical models.

However, the black-white differential in household income is not nearly as extreme as the racial differential in neighborhood income, as shown in figure 3, which presents distributions of the Wodtke neighborhood disadvantage index for white and black mothers.

**Figure 2.** Density Distribution, Income to Poverty Ratio

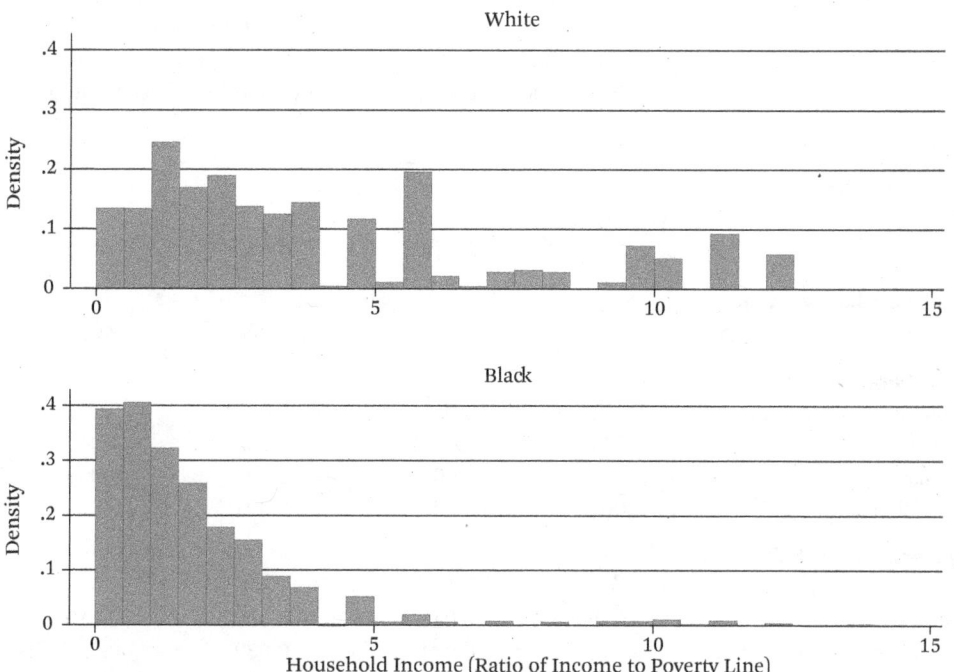

*Source:* Authors' compilation of data from the Fragile Families and Child Wellbeing Survey.

**Figure 3.** Density Distribution, Wodtke Index

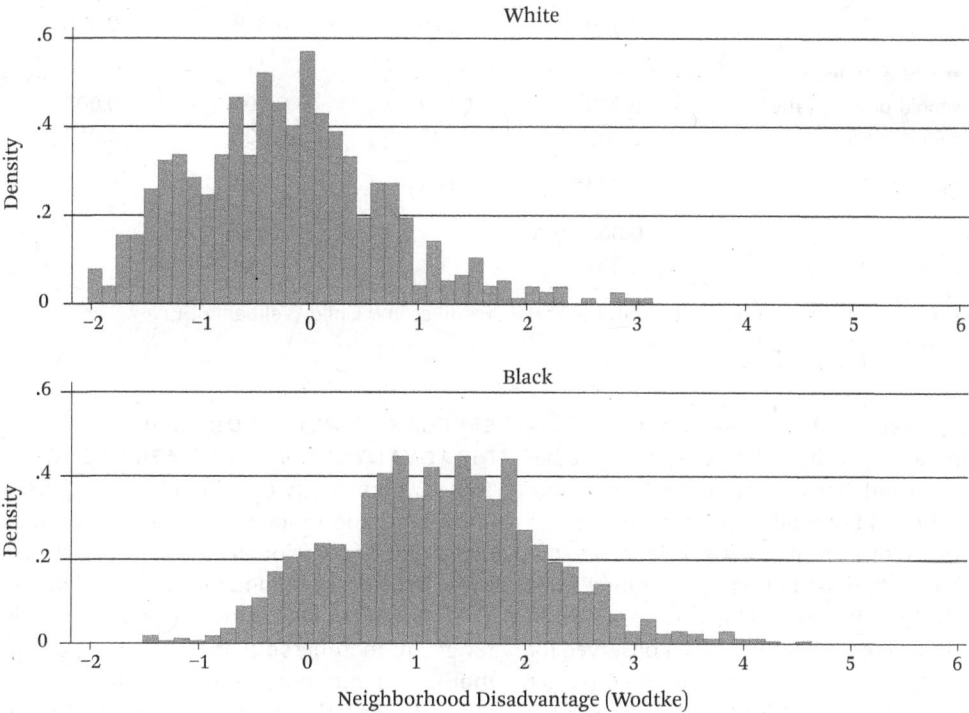

*Source:* Authors' compilation of data from the Fragile Families and Child Wellbeing Survey.

**Table 2.** OLS Regression, Effect of Neighborhood Disadvantage

| Independent Variables | Controlling for Social Background | | Controlling for Social Background and Neighborhood Disadvantage | |
|---|---|---|---|---|
| | B | SE | B | SE |
| **Mother's race-ethnicity** | | | | |
| White | — | — | — | — |
| Black | 0.052** | 0.018 | 0.074*** | 0.020 |
| **Neighborhood disadvantage** | | | | |
| Wodtke index | — | — | −0.023* | 0.009 |
| **Mother's characteristics** | | | | |
| Age at telomere collection | −0.003+ | 0.001 | −0.003+ | 0.001 |
| Foreign born | 0.041 | 0.043 | 0.032 | 0.043 |
| Body mass index | −0.001 | 0.008 | 0.004 | 0.008 |
| Moves during study | 0.000 | 0.003 | −0.001 | 0.003 |
| **Mother's education at birth** | | | | |
| Less than high school | — | — | — | — |
| High school | 0.015 | 0.019 | 0.009 | 0.019 |
| Some college | 0.043* | 0.021 | 0.032 | 0.021 |
| College or more | 0.024 | 0.034 | 0.006 | 0.035 |
| **Mother-father relationship at birth** | | | | |
| Married | — | — | — | — |
| Cohabiting | 0.028 | 0.024 | 0.031 | 0.024 |
| Other | 0.025 | 0.025 | 0.028 | 0.025 |
| **Mother's SES at birth** | | | | |
| Household poverty ratio | 0.003 | 0.004 | 0.001 | 0.004 |
| Household welfare use | −0.008 | 0.017 | −0.005 | 0.017 |
| Constant | 1.847*** | 0.061 | 1.859*** | 0.061 |
| $R^2$ | 0.008 | | 0.010 | |
| Number of cases | 1,661 | | 1,661 | |

*Source:* Authors' compilation of data from the Fragile Families and Child Wellbeing Survey.
+$p < .1$; *$p < .05$; **$p < .01$; ***$p < .001$

Whereas neighborhood disadvantage indices for the vast majority of white mothers lie between −1.0 and +1.0, indicating low to moderate levels of neighborhood disadvantage, the vast majority of black mothers display indices that are above 1.0, most falling in the range from 1.0 to 4.0 but with some values of 5.0 or greater, index values that are almost never observed for whites. Thus the racial contrast is much greater with respect to neighborhood socioeconomic status than household socioeconomic status.

## EFFECTS OF NEIGHBORHOOD DISADVANTAGE ON TELOMERE LENGTH

Table 2 presents two ordinary least squares (OLS) regression models estimated to predict the natural log of telomere length for black and white mothers in the Fragile Families dataset. The left-hand model includes dummy variables for group membership and indicators of the mother's demographics, education, relationship with the father, and socioeconomic status at the time of the child's birth. The right-hand equation contains the same independent variables with the addition of the Wodtke Index of neighborhood disadvantage. Looking at the left-hand columns we see that in the absence of a control for neighborhood disadvantage the average TL for black mothers remains significantly greater than that of white mothers ($p < .01$), consistent with the data shown in figure 1. In addition, with the notable exception of having some college education, socioeconomic status does not seem to play a significant role in determining TL among respondents, a finding that was robust across different model specifications we considered.

The right-hand equation adds in neighborhood disadvantage, which is significantly associated with shorter TL ($p < .05$). According to the estimated model, each point increase in the index of neighborhood disadvantage is associated with a decline of 0.023 logarithmic points of TL. Including neighborhood disadvantage in the model slightly increases the black-white gap in TL, though the shift is not significant. Although this model estimates a single coefficient for neighborhood disadvantage, we might anticipate that whites and blacks experience neighborhood disadvantage differently. To test this possibility, we estimated an additional model with an interaction term that allowed the effect of neighborhood disadvantage to vary between races but we did not find a significant interaction. We came to the same conclusion when we estimated the entire model separately for black and white mothers and found the coefficients for neighborhood disadvantage not to be statistically different in the black and white models.

Thus neighborhood disadvantage appears to operate similarly with regard to telomere length across the races. The Fragile Families data, however, only contain information on neighborhood disadvantage for the nine years of women's lives subsequent to the baseline interview. Our analysis thus ignores whatever neighborhood circumstances women experienced before the survey date, around two-thirds of their lifetimes. Although we do not have information on the specific tract of residence for this period, in additional models not shown we use fixed effects to account for the city of residence at the time of the baseline survey and found that findings were robust to the inclusion of these city-level controls.

## CONCLUSION AND IMPLICATIONS

Research clearly establishes that segregation and poverty interact to concentrate poverty spatially. The residential segregation of any group with a high rate of poverty inevitably concentrates poverty at high levels within neighborhoods inhabited by that group. Studies also identify telomeres (nucleotide sequences located at the ends of chromosomes) as critical buffers that protect genetic material from deterioration during cell division and that telomeres naturally shorten with age to foretell senescence. However, research also reveals that long-term exposure to high levels of stress can shorten human telomeres prematurely, potentially increasing later risks of morbidity and mortality.

In the current analysis, we hypothesized that prolonged exposure to spatially concentrated disadvantage constitutes a key source of stress for African Americans and thus may help to explain persistent racial differentials in health and life expectancy that do not disappear when socioeconomic status is controlled. To support this hypothesis we used multilevel data from the Fragile Families and Child Wellbeing Study and, using an index developed by Wodtke and colleagues (2011), we documented the distinctively high concentrations of neighborhood disadvantage experienced by African Americans relative to whites and confirmed that black inequality with respect to neighborhood disadvantage far exceeds that with respect to household income.

We went on to estimate regression models that predicted telomere length while controlling for other socioeconomic and demographic characteristics. We find the Wodtke index to be a significant predictor of telomere length among both blacks and whites. Subsequent investigations reveal no significant difference between blacks and whites in the extent to which exposure to neighborhood disadvantage was associated with shorter TL. Blacks are simply exposed to far more neighborhood disadvantage than whites, thus predicting greater shortening from their baseline TL. The difference in average neighborhood disadvantage among white and black respondents (Wodtke index = –0.252 and 1.198, respectively) implies a predicted difference in telomere length of 0.04 logarithmic points. Thus an African American respondent living in an average black neighborhood would be expected to have telomeres 0.04 logarithmic points shorter than those of an identical respondent living in an average white neighborhood. Conversely, an average white respondent living in an average white neighborhood would be expected to have telomeres 0.04 logarithmic points longer than those of an identical respondent living in an average black neighborhood. Though our results rely on cross-sectional comparisons of telomere length and cannot be taken as causal, they do provide suggestive evidence that the prolonged exposure to spatially concentrated disadvantaged experienced by African Americans is associated with greater telomere attrition.

In relying on between-person comparisons of telomere length, this study faces two major challenges future work should seek to address. First, as with all cross-sectional data analyses, correlations with omitted variables threaten between-person comparisons of telomere length. Though we included a variety of potentially relevant controls, the use of cross-sectional comparisons precludes us from asserting a causal relationship between neighborhood disadvantage and telomere length. Second, the proposed theoretical model with telomeres as a mechanism linking neighborhood disadvantage to later-life health outcomes is primarily motivated by work on the health consequences of telomere attrition (that is, change in telomere length over time). However, we are unable to measure the actual process of telomere attrition with a single time point of data available. Though differences in length could imply differences in telomere attrition, they also capture mean differences between groups. The measurement of telomeres at multiple time points is becoming more common in datasets, including future waves of the Fragile Families Study itself. As these data become available, researchers should seek to determine whether differences in exposure to neighborhood disadvantage are diachronically associated with actual telomere attrition and not just associated with cross-sectional TL disparities at a point in time.

Although our results are necessarily preliminary and await replication by other researchers using other datasets, they nonetheless add to a growing body of work demonstrating how inequality can be perpetuated through the nexus of neighborhood disadvantage, and potentially through biological as well as social mechanisms. Given the salient role of neighborhoods in perpetuating poverty over the life course and across generations, the research presented here suggests that improvements in black education and income alone may not be enough to eliminate racial differentials in health and socioeconomic status as long as residential segregation remains a characteristic structural feature of American society. Moving toward a more just and equal society requires not simply reducing discrimination in the social and economic spheres, but equalizing opportunities in the residential sphere as well. As of 2010, more than half of blacks inhabiting U.S. metropolitan areas remained highly segregated and one-third were hypersegregated (Massey and Tannen 2015). As long as such conditions continue to prevail, segregation will continue to serve as the linchpin of racial stratification in the United States (Pettigrew 1979).

## REFERENCES

Blackburn, Elizabeth H., ed. 2006. *Telomeres*. Cold Spring Harbor, N.Y.: Cold Spring Harbor Monograph Series.

Blackburn, Elizabeth H., Elissa S. Epel, and Jue Lin. 2015. "Human Telomere Biology: A Contributory and Interactive Factor in Aging, Disease Risks, and Protection." *Science* 350(6265): 1103–98.

Brown, Lauren, Belinda Needham, and Jennifer Ailshire. 2016. "Telomere Length Among Older U.S. Adults: Differences by Race/Ethnicity, Gender, and Age." *Journal of Aging and Health* (July 27): 1–7. DOI: 10.1177/089826431666139.

Cathorall, Michelle L., Huaibo Xin, Andrew Peachy, Daniel L. Bibeau, Mark Schulz, and Robert Aronson. 2015. "Neighborhood Disadvantage and Variations in Blood Pressure." *American Journal of Health Education* 46(5): 266–73.

Chetty, Raj, Nathaniel Hendren, and Lawrence F. Katz. 2016. "The Effects of Exposure to Better Neighborhoods on Children: New Evidence from the Moving to Opportunity Experiment." *American Economic Review* 106(4): 855-902.

D'Mello, Matthew J. J., Stephanie A. Ross, Matthias Briel, Sonia S. Anand, Hertzel Gerstein, and Guillaume Pare. 2014. "The Association Between Shortened Leukocyte Telomere Length and Cardio-Metabolic Outcomes: A Systematic Review and Meta-Analysis." *Cardiovascular Genetics* (November 18). DOI: 10.1161/CIRCGENETICS.113.000485.

DiPrete, Thomas A., and Gregory A. Eirich. 2006. "Cumulative Advantage as a Mechanism for Inequality: A Review of Theoretical and Empirical Developments." *Annual Review of Sociology* 32(1): 271-97.

Drury, Stacy S., Emily Mabile, Zoë H. Brett, Kyle Esteves, Edward Jones, Elizabeth A. Shirtcliff, and Katherine P. Theall. 2014. "The Association of Telomere Length with Family Violence and Disruption." *Pediatrics* 134(1): e128-37.

Epel, Elissa S., Elizabeth H. Blackburn, Jue Lin, Firdaus S. Dhabhar, Nancy E. Adler, Jason D. Morrow, and Richard M. Cawthon. 2004. "Accelerated Telomere Shortening in Response to Life Stress." *Proceedings of the National Academy of Sciences* 101(49): 17312-15.

Finch, Brian K., D. Phuong Do, Melonie Heron, Chloe Bird, Teresa Seeman, and Nicole Lurie. 2010. "Neighborhood Effects on Health: Concentrated Advantage and Disadvantage." *Health and Place* 16(5): 1058-60.

Fitzpatrick, Annette L., Richard A. Kronmal, Masayuki Kimura, Jeffrey P. Gardner, Bruce M. Psaty, Nancy S. Jenny, Russell P. Tracy, Sheetal Hardikar, and Abraham Aviv. 2011. "Leukocyte Telomere Length and Mortality in the Cardiovascular Health Study." *Journals of Gerontology: Series A* 66A(4): 421-29.

Geronimus, Arline T. 1992. "The Weathering Hypothesis and the Health of African American Women and Infants." *Ethnicity and Disease* 2(3): 207-21.

Geronimus, Arline T., Margaret Hicken, Danya Keene, and John Bound. 2006. "'Weathering' and Age Patterns of Allostatic Load Scores Among Blacks and Whites in the United States." *American Journal of Public Health* 96(5): 826-33.

Geronimus, Arline T., Jay A. Pearson, Erin Linnenbringer, Amy J. Schulz, Angela G. Reyes, Elissa S. Epel, Jue Lin, and Elizabeth H. Blackburn. 2015. "Race-Ethnicity, Poverty, Urban Stressors, and Telomere Length in a Detroit Community-Based Sample." *Journal of Health and Social Behavior* (April 30). DOI: 10.1177/0022146515582100.

Geruso, Michael. 2012. "Black-White Disparities in Life Expectancy: How Much Can the Standard SES Variables Explain?" *Demography* 49(2): 553-74.

Glei, Dana A., Noreen Goldman, Rosa Ana Risques, David H. Rehkopf, William H. Dow, Luis Rosero-Bixby, and Maxine Weinstein. 2016. "Predicting Survival from Telomere Length Versus Conventional Predictors: A Multinational Population-Based Cohort Study." *PloS One* 11(4): e0152486.

Goglin, Sarah E., Ramin Farzaneh-Far, Elissa S. Epel, Jue Lin, Elizabeth H. Blackburn, and Mary A. Whooley. 2016. "Change in Leukocyte Telomere Length Predicts Mortality in Patients with Stable Coronary Heart Disease from the Heart and Soul Study." *PLoS One* 11(12): e0168868.

Gustafsson, Per E., Miguel San Sebastian, Urban Janlert, Töres Theorell, Hugo Westerlund, and Anne Hammarström. 2014. "Life-Course Accumulation of Neighborhood Disadvantage and Allostatic Load: Empirical Integration of Three Social Determinants of Health Frameworks." *American Journal of Public Health* 104(5): 904-10.

Hackman, Daniel A., Laura M. Betancourt, Nancy L. Brodsky, Hallam Hurt, and Martha J. Farah. 2012. "Neighborhood Disadvantage and Stress Reactivity." *Frontiers in Human Neuroscience* 6(277): 1-11.

Hanson, Matthew E. B., Steven C. Hunt, Rivka C. Stone, Kent Horvath, Utz Herbig, Alessia Ranciaro, Jibril Hirbo, William Beggs, Alexander P. Reiner, James G. Wilson, Masayuki Kimura, Immaculata De Vivo, Maxine M. Chen, Jeremy D. Kark, Daniel Levy, Thomas Nyambo, Sarah A. Tishkoff, and Abraham Aviv. 2016. "Shorter Telomere Length in Europeans Than in Africans Due to Polygenetic Adaptation." *Human Molecular Genetics* 25(11): 2324-30.

Harris, Sarah E., Riccardo E. Marioni, Carmen Martin-Ruiz, Alison Pattie, Alan J. Gow, Simon R. Cox, Janie Corley, Thomas von Zglinicki, John M. Starr, and Ian J. Deary. 2016. "Longitudinal Telomere Length Shortening and Cognitive and Physical Decline in Later Life: The Lothian Birth Cohorts 1936 and 1921." *Mechanisms of Ageing and Development* 154 (March): 43-48.

Haycock, Philip C., Emma E. Heydon, Stephen Kaptoge, Adam S. Butterworth, Alex Thompson, and Peter Willeit. 2014. "Leucocyte Telomere Length and Risk of Cardiovascular Disease: Systematic Review and Meta-Analysis." *British Medical Journal* 349 (July 8): g4227.

Hunt, Steven C., Wei Chen, Jeffrey P. Gardner, Masayuki Kimura, Sathanur R. Srinivasan, John H. Eckfeldt, Gerald S. Berenson, and Abraham Aviv. 2008. "Leukocyte Telomeres Are Longer in African Americans Than in Whites: The National Heart, Lung, and Blood Institute Family Heart Study and the Bogalusa Heart Study." *Aging Cell* 7(4): 451–58.

Jargowsky, Paul A. 1997. *Poverty and Place: Ghettos, Barrios, and the American City*. New York: Russell Sage Foundation.

Karb, Rebecca A., Michael R. Elliott, Jennifer B. Dowd, and Jeffrey D. Morenoff. 2012. "Neighborhood-Level Stressors, Social Support, and Diurnal Patterns of Cortisol: The Chicago Community Adult Health Study." *Social Science and Medicine* 75(6): 1038–47.

King, Katherine, Jennifer Buher Kane, Peter Scarbrough, Cathrine Hoyo, and Susan Murphy. 2016. "Neighborhood and Family Environment of Expectant Mothers May Influence Prenatal Programming of Adult Cancer Risk: Discussion and an Illustrative Biomarker Example." *Biodemography and Social Biology* 62(1): 87–104.

Kipling, David. 1995. *The Telomere*. New York: Oxford University Press.

Kitagawa, Evelyn M., and Phillip M. Hauser. 1973. *Differential Mortality in the United States: A Study in Socioeconomic Epidemiology*. Cambridge, Mass.: Harvard University Press.

Kling, Jeffrey R., Jeffrey B. Liebman, and Lawrence F. Katz. 2007. "Experimental Analysis of Neighborhood Effects." *Econometrica* 75(1): 83–119.

Ludwig, Jens. 2012. "Guest Editor's Introduction: Special Issue on MTO." *Cityscape* 14(2): 1–28.

Ludwig, Jens, Lisa Sanbonmatsu, Lisa Gennetian, Emma Adam, Greg J. Duncan, Lawrence F. Katz, Ronald C. Kessler, Jeffrey R. Kling, Stacy Tessler Lindau, Robert C. Whitaker, and Thomas W. McDade. 2011. "Neighborhoods, Obesity and Diabetes: A Randomized Social Experiment." *New England Journal of Medicine* 365(16): 1509–19.

Lynch, Shannon M., M. K. Peek, Nandita Mitra, Krithika Ravichandran, Charles Branas, Elaine Spangler, Wenting Zhou, Electra D. Paskett, Sarah Gehlert, Cecilia DeGraffinreid, Timothy R. Rebbeck, and Harold Riethman. 2016. "Race, Ethnicity, Psychosocial Factors, and Telomere Length in a Multicenter Setting." *PLoS One* 11(1): e0146723. DOI:10.1371/journal.pone.01146723.

Marioni, Riccardo E., Sarah E. Harris, Sonia Shah, Allan F. McRae, Thomas von Zglinicki, Carmen Martin-Ruiz, Naomi R. Wray, Peter M. Visscher, and Ian J. Deary. 2016. "The Epigenetic Clock and Telomere Length are Independently Associated with Chronological Age and Mortality." *International Journal of Epidemiology* 45(2): 424–34.

Martinez-Ruiz, Carmen M., Jacobijn Gussekloo, Diana van Heemst, Thomas von Zglinicki, and Rudi G. J. Westendorp. 2005. "Telomere Length in White Blood Cells Is Not Associated with Morbidity or Mortality in the Oldest-Old: A Population-Based Study." *Aging Cell* 4(6): 287–90.

Massey, Douglas S. 1990. "American Apartheid: Segregation and the Making of the Underclass." *American Journal of Sociology* 95(2): 1153–88.

———. 2013. "Inheritance of Poverty or Inheritance of Place? The Emerging Consensus on Neighborhoods and Stratification." *Contemporary Sociology* 42(5): 690–97.

Massey, Douglas S., Len Albright, Rebecca Casciano, Elizabeth Derickson, and David Kinsey. 2013. *Climbing Mount Laurel: The Struggle for Affordable Housing and Social Mobility in an American Suburb*. Princeton, N.J.: Princeton University Press.

Massey, Douglas S., and Susan Clampet-Lundquist. 2008. "Neighborhood Effects on Economic Self-Sufficiency: A Reconsideration of the Moving to Opportunity Experiment." *American Journal of Sociology* 114(1): 107–43.

Massey, Douglas S., and Mitchell E. Eggers. 1992. "A Longitudinal Analysis of Urban Poverty: Blacks in U.S. Metropolitan Areas Between 1970 and 1980." *Social Science Research* 21(2): 175–203.

Massey, Douglas S., and Mary J. Fischer. 2000. "How Segregation Concentrates Poverty." *Ethnic and Racial Studies* 23(4): 670–91.

Massey, Douglas S., and Jacob S. Rugh. forthcoming. "Zoning, Affordable Housing, and Segregation in U.S. Metropolitan Areas." In *The Fight for Fair Housing: Causes, Consequences and Future Implications of the 1968 Federal Fair Housing Act*, edited by Gregory Squires. New York: Taylor and Francis.

Massey, Douglas S., and Jonathan Tannen. 2015. "A Research Note on Trends in Black Hypersegregation." *Demography* 52(3): 1025–34.

Mathur, Maya B., Elissa Epel, Shelley Kind, Manisha Desai, Christine G. Parks, Dale P. Sandler, Nayer Khazeni. 2016. "Perceived Stress and Telomere Length: A Systematic Review, Meta-Analysis, and Methodologic Considerations for Advancing the Field." *Brain, Behavior, and Immunity* 54 (May): 158-69.

Mitchell, Colter, John Hobcraft, Sara S. McLanahan, Susan Rutherford Siegel, Arthur Berg, Jeanne Brooks-Gunne, Irwin Garfinkel, and Daniel Notterman. 2014. "Social Disadvantage, Genetic Sensitivity, and Children's Telomere Length." *Proceedings of the National Academy of Sciences* 111(16): 5944-49.

Needham, Belinda L., David Rehkopf, Nancy Adler, Steven Gregorich, Jue Lin, Elizabeth H. Blackburn, and Elissa S. Epel. 2015. "Leukocyte Telomere Length and Mortality in the National Health and Nutrition Examination Survey, 1999-2002." *Epidemiology* 26(4): 528-35.

Orr, Larry, Judith D. Feins, Robin Jacob, Erik Beecroft, Lisa Sanbonmatsu, Lawrence F. Katz, Jeffrey B. Liebman, and Jeffrey R. Kling. 2003. *Moving to Opportunity: Interim Impacts Evaluation*. Washington: U.S. Department of Housing and Urban Development.

Park, Minjung, Josine E. Verhoeven, Pim Cuijpers, Charles F. Reynolds III, Brenda W. J. H. Penninx. 2015. "Where You Live May Make You Old: The Association Between Perceived Poor Neighborhood Quality and Leukocyte Telomere Length." *PLoS One* 10(6): e0128460. DOI:10.1371/journal.pone.0128460.

Pettigrew, Thomas. 1979. "Racial Change and Social Policy." *Annals of the American Academy of Political and Social Science* 441(1): 114-31.

Quillian, Lincoln. 2012. "Segregation and Poverty Concentration: The Role of Three Segregations." *American Sociological Review* 77(3): 354-79.

Rothwell, Jonathan, and Douglas S. Massey. 2014. "Geographic Effects on Intergenerational Income Mobility." *Economic Geography* 91(1): 83-106.

Rubinowitz, Leonard S., and James E. Rosenbaum. 2000. *Crossing the Class and Color Lines: From Public Housing to White Suburbia*. Chicago: University of Chicago Press.

Rudolph, Kara E., Wand Gary S., Elizabeth A. Stuart, Thomas A. Glass, Andrea H. Marques, Roman Duncko, and Kathleen R. Merikangas. 2014. "The Association Between Cortisol and Neighborhood Disadvantage in a U.S. Population-Based Sample of Adolescents." *Health and Place* 25(1): 68-77.

Sampson, Robert J. 2012. *Great American City: Chicago and the Enduring Neighborhood Effect*. Chicago: University of Chicago Press.

Sampson, Robert J., Jeffrey Morenoff and T. Gannon-Rowley. 2002. "Assessing Neighborhood Effects: Social Processes and New Directions in Research." *Annual Review of Sociology* 28(1): 443-78.

Sanbonmatsu, Lisa, Jens Ludwig, Lawrence F. Katz, Lisa A. Gennetian, Greg J. Duncan, Ronald C. Kessler, Emma Adam, Thomas W. McDade, Stacy Tessler Lindau, Matthew Sciandra Fanghua Yang, Ijun Lai, William Congdon, Joe Amick, Ryan Gillette, Michael A. Zabek, Jordan Marvakov, Sabrina Yusuf, and Nicholas A. Potter. 2011. *Moving to Opportunity for Fair Housing Demonstration Program: Final Impacts Evaluation*. Washington: U.S. Department of Housing and Urban Development.

Sanders, Jason L., and Anne B. Newman. 2013. "Telomere Length in Epidemiology: A Biomarker of Aging, Age-Related Disease, Both, or Neither?" *Epidemiological Reviews* 35(1): 112-31.

Sapolsky, Robert M. 2004. "Organismal Stress and Telomeric Aging: An Unexpected Connection." *Proceedings of the National Academy of Sciences* 101(50): 17323-24.

Schutte, Nicola S., and John M. Malouff. 2014. "The Relationship Between Perceived Stress and Telomere Length: A Meta-Analysis." *Stress and Health* 32(4): 313-19.

Shalev, Idan, Terrie E. Moffitt, Karen Sugden, Brittany Williams, Renate M. Houts, Andrea Danese, Jonathan Mill, Louise Aresneault, and Avshalom Caspi. 2013. "Exposure to Violence During Childhood Is Associated with Telomere Erosion from 5 to 10 Years of Age: A Longitudinal Study." *Molecular Psychiatry* 18(5): 576-681.

Sharkey, Patrick. 2013. *Stuck in Place: Urban Neighborhoods and the End of Progress toward Racial Equality*. Chicago: University of Chicago Press.

Theall, Katherine P., Zoë H. Brett, Elizabeth A. Shirtcliff, Erin C. Dunn, and Stacy S. Drury. 2013. Neighborhood Disorder and Telomeres: Connecting Children's Exposure to Community Level Stress and Cellular Response." *Social Science and Medicine* 85(1): 50-58.

Walsemann, Katrina M., Gilbert C. Gee, and Arline Geronimus. 2009. "Ethnic Differences in Trajectories of Depressive Symptoms." *Journal of Health and Social Behavior* 50(1): 82–98.

Wilhide, Eli. 2014. *Understanding Telomeres: The Science of Aging Well*. Seattle, Wash.: Amazon Digital Services.

Willeit, Peter, Johann Willeit, and Agnes Mayr. 2010. "Telomere Length and Risk of Incident Cancer and Cancer Mortality." *Journal of the American Medical Association* 304(1): 69–75.

Wilson, William J. 1987. *The Truly Disadvantaged: The Inner City, the Underclass, and Public Policy*. Chicago: University of Chicago Press.

Wodtke, Geoffrey T., David J. Harding, and Felix Elwert. 2011. "Neighborhood Effects in Temporal Perspective: The Impact of Long-Term Exposure to Concentrated Disadvantage on High School Graduation." *American Sociological Review* 76(5): 713–36.

——. 2016. "Neighborhood Effect Heterogeneity by Family Income and Developmental Period." *American Journal of Sociology* 121(4): 1168–222.

Yu, Ruby, Nelson Tang, Jason Leung, and Jean Woo. 2015. "Telomere Length Is Not Associated with Frailty in Older Chinese Elderly: Cross-Sectional and Longitudinal Analysis." *Mechanisms of Ageing and Development* 152 (December): 74–79.

# Perceived Discrimination and Adolescent Sleep in a Community Sample

BRIDGET J. GOOSBY, JACOB E. CHEADLE, WHITNEY STRONG-BAK, TAYLOR C. ROTH, AND TIMOTHY D. NELSON

*Sleep is a key restorative process, and poor sleep is linked to disease and mortality risk. The adolescent population requires more sleep on average than adults but are most likely to be sleep deprived. Adolescence is a time of rapid social upheaval and sensitivity to social stressors including discrimination. This study uses two weeks of daily e-diary measures documenting discrimination exposure and concurrent objective sleep indicators measured using actigraphy. We assess associations between daily discrimination and contemporaneous sleep with a diverse sample of adolescents. This novel study shows youth with higher average discrimination reports have worse average sleep relative to their counterparts. Interestingly, youth reporting daily discrimination have better sleep the day of the report than youth who do not.*

**Keywords:** sleep, adolescence, discrimination, actigraphy

Sleep is an important restorative process instrumental in regulating physiologic systems, cognition, and behavioral outcomes (Balbo, Leproult, and Van Cauter 2010; Kliewer and Lepore 2014). Sleep quality and duration are associated with an array of morbidities including metabolic conditions, cardiovascular disease, and major depression (Irwin 2015). Because adolescents are a population vulnerable to poor sleep during a key developmental period of significant physiological and environmental change, they are an important group to systematically assess with regard to sleep patterns and social conditions linked to chronic

---

**Bridget J. Goosby** and **Jacob E. Cheadle** are Happold Associate Professors of Sociology and co-directors of the LifeHD: *Life in Frequencies Health Disparities* Research Lab at the University of Nebraska–Lincoln. **Whitney Strong-Bak** is a doctoral candidate and graduate research assistant in the School Psychology Program. **Taylor C. Roth** is a doctoral student and graduate research assistant in the department of psychology at the University of Nebraska–Lincoln. **Timothy D. Nelson** is associate professor of psychology and director of the Pediatric Health Lab at the University of Nebraska–Lincoln.

© 2018 Russell Sage Foundation. Goosby, Bridget J., Jacob E. Cheadle, Whitney Strong-Bak, Taylor C. Roth, and Timothy D. Nelson. 2018. "Perceived Discrimination and Adolescent Sleep in a Community Sample." *RSF: The Russell Sage Foundation Journal of the Social Sciences* 4(4): 43–61. DOI: 10.7758/RSF.2018.4.4.03. This research was supported by grant K01 HD 064537 from the Eunice Kennedy Shriver Institute of Child Health and Human Development (Bridget Goosby, PI) and by the University of Nebraska Social Sciences and Behavioral Research Consortium (SBSRC). We appreciate the helpful comments from Thomas McDade and Kathleen Mullan Harris. Direct correspondence to: Bridget J. Goosby at bgoosby2@unl.edu, University of Nebraska–Lincoln, Department of Sociology, 741 Oldfather Hall, Lincoln, NE 68588; Jacob E. Cheadle at jcheadle2@unl.edu, University of Nebraska–Lincoln, Department of Sociology, 732 Oldfather Hall, Lincoln, NE 68588; Whitney Strong-Bak at whitney.strong@huskers.unl.edu, Munroe-Meyer Institute, 985450 Nebraska Medical Center, Omaha, NE 68198; Taylor C. Roth at taylor.roth@huskers.unl.edu, University of Nebraska–Lincoln, Department of Psychology, 238 Burnett Hall, Lincoln, NE 68588; and Timothy D. Nelson at tnelson3@unl.edu, University of Nebraska–Lincoln, Department of Psychology, 319 Burnet Hall, Lincoln, NE 68588.

Open Access Policy: *RSF: The Russell Sage Foundation Journal of the Social Sciences* is an open access journal. This article is published under a Creative Commons Attribution-NonCommercial-NoDerivs 3.0 Unported License.

disease risk (Becker, Langberg, and Byars 2015; Park et al. 2016). A growing literature indicates that sleep may function as a key mechanistic pathway through which exposure to social stressors such as discrimination or other social exclusionary experiences decrease health (Lewis et al. 2013; Hicken et al. 2013). This research, however, primarily focuses on adult populations with inferences based mostly on self-reported rather than objective sleep measures. This study fills the gap in existing sleep research by examining adolescents, a key at-risk group for poor sleep and stressful social dynamics, using a lengthy window of objective actigraphy-based sleep measures.

Adolescence is a critical time to study the impact of social stressors on sleep because they are more likely, on average, to report difficulty falling asleep, staying asleep, and to be chronically sleep deprived (Yip 2014; Carskadon 1990). For adolescents, sleep is instrumental in the ability to regulate negative emotions and coping with stressful conditions (Dahl 1999; El-Sheikh et al. 2010). Although frequency of day-to-day discrimination exposure as well as accumulated discrimination has been linked to poorer mental and physical health outcomes, less is known about the role of discrimination for sleep patterns among adolescents (Schmitt et al. 2014; Goosby et al. 2015; Torres and Ong 2010). To address these gaps, this study uses novel pilot data from a diverse sample of adolescents combining survey data, daily electronic-diaries (e-diaries), and actigraphy-based sleep measures to address the following questions (Eufemia et al. 2012): In early to mid-adolescence, do experiences of discrimination or unfair treatment affect sleep (both quantity and quality) consistently over time? Do daily fluctuations in such experiences influence nightly sleep variability?

## LITERATURE REVIEW
Public health concern is growing over sleep quality and duration, also known as sleep health, in the United States. Nearly 25 percent of the U.S. population report insomnia complaints and 10 percent meet clinical criteria for insomnia (see Irwin 2015). Due to the importance of sleep for numerous health and behavioral outcomes, interest in studying sleep quality and duration is considerable (Kingsbury, Buxton, and Emmons 2013; Gregory and Sadeh 2012; Irwin 2015). Moreover, increasing evidence suggests that sleep characteristics differ across populations and are linked to social and environmental conditions.

Sleep patterns appear to vary by sociodemographic factors that include age, socioeconomic conditions, race and ethnicity, and education (Hale, Emanuele, and James 2015). Adolescents, for example, as a group require more sleep on average (approximately nine hours) but are less likely to actually get adequate sleep than adults (Becker, Langberg, and Byars 2015). People living in economically disadvantaged and segregated neighborhoods also have poorer sleep quality, in part due to the excess noise and crowding found frequently in such environments (Hale, Emanuele, and James 2015; Massey 2004). Race differences are also documented, particularly among African Americans relative to whites; African Americans are a population at higher risk for living in or near economically disadvantaged neighborhoods and at higher risk for disruptive chronic stressors (Williams 2012). Consequently, this population commonly shows signs of harmful sleep patterns by sleeping both shorter and longer durations than the recommended average and accompanied by poorer sleep quality that is less restorative (Kingsbury, Buxton, and Emmons 2013; Mezick et al. 2008; Profant, Ancoli-Israel, and Dimsdale 2002).

Yet much of the literature has used subjective sleep reports rather than objective measures of sleep, and that subjective reports have relatively low reliability relative to more objective measures is well documented (Short et al. 2012, 2013). Respondents asked retrospectively about their sleep duration, for example, are more likely to overestimate duration and underestimate number of awakenings during the night; adolescents in particular may tend to only report more salient, recent information (Wolfson et al. 2003). Daily diaries are another self-report approach to measuring sleep that has the advantage of capturing day-to-day variation usually over an extended period to characterize sleep. Use of temporally proximal data on sleep habits across a range of days is more strongly correlated with laboratory-based gold standard measures of sleep quality than one-shot, long-term subjective self-reports (Wolfson et al. 2003). Among self-report measures, sleep diaries appear to provide the most reliable sleep measures, particularly among adolescents (Short et al. 2013). Sleep diaries, however, tend to overestimate total objective sleep time and underestimate awakening frequency during the night because individuals may not always be aware of waking during the night or other factors that may make sleep more or less restful (Short et al. 2012; Wolfson et al. 2003).

Although self-reported measures of sleep can provide meaningful information and in some cases be correlated with objective sleep measures, they are not as reliable in accurately measuring total sleep duration, waking after sleep onset, or activity during sleep. In nonlaboratory settings, the current state-of-the-art method for objectively measuring sleep dimensions is actigraphy (Short et al. 2012). Actigraphy uses accelerometers placed on the wrist to document sleeping and waking states (Marino et al. 2013). Though actigraphy cannot measure specific sleep architecture or sleep staging, it has been validated to accurately measure distinctions between sleeping and waking along with total sleep time (TST) in both sleep disordered and general populations (Ancoli-Israel et al. 2003). Actigraphs are particularly useful for nonlaboratory studies because they can be worn for extended periods for tracking sleep patterns, which cannot be feasibly measured in sleep labs. Despite the convenience of actigraphy for measuring sleep in the field, use of it is not yet as common in studies of adolescence. We broadly characterize adolescents' sleep using a rich set of actigraphy measures taken nightly over a two-week period, emphasizing a key exclusionary social experience, discrimination, and relationships to different features of sleep.

## Discrimination and Sleep

The need for social bonding and connection is among the most basic of all human needs (Baumeister and Leary 1995), and our health suffers when our needs for social connection are not satisfied (Cacioppo and Patrick 2009). Social exclusion has widespread implications for health, health behaviors generally, and sleep specifically (Hawkley et al. 2003; Duclos, Wan, and Jiang 2014; on sleep, Pereira, Meier, and Elfering 2013; Sladek and Doane 2014). A key dimension of social exclusion is the perception of discrimination or unfair, prejudicial, and exclusionary treatment based on certain characteristics or stigmatized identities such as race, obesity, gender, and sexuality (among others). Specifically, discrimination has been linked to a variety of health outcomes including poorer self-rated health (Krieger et al. 2011), high blood pressure (Lewis et al. 2009), vascular resistance (Guyll, Matthews, and Bromberger 2001), adiposity (Lewis et al. 2011), increased inflammation (Lewis et al. 2010), and higher allostatic load (Brody et al. 2014). As early as adolescence, discrimination is linked to worse self-rated health (Priest et al. 2013), depressive symptoms (Hope, Hoggard, and Thomas 2015), anger (Wong, Eccles, and Sameroff 2003), as well as elevated systolic and diastolic blood pressure, and higher C-reactive protein (CRP) (Goosby et al. 2015). Although less is known about the links between discrimination and sleep quality than some other stressors, research suggests that even the anticipation and rumination on social exclusion can decrease sleep quality (Hicken et al. 2013; Åkerstedt 2006; Åkerstedt, Kecklund, and Axelsson 2007).

In findings from sleep lab clinical studies, discrimination exposure predicts less time in restorative sleep stages and greater daytime fatigue in adults (Thomas et al. 2006). In nonclinical, larger scale surveys, differences in subjective sleep quality and wakefulness after falling asleep among African Americans relative to whites are attenuated (though not eliminated) by reports of chronic discrimination (Lewis et al. 2013) and racism-related vigilance (Hicken et al. 2013). Although the evidence from adults points to a key role for perceived discrimination in reducing sleep quality, less is known about links between discrimination and adolescent sleep. Limited available evidence suggests that the same pattern for adults may also hold for youth; adolescents who retrospectively report experiencing higher levels of discrimination over the past year reported lower sleep quality and quantity in their daily sleep diary reports (Yip 2014).

Discrimination exposure and sleep are dy-

**Figure 1.** CCFW Study Design and Discrimination Measures

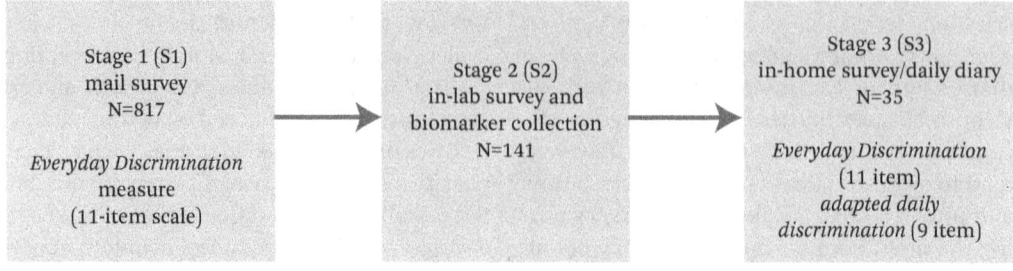

*Source:* Authors' compilation.

namic processes, but most studies in this area have so far relied heavily on retrospective measures of both discrimination and self-reported sleep quality. Despite the cross-sectional nature of these studies, the links between discrimination and sleep, as well as for other health outcomes, are robust. In a study of Latino youth, researchers Lucas Torres and Anthony Ong use daily diary information documenting both discrimination events and depressive symptoms found a day lag among youth who reported discrimination for subsequent elevated depressive symptoms (2010). Both this study and Tiffany Yip's of 2014 suggest that the accumulation of chronic discrimination may have long-term implications for subsequent sleep; however, neither study examined daily discrimination experiences and sleep contemporaneously, thus leaving an open question regarding whether discrimination can have more immediate consequences for youth sleep patterns.

Our study aims to address these gaps in the literature by first assessing the temporal relationship between daily experiences of discrimination and subsequent objective dimensions of sleep among a sample of adolescents. We explore sleep both as average sleep trends over a two-week period and as day-to-day fluctuations in sleep. Our first hypothesis (H1) posits that the accumulation of discriminatory experiences is related to poorer average sleep. Our second hypothesis (H2) states that adolescent sleep will be poorer on days that adolescents perceive they have been discriminated against.

### DATA AND METHODS

Data in this study come from the Community Connections and Family Wellness Study, which was designed to assess the intergenerational health and well-being of parent-child dyads and was originally conceived of as a two-part pilot study comprising a mail survey screening for an in-lab component to develop and assess recruitment protocols for a larger social neuroscience project (Falk et al. 2013). Sampling and data collection methods included three stages ranging over two years. Figure 1 outlines the stages (S1–S3) of data collection for this multistage sample. In stage 1, in collaboration with a local school system in a mid-sized Midwestern city, we contacted a subset of 2,181 (1,000 white, 1,181 African American or biracial) middle- and high school students ages eleven through fourteen in the school district during the fall of 2014. Two survey packets, one for the parent or guardian and another for the student, were mailed to each family in summer 2014 with a $2 incentive for each. A total of 817 parent-guardian and child dyads completed the mail surveys in stage 1.

The stage 2 data collection took place from December 2014 to June 2015 with a subset of 141 parent-child pairs from stage 1 who expressed interest in participating in future studies. These participants were invited to visit a laboratory space on a local college campus where anthropometrics, biospecimens, experimental, and additional survey data were collected. Participants in this phase of the study were restricted to families of white, African American, and biracial youth with one African American parent. A $20 incentive was given to each participant along with meal vouchers for participants who were interested in visiting campus (based on responses to an incentive question during stage 1). The overall response rate for participation in the stage 2 portion of the study was 32.4 percent.

Approximately a year later, a subset of forty parent-youth dyads from the in-lab participant pool were recruited for a third stage (stage 3) in-home data collection between February and May 2016. At the initial home visit, after parental consent and child assent, the parent and child independently completed baseline survey measures of health, daily experiences, diet, sleep behavior, and anthropometric measurements. Participants were then trained to use ActiGraph Black/wActiSleep BT and Red/wGTX-BT wristbands and the daily online e-diary procedure (Eufemia et al. 2012). Both the parent and youth were sent an email nightly with a link to their e-diary, which was formatted for use on either a computer or smart device. Both the parent and youth were asked to wear the actigraph wristband all day and night for fourteen consecutive days to measure sleep activity. At the end of the period, parents and youth returned the actigraph wristbands and, to facilitate recruitment and retention of participants, were compensated with cash (up to $200 for the family based on adherence to the study protocol). High rates of protocol adherence (approximately 90 percent) were obtained with both e-diary and actigraph protocols.

Of the 113 families contacted for participation, fifty-eight could not be reached or did not return messages, and thirteen refused, had moved, or were otherwise ineligible. Based on the race of the child, twenty-one of the families were white, four were African American, and fifteen were biracial (one biological African American parent). However, because of missing sleep and biological data, only thirty-five families were used in these analyses. The distribution across race groups in the current analytic sample was twenty-one white, four African American, and ten biracial adolescents. Of these, sixteen were male and nineteen were female. For this study, African American and biracial youth were combined into one category because of the small sample sizes.

## MEASURES

Sleep measures are derived from the mathematical decomposition of accelerometer data recorded continuously on the actigraph wristbands. The devices were configured to collect data at 60hz with the idle sleep mode enabled. The actigraphy measures were calculated using the ActiLife 6 software package (ActiGraph 2012). The actigraph data were segmented into sixty-second epochs and wear time validation was assessed using Troiano's algorithm (Troiano et al. 2008). Sleep analyses then utilized Sadeh's algorithms and were manually adjusted using bed and wake time information collected in the nightly e-diary (Sadeh 2011; Sadeh, Sharkey, and Carskadon 1994).

We present a diverse number of sleep measures, including multiple measures of both sleep duration and quality, in this study. Descriptions are presented in table 1 for reference. Example data are presented in figure 2 for illustrative purposes. The lightly shaded sleep period denotes the time in bed and the darker shaded period denotes the time asleep. The top chart in figure 2 shows a highly efficient night of sleep with only short interruptions as indicated by physical movement. The second chart shows much less efficient and poorer sleep with longer periods of disrupted wakefulness and delayed sleep onset. In addition to the actigraphy data, the bottom row of table 1 describes a sleep factor score that was constructed after conducting exploratory factor analysis of the following sleep quality items: sleep efficiency, waking after sleep onset (WASO), average awakening length, movement index, and sleep fragmentation. The scale was then validated using a confirmatory factor analysis to provide an overall *sleep quality* measure. All sleep measures in the statistical analysis were standardized over the entire sleep distribution to facilitate effect size comparisons.

## Discrimination

The key predictor of sleep in this study, measures of discrimination, are operationalized three ways. First, the Williams Everyday Discrimination Scale (EDiS) adapted for adolescents was collected during the initial stage 3 home visit before the actigraphy sleep data was collected (Williams et al. 1997). The EDiS comprised eleven ordinal items categorized from never (0) to almost every day (5). Items were prefaced with the question "In your day-to-day life, how often do you experience the follow-

**Table 1.** Description of Sleep Measures

| Measure | Description |
| --- | --- |
| Latency | Sleep latency is the time it takes to fall asleep, as measured by the difference between bedtime and the onset of sleep (measured in minutes). |
| Efficiency | Sleep efficiency is the number of minutes scored as being asleep divided by the total number of minutes in bed. 85% sleep efficiency is typically considered normal sleep efficiency, so higher values indicated better sleep for the amount of time spent in bed. |
| Total minutes | Total minutes spent in bed. |
| Total sleep time | Total sleep time is the number of minutes scored as being asleep. |
| WASO | Wake after sleep onset (WASO) is the total number of minutes awake after the initial onset of sleep. Larger values indicate poorer sleep. |
| Awakening frequency | The number of different awakening episodes after the initial onset of sleep. Higher values indicate more awakenings and poorer sleep. |
| Average awakening length | The average length, in minutes, of all awakening episodes. Higher values indicate greater time spent awake for each awakening episode, which reflects poorer sleep. |
| Movement index | The movement index is the percentage of epochs with y-axis counts greater than zero in the sleep period. Thus higher values indicate more movement and suggest less restful sleep. |
| Fragmentation index | The fragmentation index is a measure of restlessness and interruption of sleep. It is calculated by the percentage of one minute sleep periods versus all sleep periods. Higher values indicate more frequent interruption of sleep (and, therefore, poorer sleep). |
| Sleep fragmentation index | The sum of the movement and fragmentation indices. Higher values suggest greater microarousals and poorer sleep quality. |
| Poor sleep factor | CFA-derived factor score summarizing poor sleep quality using the total actigraphy counts summed together over the sleep period, efficiency, WASO, average awakening length, movement index, and sleep fragmentation. |

*Source:* Authors' compilation.

ing?" The scale covered a range of social exclusionary and unfair treatment situations that included being treated with less courtesy and less respect, receiving poorer service at restaurants and stores than other people, being insulted or treated poorly by teachers, and being threatened and harassed. Factor loadings were all greater than 0.6 and Cronbach's = 0.9. The mean was calculated across items and scores were standardized across participants. Importantly, the EDiS is one of the most widely used scales in the area of health disparities research (Paradies 2006). It is also shown to have good reliability, validity, and measurement invariance across African American and white populations (on validity, Benjamins 2012; on measurement, Shariff-Marco et al. 2011; Kim, Sellbom, and Ford 2014). In short, a key advantage of EDiS to measures of, for example, racism-related discrimination is that the EDiS captures discrimination-based social exclusion for a variety of groups, including white respondents.

Next, a series of binary items based on the EDiS were included in the *daily e-diaries* to indicate whether specific types of mistreatment had occurred over the course of the day. These items captured unfair or poor treatment at school, store, restaurant, or other public space. Five questions measured specific types of mistreatment drawn directly from EDiS, such as "Over the course of the day, did you feel like

**Figure 2.** Actigraph Sleep Data, Good (Top) and Poor (Bottom) Nights of Sleep

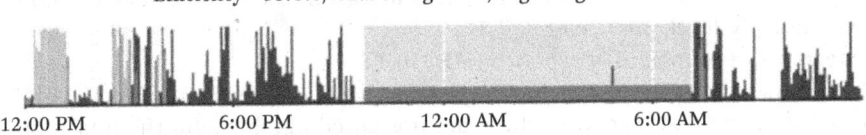

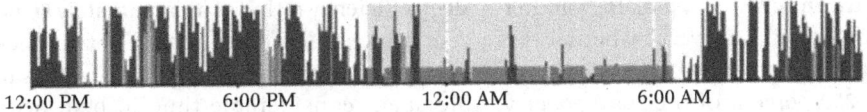

*Source:* Authors' calculations.
*Note:* Movement activity where lightly shaded area denotes period in bed and darker shaded area denotes time asleep.

you were called names or were insulted?" Four additional EDiS items asked whether participants felt that others thought they were not smart, were afraid of them, thought that they were dishonest, and better than them over the course of the day. These items are operationalized as a sum score at the daily level. The third measure is based on the average daily number of experiences, standardized across participants to facilitate comparison with the traditional EDiS instrument.

### Controls

Biomarkers from dried blood spots from capillary whole blood were collected during the stage 2 in-lab data collection and were included in the current analyses as controls for potential markers of prior chronic disease risk. Blood spots were assayed for hemoglobin a1c (HbA1c), high sensitivity CRP, and Epstein-Barr virus (EBV) titers. Samples were stored at –20 degree freezer at the University of Nebraska and shipped overnight to the University of Washington Department of Laboratory Medicine for assays (Mark H. Wener, MD, director, Seattle, Washington). Hemoglobin Hba1c, a marker of the percentage average blood glucose over two to three months, is an indicator of diabetes risk, a condition correlated with poor sleep. The raw percentage Hba1c levels of respondents were derived from dried blood from 3.2mm punch disc eluted in a buffer. The raw percentages were converted to the blood equivalent (B-E) value, which is the equivalent of conventional venous liquid blood samples. These values were used in this study and are used to determine cutoffs for normal (< 5.7 percent), prediabetic (5.7–6.4 percent), and diabetic (> = 6.5 percent) range (Potter, UW lab personal correspondence). CRP is a cell-mediated inflammatory marker that is strongly correlated with cardiovascular disease risk. CRP concentrations were also assayed from a 3.2mm punch disc and eluted in a buffer. CRP values converted to serum equivalents using established clinical metrics (for example, NHANES) range from low (< 3 mg/L), elevated (3 < 10 mg/L) to high (10 <) values likely due to acute infection (Pearson et al. 2003). Epstein-Barr antibodies (anti-EBV VCA IgG Ab), whose elevated presence is an indicator stress induced immunosuppression (McClure et al. 2010), were assayed and converted to plasma equivalent values as well. Little is known about its link to sleep. Both CRP and EBV were transformed using a hyperbolic sine transformation that is very similar to a log transformation (Burbidge, Magee, and Robb 1988). All scores were then standardized for use in statistical analyses.

Additional measures include waist-hip ratio from stage 2, standardized across participants to adjust for body size when the biological data were collected (Dalton et al. 2003). From the stage 3 e-diaries, daily *somatic complaints* as well as the two-week somatic complaint average was calculated from four ordinal items—

none (1) to a lot (4)—capturing poor appetite, aches or pains or muscle-joint soreness, being tired for no reason, stomach ache or upset, and headaches. At the daily level, *poor self-rated health* (five categories, very good to very poor) is included as a standardized measure, along with a standardized person-average over the two-week study period. Finally, all models include an indicator for whether the child was biracial or African American, female, whether the focal parent is married, and whether the family income was greater than $45,000, approximately 250 percent of the state poverty level collected at stage 1 (CFIN 2012). The number and age of children in the household were also included.

## Analytic Strategy

The sleep measures comprise the key dependent variables of the analysis and have two key forms of dependency. First, the data are nested within individual participants. For this reason, the basic model is a two-level random-intercept model with each day's sleep nested within each participant (Raudenbush and Bryk 2002). The daily e-diary measures (discrimination, somatic complaints, SRH) are used to predict sleep that night; the remaining parameters reflect associations with average sleep over the study period. Because the child-means are controlled at the between participant level of the model, the daily measures are orthogonal to the between-subject random intercept and can be interpreted as within-person estimates (Allison 2005). Second, the within-subjects data are neither independent nor exchangeable after accounting for the nesting structure. Rather, an ordered dependency is captured using an autoregressive AR(1) residual structure (Chi and Reinsel 1989).

The models are presented in two ways. First, a between-subjects model including EDiS but not the daily e-diary measures is presented. This model captures the association between sleep and *retrospective* reports of perceived discrimination in day-to-day life collected during the in-home visit. Second, EDiS is removed from the equation and the *daily* e-diary discrimination measures and their over-time average are included. The control and biological measures are included in all models reported.[1]

## RESULTS

Descriptive statistics for the sleep variables are presented in table 2 for the total sample, by race and by gender. In general, participants fell asleep within two minutes and with a sleep efficiency rating of approximately 80 percent, which is less than normal healthy sleep efficiency (85 percent). The youth in this sample spent considerable time in bed, nearly (521/60 = ) 8.7 hrs and had a TST of nearly seven hours (413/60), well below the recommended sleep time for this age range of approximately nine hours. The wake after sleep onset averaged around ninety minutes and awakenings per night, of approximately two minutes each, totaled about twenty-three. Differences between groups were minimal other than an indication that biracial and African American youth had more fragmented or restless sleep than white youth, which falls in line with prior literature that finds African Americans have lower average sleep time and more disrupted sleep quality (Hale and Do 2007; Krueger and Friedman 2009).

Table 3 presents the descriptive demographic and health characteristics along with averages of both daily and retrospective discrimination levels reported in the sample. The youth in this sample were relatively disadvantaged, about half coming from homes making less than $45,000 per year. Overall, retrospective EDiS average across items was low with the 1-value category reflecting "less than once a year" and the two-value category reflecting "a few times a year." However, youth reported 0.6 events per day, on average, suggesting that the retrospective EDiS may underreport the amount of discriminatory experiences that young people perceive when the questions are posed more closely in time to those experiences. It is also important that youths' average retrospective reports of discrimination using the EDiS showed similar average trends to our initial stage 1 sample of youth from which this

---

1. We have omitted day of the week from these analyses because inclusion of weekday indicators did meaningfully affect the reported results or inferences. These results are available on request.

**Table 2.** Descriptive Statistics of Sleep Measures

|  | Full Analytic Sample | | | | Race | | Gender | |
| --- | --- | --- | --- | --- | --- | --- | --- | --- |
|  | Mean | SD | Min | Max | White | Biracial | Male | Female |
| Latency | 2.04 | 1.87 | 0 | 6 | 2.14 | 1.89 | 2.21 | 1.91 |
| Efficiency | 79.87 | 11.06 | 45 | 100 | 79.57 | 80.33 | 79.23 | 80.40 |
| Total minutes | 520.91 | 101.40 | 120 | 800 | 524.57 | 515.37 | 525.85 | 516.82 |
| TST | 413.57 | 87.28 | 75 | 650 | 414.75 | 411.78 | 415.00 | 412.38 |
| WASO | 90.44 | 55.33 | 0 | 250 | 92.92 | 86.69 | 92.26 | 88.94 |
| Awakening frequency | 22.72 | 9.33 | 0 | 51 | 22.70 | 22.76 | 23.27 | 22.27 |
| Average awakening length | 1.95 | 0.60 | 0 | 4 | 1.98 | 1.90 | 1.95 | 1.95 |
| Movement index | 17.82 | 8.74 | 0 | 45 | 17.99 | 17.56 | 18.51 | 17.25 |
| Fragmentation index | 11.65 | 7.95 | 0 | 38 | 10.84 | 12.89 | 11.39 | 11.87 |
| Sleep frag. index | 29.47 | 13.82 | 0 | 70 | 28.79 | 30.50 | 30.02 | 29.02 |
| Poor sleep factor score | 0.01 | 0.88 | -2 | 3 | 0.04 | -0.02 | 0.07 | -0.03 |

*Source:* Community Connections and Family Wellness Study sleep data.

**Table 3.** Descriptive Statistics of Predictor Variables

|  | Full Analytic Sample | | | | Race | | Gender | |
| --- | --- | --- | --- | --- | --- | --- | --- | --- |
|  | Mean | SD | Min | Max | White | Biracial | Male | Female |
| **Between youth measures** | | | | | | | | |
| EDiS | 1.22 | 1.08 | 0.00 | 3.91 | 1.20 | 1.24 | 1.15 | 1.27 |
| African American or biracial | 0.40 |  | 0.00 | 1.00 |  |  | 0.43 | 0.37 |
| Female | 0.55 |  | 0.00 | 1.00 | 0.57 | 0.51 |  |  |
| Age | 13.66 | 1.12 | 12.00 | 16.00 | 13.62 | 13.72 | 13.49 | 13.80* |
| Parent married | 0.61 |  | 0.00 | 1.00 | 0.63 | 0.58 | 0.57 | 0.65+ |
| Number of children | 3.18 | 1.49 | 1.00 | 8.00 | 3.14 | 3.23 | 3.28 | 3.09 |
| Income greater than $45,000 | 0.50 |  | 0.00 | 1.00 | 0.53 | 0.44* | 0.57 | 0.43* |
| **Biological between youth measures** | | | | | | | | |
| CRP | 0.83 | 0.75 | 0.05 | 2.41 | 0.89 | 0.75* | 1.20 | 0.53* |
| Hba1c | 5.36 | 0.47 | 4.60 | 7.30 | 5.22 | 5.56* | 5.40 | 5.32+ |
| EBV | 3.25 | 1.24 | 0.88 | 5.26 | 3.05 | 3.57* | 3.00 | 3.47* |
| Waist-hip ratio | 0.84 | 0.10 | 0.67 | 1.02 | 0.85 | 0.84 | 0.90 | 0.79* |
| **Daily diary questions** | | | | | | | | |
| Discrimination (t, count) | 0.57 | 1.26 | 0.00 | 7.00 | 0.51 | 0.68* | 0.50 | 0.64 |
| Discrimination (t, avg.) | 0.55 | 0.76 | 0.00 | 3.64 | 0.49 | 0.65 | 0.48 | 0.61+ |
| Somatic complaints (t) | 1.37 | 0.47 | 1.00 | 4.00 | 1.45 | 1.26* | 1.16 | 1.55* |
| Somatic complaints (t, avg.) | 1.37 | 0.37 | 1.00 | 2.46 | 1.45 | 1.26* | 1.16 | 1.55* |
| Poor SRH (t, z) | 2.11 | 0.90 | 1.00 | 5.00 | 2.15 | 2.06 | 1.90 | 2.28* |
| Poor SRH (t, avg.) | 2.11 | 0.67 | 1.00 | 3.31 | 2.15 | 2.06 | 1.90 | 2.28* |

*Source:* Community Connections and Family Wellness Study sleep data.
*Note:* Full analytic sample repeated observations = 475, white observations = 286, biracial observations = 189, male observations = 215, female observations = 260, across 35 participants.
EDiS denotes Williams Everyday Discrimination scale taken during the in-home survey.
CRP (C-reactive Protein) units- mg/L; Hba1c (hemoglobin a1c) units- % glycosolated hemoglobin over 2–3 month period; EBV (Epstein Barr antibodies)—AU/mL.
t-test comparisons indicated at +$p < .1$, *$p < .05$

**Figure 3.** Kernel Density Plot Everyday Discrimination Distribution

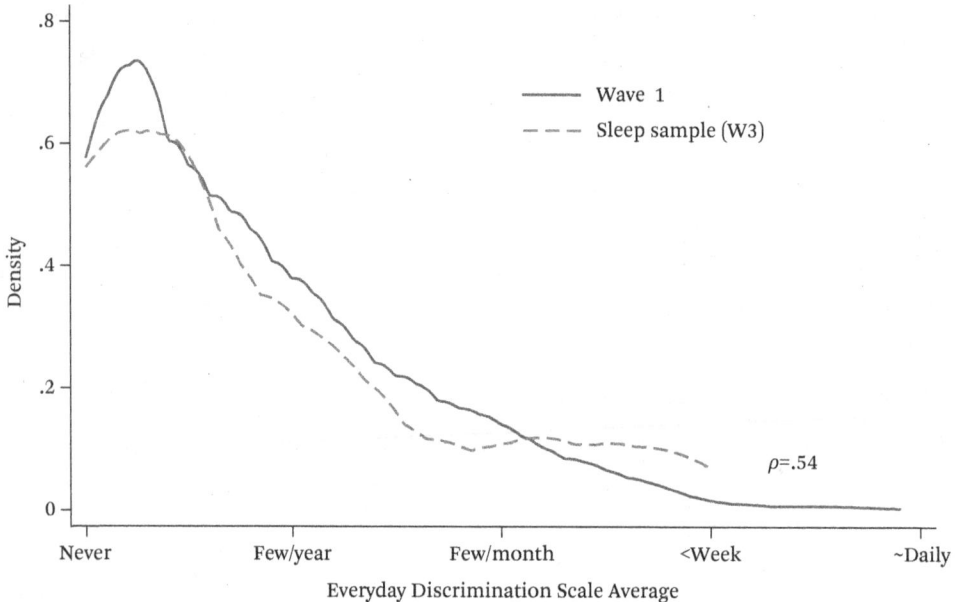

*Source:* Authors' calculations.
*Note:* Wave 1, N = 688. Analysis Sample, N = 35.

sample was drawn upon, who reported discrimination (see figure 3). Daily discrimination report counts were higher for biracial or African American youth, but they had fewer somatic complaints. Females reported both more somatic complaints and poorer self-rated health. Both biracial and female youth were more likely to come from disadvantaged families. The biracial youth had lower CRP values, as did females, but biracial and African American youth had higher average Hba1c and EBV antibody levels.

### Sleep Analysis

A summary sleep analysis using the poor sleep factor score summary measure is presented in table 4. As indicated in table 1, this measure includes an array of highly intercorrelated sleep measures capturing many different features of actigraphy-based sleep assessment. Model A1 includes the home assessment of EDiS (retrospective reports) and model A2 replaces this measure with the *daily* e-diary reports. Each standard deviation of EDiS (about one point on the ordinal average scale) is associated with a nearly 0.3 standard deviation ($p < .01$) increase in poor sleep quality. Notably, the EDiS assessment is similar though smaller in magnitude than the two-week accumulation reported in model A2 ($b = 0.352$, $p < .001$). Together, these results suggest that the experience or perception of discrimination is positively associated with systematically poorer sleep. Surprisingly, however, the results also suggest that sleep may actually improve during the days when these negative experiences take place ($b = -.126$, $p < .01$), in contrast to expectations. Given the nature of this effect, it indicates that youth who experience or perceive more discrimination have *poorer average* sleep. These youth, however, sleep slightly better on days when those events are reported, but not better overall relative to youth who do not experience such events. Thus, these global sleep findings are consistent with hypotheses 1 but contradict hypothesis 2.

These models are reproduced in table 5 for sleep latency, overall sleep efficiency, total minutes in bed, and total sleep time. Indications are that, over time, discrimination is associated with increased sleep latency, lower efficiency, and more time in bed with lower TST. Effi-

**Table 4.** Random Intercept Models, Poor Sleep Factor Score (z)

|  | A1 | | A2 | |
| --- | --- | --- | --- | --- |
|  | B | SE | B | SE |
| **Between youth measures** | | | | |
| EDiS (z) | 0.289** | [0.089] | | |
| African American or biracial | −0.245 | [0.190] | −0.130 | [0.182] |
| Female | 0.002 | [0.093] | 0.048 | [0.085] |
| Age (centered) | −0.217 | [0.221] | −0.441+ | [0.234] |
| Parent married | 0.218 | [0.194] | 0.314+ | [0.178] |
| Number of children | 0.027 | [0.060] | 0.114+ | [0.064] |
| Income greater than $45,000 | −0.063 | [0.193] | −0.278 | [0.180] |
| **Biological between youth measures** | | | | |
| CRP (z) | −0.034 | [0.111] | 0.143 | [0.107] |
| Hba1c (z) | 0.195* | [0.089] | 0.184* | [0.082] |
| EBV (z) | 0.031 | [0.094] | −0.083 | [0.086] |
| Waist-hip ratio (z) | −0.003 | [0.116] | −0.102 | [0.102] |
| **Daily diary questions** | | | | |
| Discrimination (t, count) | | | −0.126** | [0.042] |
| Discrimination (t, avg, z) | | | 0.352*** | [0.088] |
| Somatic complaints (t, z) | | | 0.142* | [0.069] |
| Somatic complaints (t, avg, z) | | | 0.103 | [0.129] |
| Poor SRH (t, z) | | | 0.045 | [0.062] |
| Poor SRH (t, avg, z) | | | 0.064 | [0.105] |
| Intercept | −0.293 | [0.322] | −0.066 | [0.288] |
| **Variance components** | | | | |
| Between subject (ln) | −0.933*** | [0.183] | −1.053*** | [0.188] |
| Residual (ln) | −0.096** | [0.036] | −0.118*** | [0.035] |
| AR1 (rho) | 0.136* | [0.057] | 0.094+ | [0.057] |

*Source:* Community Connections and Family Wellness Study sleep data.
+$p < .10$; *$p < .05$; **$p < .01$; ***$p < .001$

ciency, in particular is lower ($b = 0.3$) for those who experience more discrimination, but there are signs of greater sleep efficiency on specific days when discrimination events took place. As before, the daily discrimination measures contradict the hypothesis that negative experiences during the day decrease sleep quality. Instead these results suggest that youth who experience more discrimination generally have poorer sleep, but that sleep recovers relative to personal baseline on days when those experiences take place.

Results for waking from sleep over the night (WASO, awakening frequency, average awakening length) in table 6 and for the sleep indices (movement, fragmentation, sleep fragmenta-tion) in table 7 are consistent with the trends reported in tables 4 and 5. Retrospective EDiS is associated with poorer sleep characteristics and is generally smaller but similar in magnitude to the standardized average of the daily reports. Moreover, on days when discrimination events are reported, youth tend to report better sleep quality as well. Overall, the sleep findings are consistent with hypotheses 1, that discrimination is associated with average sleep quality across a range of sleep measures capturing time in bed. Contradictory to hypothesis 2, however, sleep quality did not decrease on days when discrimination was reported. In fact, signs of a small recovery relative to individual baseline were again evident. Notably, retrospec-

**Table 5.** Random Intercept Models, Sleep Latency, Efficiency, Minutes in Bed, and Total Sleep Time

| | Latency (z) | | Efficiency (z) | | Total Minutes (z) | | TST (z) | |
|---|---|---|---|---|---|---|---|---|
| | B1 | B2 | C1 | C2 | D1 | D2 | E1 | E2 |
| **Between youth measures** | | | | | | | | |
| EDiS (z) | 0.130+ | | -0.302** | | 0.022 | | -0.172* | |
| African American or biracial | -0.184 | -0.069 | 0.253 | 0.145 | -0.149 | -0.134 | 0.023 | -0.030 |
| Female | -0.043 | 0.007 | 0.026 | -0.003 | -0.062 | -0.013 | -0.051 | -0.028 |
| Age (centered) | -0.312+ | -0.394* | 0.252 | 0.552* | -0.024 | 0.151 | 0.114 | 0.439* |
| Parent married | 0.078 | 0.147 | -0.260 | -0.345+ | -0.133 | -0.109 | -0.312+ | -0.345* |
| Number of children | -0.004 | 0.074 | -0.018 | -0.093 | -0.059 | -0.035 | -0.070 | -0.096+ |
| Income less than $45,000 | 0.006 | -0.117 | 0.021 | 0.215 | 0.099 | 0.030 | 0.143 | 0.211 |
| **Biological between youth measures** | | | | | | | | |
| CRP (z) | -0.163+ | -0.012 | 0.119 | -0.018 | 0.037 | 0.149+ | 0.096 | 0.103 |
| Hba1c (z) | 0.014 | 0.004 | -0.178* | -0.175* | 0.093 | 0.071 | -0.022 | -0.038 |
| EBV (z) | -0.022 | -0.093 | -0.044 | 0.059 | 0.033 | -0.002 | 0.018 | 0.053 |
| Waist-hip ratio (z) | 0.016 | -0.017 | -0.016 | 0.100 | 0.009 | 0.029 | 0.002 | 0.090 |
| **Daily diary questions** | | | | | | | | |
| Discrimination (t, count) | | -0.034 | | 0.114** | | -0.082+ | | 0.001 |
| Discrimination (t, avg, z) | | 0.158* | | -0.307*** | | 0.162* | | -0.063 |
| Somatic complaints (t, z) | | 0.131+ | | -0.121+ | | -0.138+ | | -0.198** |
| Somatic complaints (t, avg, z) | | 0.111 | | -0.111 | | 0.119 | | 0.046 |
| Poor SRH (t, z) | | -0.001 | | -0.047 | | 0.060 | | 0.003 |
| Poor SRH (t, avg, z) | | -0.064 | | -0.134 | | -0.196* | | -0.237** |
| Intercept | 0.056 | -0.016 | 0.314 | 0.001 | 0.294 | 0.216 | 0.490+ | 0.225 |
| **Variance components** | | | | | | | | |
| Between subject (ln) | -1.524*** | -1.953** | -0.934*** | -1.034*** | -1.373*** | -1.568*** | -1.103*** | -1.284*** |
| Residual (ln) | -0.035 | -0.039 | -0.126*** | -0.148*** | -0.050 | -0.061+ | -0.108** | -0.119*** |
| AR1 (rho) | 0.108* | 0.109* | 0.148** | 0.097+ | 0.041 | 0.029 | 0.001 | -0.024 |

*Source:* Community Connections and Family Wellness Study sleep data.
+$p < .10$; *$p < .05$; **$p < .01$; ***$p < .001$

tive EDiS scores strongly predicts daily reports ($b = 0.70$, $p < .001$; full results not shown, and coefficient is partially standardized with respect to EDiS), suggesting that despite signs of recovery, youth who report discrimination tend to on average have worse sleep. Moreover, the poor sleep factor score on the prior night does not predict daily reports of discrimination ($b = -.08$, $p = .014$; results not shown), suggesting that reports of discrimination are not an outcome of poor sleep quality or poor mood (zCESD: $b = -.13$, $p = .164$).

## DISCUSSION

This study examines the links between everyday discrimination, daily variations in discrimination exposure, and objective daily measures of sleep using actigraphy among a diverse sample of adolescents. It contributes to the existing literature documenting the harmful consequences of discrimination for health outcomes by demonstrating the associations between discriminatory and exclusionary experiences for objective daily measures of sleep quality in adolescence. To our knowledge, this is the first

**Table 6.** Random Intercept Models, Waking, Frequency, Awake Time

|  | WASO (z) | | Awakening Frequency (z) | | Average Awake Time (z) | |
| --- | --- | --- | --- | --- | --- | --- |
|  | F1 | F2 | G1 | G2 | H1 | H2 |
| **Between youth measures** | | | | | | |
| EDiS (z) | 0.218* |  | 0.217** |  | 0.161* |  |
| African American or biracial | -0.295 | -0.204 | -0.392** | -0.312* | -0.142 | -0.073 |
| Female | -0.041 | -0.024 | 0.001 | 0.028 | -0.096 | -0.091 |
| Age (centered) | -0.100 | -0.358 | -0.292+ | -0.494** | 0.070 | -0.144 |
| Parent married | 0.187 | 0.256 | 0.146 | 0.182 | 0.069 | 0.131 |
| Number of children | 0.016 | 0.079 | 0.024 | 0.060 | 0.021 | 0.077 |
| Income less than $45,000 | -0.019 | -0.164 | -0.128 | -0.229 | 0.109 | -0.013 |
| **Biological between youth measures** | | | | | | |
| CRP (z) | -0.009 | 0.089 | -0.008 | 0.080 | -0.014 | 0.056 |
| Hba1c (z) | 0.201* | 0.202* | 0.364*** | 0.365*** | 0.036 | 0.038 |
| EBV (z) | 0.052 | -0.023 | 0.162* | 0.104 | 0.042 | -0.018 |
| Waist-hip ratio (z) | -0.003 | -0.090 | -0.099 | -0.185* | 0.064 | 0.001 |
| **Daily diary questions** | | | | | | |
| Discrimination (t, count) |  | -0.116** |  | -0.026 |  | -0.053 |
| Discrimination (t, avg, z) |  | 0.251** |  | 0.110 |  | 0.184* |
| Somatic complaints (t, z) |  | 0.023 |  | -0.143* |  | 0.098 |
| Somatic complaints (t, avg, z) |  | 0.158 |  | 0.246* |  | 0.064 |
| Poor SRH (t, z) |  | 0.045 |  | 0.094 |  | -0.061 |
| Poor SRH (t, avg, z) |  | 0.101 |  | 0.039 |  | 0.164+ |
| Intercept | -0.224 | 0.004 | -0.041 | 0.208 | -0.329 | -0.200 |
| **Variance components** | | | | | | |
| Between subject (ln) | -1.011*** | -1.106*** | -1.498*** | -1.460*** | -1.452*** | -1.742*** |
| Residual (ln) | -0.082* | -0.097** | -0.104** | -0.113** | -0.050 | -0.057 |
| AR1 (rho) | 0.127* | 0.096+ | 0.129* | 0.120* | 0.210*** | 0.199*** |

*Source:* Community Connections and Family Wellness Study sleep data.
+$p < .10$; *$p < .05$; **$p < .01$; ***$p < .001$

study to concurrently measure both retrospective reports of Everyday Discrimination (EDiS) and daily diary reports of discrimination with concurrent objective sleep measures.

The findings support our first hypothesis that *average* sleep would be linked to discrimination. In fact, average discrimination, operationalized using the retrospective EDiS scale was associated with poorer sleep outcomes across all but two included measures. In general, youth who report more discrimination had shorter sleep duration and poorer sleep quality. Specifically, on indicators of sleep duration, youth who reported discrimination took longer to fall asleep (latency), had less efficient sleep, and spent more time in bed but less time asleep. In terms of sleep quality, youth who reported discrimination had more awakenings after sleep onset, longer duration awake during a sleep disruption, moved more while asleep and had more fragmented sleep. This study falls in line with research using gold standard laboratory techniques finding evidence among adults that discrimination exposure is linked to less time in restorative slow wave sleep (stage 4) (Thomas et al. 2006).

Hypothesis 2 posited that day-to-day variation in perceived discrimination would be adversely associated with sleep variability around the person-average. Thus hypothesis 2 is a

**Table 7.** Random Intercept Models, Movement, Fragmentation Index, Sleep Fragmentation Index

|  | Movement Index (z) | | Fragmentation Index (z) | | Sleep Fragmentation Index (z) | |
| --- | --- | --- | --- | --- | --- | --- |
|  | I1 | I2 | J1 | J2 | K1 | K2 |
| **Between youth measures** | | | | | | |
| EDiS (z) | 0.283** | | 0.110 | | 0.239** | |
| African American or biracial | -0.208 | -0.092 | 0.140 | 0.192 | -0.046 | 0.054 |
| Female | 0.021 | 0.077 | -0.035 | -0.051 | -0.009 | 0.015 |
| Age (centered) | -0.227 | -0.402+ | 0.105 | -0.141 | -0.098 | -0.350+ |
| Parent married | 0.201 | 0.300+ | 0.113 | 0.157 | 0.183 | 0.268+ |
| Number of children | 0.033 | 0.123* | -0.005 | 0.034 | 0.017 | 0.095 |
| Income less than $45,000 | -0.086 | -0.308+ | -0.010 | -0.083 | -0.048 | -0.226 |
| **Biological between youth measures** | | | | | | |
| CRP (z) | -0.015 | 0.182+ | -0.019 | -0.006 | -0.018 | 0.108 |
| Hba1c (z) | 0.171+ | 0.155+ | 0.153* | 0.164** | 0.196* | 0.192** |
| EBV (z) | 0.013 | -0.106 | 0.023 | -0.009 | 0.033 | -0.060 |
| Waist-hip ratio (z) | -0.006 | -0.095 | 0.038 | -0.020 | 0.014 | -0.075 |
| **Daily diary questions** | | | | | | |
| Discrimination (t, count) | | -0.119** | | -0.108* | | -0.134** |
| Discrimination (t, avg, z) | | 0.362*** | | 0.160* | | 0.315*** |
| Somatic complaints (t, z) | | 0.179** | | 0.016 | | 0.120+ |
| Somatic complaints (t, avg, z) | | 0.072 | | 0.102 | | 0.101 |
| Poor SRH (t, z) | | 0.043 | | -0.090 | | -0.021 |
| Poor SRH (t, avg, z) | | 0.027 | | 0.216* | | 0.141 |
| Intercept | -0.299 | -0.116 | -0.325 | -0.156 | -0.369 | -0.156 |
| **Variance components** | | | | | | |
| Between subject (ln) | -0.943*** | -1.078*** | -1.349*** | -1.613*** | -1.050*** | -1.233*** |
| Residual (ln) | -0.109** | -0.132*** | -0.074* | -0.081* | -0.093** | -0.111** |
| AR1 (rho) | 0.107+ | 0.068 | 0.078 | 0.093+ | 0.121* | 0.094+ |

*Source:* Community Connections and Family Wellness Study data.
+$p < .10$; *$p < .05$; **$p < .01$; ***$p < .001$

within-person hypothesis, suggesting discrimination as a potential source of individual variability in sleep quality. This hypothesis was consistently contradicted by our results, which suggest that contemporaneous exposure is linked to improved sleep efficiency, longer total sleep time, less time awake after sleep onset, and decreased movement and sleep fragmentation. Given that youth more likely to report discrimination having happened over the course of the day are generally more likely to report accumulated everyday discrimination, these results suggest a partial recovery in sleep quality following the negative experience. It is important, however, that despite daily indications of improved sleep on the day of the event, the *average sleep* duration and quality remain lower in youth who report discriminatory events. In general, around three discriminatory experiences in one day would be required to make up for the average decrease in sleep quality over days across those sleep features given the effect sizes estimated.

In her study measuring discrimination exposure and minority youth psychological well-being, Yip posits that for minority youth who experience discrimination, sleep may in fact be a health coping mechanism that lessens the deleterious impact of discrimination in the short term (2014). Her study finds that youth who experience discrimination and have better daily sleep quality experience higher self-esteem and lower depressive symptoms. It does not, however, contemporaneously measure both daily sleep and discrimination exposure contemporaneously, pointing to the need for more research with larger and more diverse samples using designs similar to those in this study.

An important unmeasured component in this study that may shed light on our surprising results and merits examination is the role of active coping style in the face of social stressors. Sleep is an essential component for healthy adolescent development, yet variations in how coping styles impact sleep or how sleep can be used as a coping tool have yet to be systematically examined. *Escape to sleep* describes how individuals who have disengaged coping styles may use sleep to regulate exposure to adverse stressful emotions or social conditions. Conversely, individuals who engage in more emotionally focused coping may interpret sleep as a loss of mastery and thus are more prone to heightened arousal and sleep disruption (Sadeh, Keinan, and Daon 2004). Although this study does not include specific measures of coping styles, integrating behavioral and emotional coping among diverse populations is an important direction to take future research in this area.

Despite the novelty of these findings, this study is limited in several important ways. First, although actigraphy provides validated objective measures of sleep quality and duration, validation studies indicate that actigraphs can suffer from low specificity or accuracy when detecting wakefulness, which may affect a number of sleep indices (Sadeh 2011). However, it has been suggested that aggregate data over at least four to five nights can compensate for this issue. This study includes fourteen days of data. Second, the sample size is both small and is based on convenience sample in a single community. Obviously, more powerful samples, and samples constructed using state-of-the-art sampling methodologies are important for better characterizing sleep variability and enhancing generalizability to broader populations. Finally, though racial and ethnic heterogeneity was also low, the racial diversity in this sample is mostly biracial youth with an African American parent, which is novel. More diversity, however, is needed for understanding how the experience of discrimination shapes sleep and health over the early life course.

Overall, discrimination is consistently related to poorer sleep and poor sleep appears to be related to an important long-term health marker already by adolescence. Moreover, supplementary analyses indicated that sleep did not predict discrimination reports the following day, and measures of depressive symptoms did not predict sleep or mediate the discrimination parameters. Taken together, these results support the small but growing literature demonstrating the harmful consequences of discrimination for sleep health and the extensive literature demonstrating the association between discrimination and health risk (Slopen, Lewis, and Williams 2016; Williams 2012).

# REFERENCES

ActiGraph. 2012. "ActiLife 6 User's Manual." *ActiGraph* SFT12DOC13(A).

Åkerstedt, Torbjörn. 2006. "Psychosocial Stress and Impaired Sleep." *Scandinavian Journal of Work, Environment & Health* 32(6): 493–501.

Åkerstedt, Torbjörn, Göran Kecklund, and John Axelsson. 2007. "Impaired Sleep After Bedtime Stress and Worries." *Biological Psychology* 76(3): 170–73. DOI: 10.1016/j.biopsycho.2007.07.010.

Allison, Paul D. 2005. *Fixed Effects Regression Methods for Longitudinal Data Using SAS*. Cary, N.C.: SAS Institute, Inc.

Ancoli-Israel, S., Roger Cole, Cathy Alessi, Mark Chambers, William Moorcroft, and Charles P. Pollak. 2003. "The Role of Actigraphy in the Study of Sleep and Circadian Rhythms." *Sleep* 26(3): 342–92.

Balbo, Marcella, Rachel Leproult, and Eve Van Cauter. 2010. "Impact of Sleep and Its Disturbances on Hypothalamo-Pituitary-Adrenal Axis Activity." *International Journal of Endocrinology* 2010. DOI: 10.1155/2010/759234.

Baumeister, Roy F., and Mark R. Leary. 1995. "The Need to Belong: Desire for Interpersonal Attachments as a Fundamental Human Motivation." *Psychological Bulletin* 117(3): 497–529.

Becker, Stephen P., Joshua M. Langberg, and Kelly C.

Byars. 2015. "Advancing a Biopsychosocial and Contextual Model of Sleep in Adolescence: A Review and Introduction to the Special Issue." *Journal of Youth and Adolescence* 44(2): 239–70. DOI: 10.1007/s10964-014-0248-y.

Benjamins, M. R. 2012. "Race/Ethnic Discrimination and Preventive Service Utilization in a Sample of Whites, Blacks, Mexicans, and Puerto Ricans." *Med Care* 50(10): 870–76. DOI: 10.1097/MLR.0b013e31825a8c63.

Brody, Gene H., Man-Kit Lei, David H. Chae, Tianyi Yu, Steven M. Kogan, and Steven R. H. Beach. 2014. "Perceived Discrimination Among African American Adolescents and Allostatic Load: A Longitudinal Analysis with Buffering Effects." *Child Development* 85(3): 989–1002. DOI: 10.1111/cdev.12213.

Burbidge, John B., Lonnie Magee, and A. Leslie Robb. 1988. "Alternative Transformations to Handle Extreme Values of the Dependent Variable." *Journal of the American Statistical Association* 83(401): 123–27. DOI: 10.2307/2288929.

Cacioppo, John T., and William Patrick. 2009. *Loneliness: Human Nature and the Need for Social Connection*. New York: W. W. Norton.

Carskadon, Mary A. 1990. "Patterns of Sleep and Sleepiness in Adolescents." *Journal of Adolescent Health* 17(1): 5–12.

CFIN. 2012. *The Face of Poverty Today in Lincoln, NE*. Lincoln, Neb.: Center for People in Need.

Chi, Eric M., and Gregory C. Reinsel. 1989. "Models for Longitudinal Data with Random Effects and AR(1) Errors." *Journal of the American Statistical Association* 84(406): 452–59. DOI: 10.1080/01621459.1989.10478790.

Dahl, Ronald E. 1999. "The Consequences of Insufficient Sleep for Adolescents." *Phi Delta Kappan* 80(5): 354–59.

Dalton, M., A. J. Cameron, P. Z. Zimmet, J. E. Shaw, D. Jolley, D. W. Dunstan, T. A. Welborn, and Committee on Behalf of the AusDiab Steering. 2003. "Waist Circumference, Waist-Hip Ratio and Body Mass Index and Their Correlation with Cardiovascular Disease Risk Factors in Australian Adults." *Journal of Internal Medicine* 254(6): 555–63. DOI: 10.1111/j.1365-2796.2003.01229.x.

Duclos, Rod, Echo Wen Wan, and Yuwei Jiang. 2014. "Show Me the Money! Effects of Social Exclusion on Financial Risk-Taking." *Journal of Consumer Research* 40(1): 122–35.

El-Sheikh, Mona, Ryan J. Kelly, Joseph A. Buckhalt, and J. Benjamin Hinnant. 2010. "Children's Sleep and Adjustment over Time: The Role of Socioeconomic Context." *Child Development* 81(3): 870–83. DOI: 10.1111/j.1467-8624.2010.01439.x.

Eufemia, Jacob, Jennifer Stinson, Joana Duran, Ankur Gupta, Mario Gerla, Mary Ann Lewis, and Lonnie Zeltzer. 2012. "Usability Testing of a Smartphone for Accessing a Web-Based E-Diary for Self-Monitoring of Pain and Symptoms in Sickle Cell Disease." *Journal of Pediatric Hematology and Oncology* 34(5): 326–35. DOI: 10.1097/MPH.0b013e318257a13c.

Falk, Emily B., Luke W. Hyde, Colter Mitchell, Jessica Faul, et al. 2013. "What Is a Representative Brain? Neuroscience Meets Population Science." *Proceedings of the National Academy of Sciences* 110(44): 17615–22.

Goosby, Bridget J., Sarah Malone, Elizabeth A. Richardson, Jacob E. Cheadle, and Deadric T. Williams. 2015. "Perceived Discrimination and Markers of Cardiovascular Risk Among Low-Income African American Youth." *American Journal of Human Biology* 27(4): 546–52. DOI: 10.1002/ajhb.22683.

Gregory, Alice M., and Avi Sadeh. 2012. "Sleep, Emotional and Behavioral Difficulties in Children and Adolescents." *Sleep Medicine Reviews* 16(2): 129–36. DOI: 10.1016/j.smrv.2011.03.007.

Guyll, Max, Karen A. Matthews, and Joyce T. Bromberger. 2001. "Discrimination and Unfair Treatment: Relationship to Cardiovascular Reactivity Among African American and European American Women." *Health Psychology* 20(5): 315–25. DOI: 10.1037/0278-6133.20.5.315.

Hale, Lauren, and D. Phuong Do. 2007. "Racial Differences in Self-Reports of Sleep Duration in a Population-Based Study." *Sleep* 30(9): 1096–103.

Hale, Lauren, Erin Emanuele, and Sarah James. 2015. "Recent Updates in the Social and Environmental Determinants of Sleep Health." *Current Sleep Medicine Reports* 1(4): 212–17. DOI: 10.1007/s40675-015-0023-y.

Hawkley, Louise C., Mary H. Burleson, Gary G. Berntson, and John T. Cacioppo. 2003. "Loneliness in Everyday Life: Cardiovascular Activity, Psychosocial Context, and Health Behaviors." *Journal of Personality Social Psychology* 85(1): 105–20.

Hicken, Margaret T., Hedwig Lee, Jennifer Ailshire, Sarah A. Burgard, and Deadric R. Williams. 2013. "'Every Shut Eye, Ain't Sleep': The Role of Racism-Related Vigilance in Racial/Ethnic Disparities in Sleep Difficulty." *Race and Social Problems* 5(2): 100–12. DOI: 10.1007/s12552-013-9095-9.

Hope, Elan C., Lori S. Hoggard, and Alvin Thomas. 2015. "Emerging into Adulthood in the Face of Racial Discrimination: Physiological, Psychological, and Sociopolitical Consequences for African American Youth." *Translational Issues in Psychological Science* 1(4): 342–51. DOI: 10.1037/tps0000041.

Irwin, Michael R. 2015. "Why Sleep Is Important for Health: A Psychoneuroimmunology Perspective." *Annual Review of Psychology* 66(1): 143–72. DOI: 10.1146/annurev-psych-010213-115205.

Kim, Giyeon, Martin Sellbom, and Katy-Lauren Ford. 2014. "Race/Ethnicity and Measurement Equivalence of the Everyday Discrimination Scale." *Psychological Assessment* 26(3): 892–900. DOI: 10.1037/a0036431.

Kingsbury, John H., Orfeu M. Buxton, and Karen M. Emmons. 2013. "Sleep and Its Relationship to Racial and Ethnic Disparities in Cardiovascular Disease." *Current Cardiovascular Risk Reports* 7(5): 387–94. DOI: 10.1007/s12170-013-0330-0.

Kliewer, Wendy, and Stephen J. Lepore. 2014. "Exposure to Violence, Social Cognitive Processing, and Sleep Problems in Urban Adolescents." *Journal of Youth and Adolescence* 44(2): 507–17. DOI: 10.1007/s10964-014-0184-x.

Krieger, Nancy, Anna Kosheleva, Pamela D. Waterman, Jarvis T. Chen, and Karestan Koenen. 2011. "Racial Discrimination, Psychological Distress, and Self-Rated Health Among US-Born and Foreign-Born Black Americans." *American Journal of Public Health* 101(9): 1704–13. DOI: 10.2105/AJPH.2011.300168.

Krieger, Nancy, Kevin Smith, Deepa Naishadham, Cathy Hartman, and Elizabeth M. Barbeau. 2005. "Experiences of Discrimination: Validity and Reliability of a Self-Report Measure for Population Health Research on Racism and Health." *Social Science & Medicine* 61(7): 1576–96. DOI: 10.1016/j.socscimed.2005.03.006.

Krueger, Patrick M., and Elliot M. Friedman. 2009. "Sleep Duration in the United States: A Cross-Sectional Population-Based Study." *American Journal of Epidemiology* 169(9): 1052–63. DOI: 10.1093/aje/kwp023.

Lewis, Tené T., Allison E. Aiello, Sue Leurgans, Jeremiah Kelly, and Lisa L. Barnes. 2010. "Self-Reported Experiences of Everyday Discrimination Are Associated with Elevated C-Reactive Protein Levels in Older African-American Adults." *Brain, Behavior, and Immunity* 24(3): 438–43. DOI:10.1016/j.bbi.2009.11.011.

Lewis, Tené T., Lisa L. Barnes, Julia L. Bienias, Daniel T. Lackland, Denis A. Evans, and Carlos F. Mendes de Leon. 2009. "Perceived Discrimination and Blood Pressure in Older African American and White Adults." *Journals of Gerontology Series A: Biological Sciences and Medical Sciences* 64A(9): 1002–08.

Lewis, Tené T., Howard M. Kravitz, Imke Janssen, and Lynda H. Powell. 2011. "Self-Reported Experiences of Discrimination and Visceral Fat in Middle-Aged African-American and Caucasian Women." *American Journal of Epidemiology* 173(11): 1223–31. DOI: 10.1093/aje/kwq466.

Lewis, Tené T., Wendy M. Troxel, Howard M. Kravitz, Joyce T. Bromberger, Karen A. Matthews, and Martica Hall. 2013. "Chronic Exposure to Everyday Discrimination and Sleep in a Multi-Ethnic Sample of Middle-Aged Women." *Health Psychology* 32(7): 810–19. DOI: 10.1037/a0029938.

Marino, Miguel, Yi Li, Michael N. Rueschman, John W. Winkelman, J. M. Ellenbogen, Jo M. Solet, Hilary Dulin, Lisa F. Berkman, and Orfeu M. Buxton. 2013. "Measuring Sleep: Accuracy, Sensitivity, and Specificity of Wrist Actigraphy Compared to Polysomnography." *Sleep* 36(11): 1747–55. DOI: 10.5665/sleep.3142.

Massey, Douglas S. 2004. "Segregation and Stratification: A Biosocial Perspective." *Du Bois Review: Social Science Research on Race* 1(1): 7–25.

McClure, Heather H., Charles R. Martinez, Jr., J. Josh Snodgrass, J. Mark Eddy, Roberto A. Jiménez, Laura E. Isiordia, and Thomas W. McDade. 2010. "Discrimination-Related Stress, Blood Pressure and Epstein-Barr Virus Antibodies Among Latin American Immigrants in Oregon, US." *Journal of Biosocial Science* 42(4): 433–61. DOI: 10.1017/S0021932010000039.

Mezick, Elizabeth J., Karen A. Matthews, Martica Hall, Patrick J. Strollo Jr., Daniel J. Buysse, Thomas W. Kamarck, Jane F. Owens, and Steven E. Reis. 2008. "Influence of Race and Socioeconomic Status on Sleep: Pittsburgh SleepSCORE Project." *Psychosomatic Medicine* 70(4): 410–16. DOI: 10.1097/PSY.0b013e31816fdf21.

Paradies, Yin. 2006. "A Systematic Review of Empirical Research on Self-Reported Racism and

Health." *International Journal of Epidemiology* 35(4): 888–901. DOI: 10.1093/ije/dyl056.

Park, Heejung, Kim M. Tsai, Ronald E. Dahl, Michael R. Irwin, Heather McCreath, Teresa Seeman, and Andrew J. Fuligni. 2016. "Sleep and Inflammation During Adolescence." *Psychosomatic Medicine* 78(6): 677–85.

Pearson, Thomas A., George A. Mensah, R. Wayne Alexander, Jeffrey L. Anderson, et al. 2003. "Markers of Inflammation and Cardiovascular Disease: Application to Clinical and Public Health Practice: A Statement for Healthcare Professionals from the Centers for Disease Control and Prevention and the American Heart Association." *Circulation* 107(3): 499–511.

Pereira, Diana, Lawrence L. Meier, and Achim Elfering. 2013. "Short-Term Effects of Social Exclusion at Work and Worries on Sleep." *Stress and Health: Journal of the International Society for the Investigation of Stress* 29(3): 240–52.

Priest, Naomi, Yin Paradies, Brigid Trenerry, Mandy Truong, Saffron Karlsen, and Yvonne Kelly. 2013. "A Systematic Review of Studies Examining the Relationship Between Reported Racism and Health and Wellbeing for Children and Young People." *Social Sciences Medicine* 95 (October): 115–27. DOI: 10.1016/j.socscimed.2012.11.031.

Profant, Judi, Sonia Ancoli-Israel, and Joel E. Dimsdale. 2002. "Are There Ethnic Differences in Sleep Architecture?" *American Journal of Human Biology* 14(3): 321–26. DOI: 10.1002/ajhb.10032.

Raudenbush, Stephen W., and Anthony S. Bryk. 2002. *Hierarchical Linear Models: Applications and Data Analysis Methods*, 2nd ed. Thousand Oaks, Calif.: Sage Publications.

Sadeh, Avi. 2011. "The Role and Validity of Actigraphy in Sleep Medicine: An Update." *Sleep Medicine Reviews* 15(4): 259–67. DOI: 10.1016/j.smrv.2010.10.001.

Sadeh, Avi, Giora Keinan, and Keren Daon. 2004. "Effects of Stress on Sleep: The Moderating Role of Coping Style." *Health Psychology* 23(5): 542–45. DOI: 10.1037/0278-6133.23.5.542.

Sadeh, Avi, Katherine M. Sharkey, and Mary A. Carskadon. 1994. "Activity-Based Sleep-Wake Identification: An Empirical Test of Methodological Issues." *Sleep* 17(3): 201–07.

Schmitt, Michael T., Nyla R. Branscombe, Tom Postmes, and Amber Garcia. 2014. "The Consequences of Perceived Discrimination for Psychological Well-Being: A Meta-Analytic Review." *Psychological Bulletin* 140(4): 1–28.

Shariff-Marco, Salma, Nancy Breen, Hope Landrine, Bryce B. Reeve, Nancy Krieger, Gilbert C. Gee, David R. Williams, Vickie M. Mays, Ninez A. Ponce, and Margarita Alegria. 2011. "Measuring Everyday Racial/Ethnic Discrimination in Health Surveys." *Du Bois Review* 8(1): 159–77.

Short, Michelle A., Michael Gradisar, Leon C. Lack, Helen R. Wright, and Mary A. Carskadon. 2012. "The Discrepancy Between Actigraphic and Sleep Diary Measures of Sleep in Adolescents." *Sleep Medicine* 13(4): 378–84. DOI: 10.1016/j.sleep.2011.11.005.

Short, Michelle A., Michael Gradisar, Leon C. Lack, Helen R. Wright, and Alex Chatburn. 2013. "Estimating Adolescent Sleep Patterns: Parent Reports Versus Adolescent Self-Report Surveys, Sleep Diaries, and Actigraphy." *Nature and Science of Sleep* 5(1): 23–26.

Sladek, Michael R., and Leah D. Doane. 2014. "Daily Diary Reports of Social Connection, Objective Sleep, and the Cortisol Awakening Response During Adolescents' First Year of College." *Journal of Youth and Adolescence* 44(2): 298–316. DOI: 10.1007/s10964-014-0244-2.

Slopen, Natalie, Tené T. Lewis, and David R. Williams. 2016. "Discrimination and Sleep: A Systematic Review." *Sleep Medicine* 18 (February): 88–95. DOI: 10.1016/j.sleep.2015.01.012.

Thomas, Kamala S., Wayne A. Bardwell, Sonia Ancoli-Israel, and Joel E. Dimsdale. 2006. "The Toll of Ethnic Discrimination on Sleep Architecture and Fatigue." *Health Psychology* 25(5): 635–42.

Torres, Lucas, and Anthon D. Ong. 2010. "A Daily Diary Investigation of Latino Ethnic Identity, Discrimination, and Depression." *Cultural Diversity and Ethnic Minority Psychology* 16(4): 561–68.

Troiano, Richard P., David Berrigan, Kevin W. Dodd, Louise C. Masse, Timothy Tilert, and Margaret McDowell. 2008. "Physical Activity in the United States Measured by Accelerometer." *Medicine & Science in Sports & Exercise* 40(1): 181–88. DOI: 10.1249/mss.0b013e31815a51b3.

Williams, David R. 2012. "Miles to Go Before We Sleep: Racial Inequities in Health." *Journal of Health and Social Behavior* 53(3): 279–95. DOI: 10.1177/0022146512455804.

Williams, David R., Yu Yan, James S. Jackson, and Norman B. Anderson. 1997. "Racial Differences in

Physical and Mental Health: Socio-Economic Status, Stress and Discrimination." *Journal of Health Psychology* 2(3): 335–51.

Wolfson, Amy R., Mary A. Carskadon, Christine Acebo, Ronald Seifter, Gahan Fallone, Susan E. Layak, and Jennifer Martin. 2003. "Evidence for the Validity of a Sleep Habits Survey for Adolescents." *Sleep* 26(3): 213–16.

Wong, Carol A., Jacquelynne S. Eccles, and Arnold Sameroff. 2003. "The Influence of Ethnic Discrimination and Ethnic Identification on African American Adolescents' School and Socioemotional Adjustment." *Journal of Personality* 71(6): 1197–232. DOI: 10.1111/1467-6494.7106012.

Yip, Tiffany. 2014. "The Effects of Ethnic/Racial Discrimination and Sleep Quality on Depressive Symptoms and Self-Esteem Trajectories Among Diverse Adolescents." *Journal of Youth and Adolescence* 44(2): 419–30. DOI: 10.1007/s10964-014-0123-x.

# The Great Recession and Immune Function

ELIZABETH MCCLURE, LYDIA FEINSTEIN, SARA FERRANDO-MARTÍNEZ, MANUEL LEAL, SANDRO GALEA, AND ALLISON E. AIELLO

*The Great Recession precipitated unprecedented home foreclosures increases, but documentation of related neighborhood changes and population health is scant. Using the Detroit Neighborhood Health Study (N = 277), we examined associations between neighborhood-level recession indicators and thymic function, a life course immunological health indicator. In covariate-adjusted multilevel models, each 10 percentage point increase in abandoned home prevalence and 1 percentage point increase in 2009 home foreclosures was associated with 1.7-year and 3.3-year increases in thymic aging, respectively. Associations attenuated after adjustment for neighborhood-level social cohesion, suggesting community ties may buffer recession-related immune aging. Effects of neighborhood stressors were strongest in middle-income households, supporting theory of excess vulnerability in this group. Future research should assess whether ongoing foreclosure and blight reduction efforts improve health for residents of recession impacted neighborhoods.*

**Keywords:** neighborhood, social determinants of health, Detroit, immunity, immunosenescence, thymic function

In December 2007, the United States began to experience one of the most stressful economic downturns in its history. This period—now referred to as the Great Recession—resulted in a disconcerting combination of job losses, fewer new jobs, and massive declines in housing and equity values that had not been seen for almost a century (Mishel et al. 2012; Gould Ellen and Dastrup 2012; Flanagan and Wilson 2013). Given the enormity of the changes in economic conditions during the Great Recession, it is not surprising that emerging evidence has linked economic stressors over this period to a range of negative health outcomes, including decreases in self-rated health, poor mental health, and substance abuse (Burgard, Seefeldt, and Zelner 2012; Riumallo-Herl et al. 2014; Mulia et al. 2014; Bacigalupe and Escolar-Pujolar 2014; McLaughlin et al. 2012; Tsai 2015; Cagney et al. 2014; Pollack et al. 2011). Other sources of stress

---

**Elizabeth McClure** is a predoctoral trainee at the Carolina Population Center and Department of Epidemiology, University of North Carolina at Chapel Hill. **Lydia Feinstein** is an epidemiologist at Social & Scientific Systems, Inc. **Sara Ferrando-Martínez** is a scientist at MedImmune. **Manuel Leal** is faculty at the Laboratory of Immunovirology, Clinic Unit of Infectious Diseases, Microbiology and Preventive Medicine, Institute of Biomedicine of Seville, IBiS, Virgen del Rocio University Hospital, Seville, Spain. **Sandro Galea** is dean of the Boston University School of Public Health. **Allison E. Aiello** is faculty at the Carolina Population Center and Department of Epidemiology, University of North Carolina at Chapel Hill.

© 2018 Russell Sage Foundation. McClure, Elizabeth, Lydia Feinstein, Sara Ferrando-Martínez, Manuel Leal, Sandro Galea, and Allison E. Aiello. 2018. "The Great Recession and Immune Function." *RSF: The Russell Sage Foundation Journal of the Social Sciences* 4(4): 62–81. DOI: 10.7758/RSF.2018.4.4.04. Direct correspondence to: Elizabeth McClure at emcclure@unc.edu; and Allison E. Aiello at aaiello@unc.edu, 2101C Mcgavran-Greenberg Hall, CB #7435, Chapel Hill, NC 27599.

Open Access Policy: *RSF: The Russell Sage Foundation Journal of the Social Sciences* is an open access journal. This article is published under a Creative Commons Attribution-NonCommercial-NoDerivs 3.0 Unported License.

were likely experienced at the community level. One of the most profound impacts was a steep rise in home foreclosures that fueled a proliferation of abandoned homes across the country. Despite the magnitude of home vacancies that followed the economic downturn, little is known about how this fundamental change in the neighborhood physical environment has impacted the health of residents in highly affected communities.

The economic impact of the Great Recession was especially profound in the state of Michigan: in the wake of the crisis, the unemployment rate doubled from an average of 6 percent before the crisis (2000–2007) to approximately 14 percent by 2009 (Bureau of Labor Statistics 2015). Even among residents fortunate enough to retain their jobs, many faced steep declines in asset values, including homes and equities. Indeed, median home values fell nearly 30 percent from their pre-crisis peak, and between 2005 and 2010 more than four hundred thousand residential units in both urban and rural areas faced a foreclosure auction filing (Michigan Foreclosure Task Force 2016). Although economic conditions worsened across the state, Detroit's economy was suffering before the Great Recession. Relative to its population peak in 1950, Detroit lost half of its residents by the beginning of the recession (Sugrue 2014). Detroit's history of racial segregation and industrial losses before the Great Recession uniquely left many neighborhoods in the city of Detroit particularly vulnerable to home foreclosures and other economic stressors (Lichter, Parisi, and Taquino 2015).

The quality of the neighborhood physical environment is increasingly being implicated as a key determinant of population health (Kawachi and Berkman 2003). Indeed, poor neighborhood physical environments contribute to the degradation of communities in the form of increased exposure to violence and reductions in social cohesion, both of which have been linked to negative health outcomes (Smith et al. 1998; Diez Roux et al. 2001; Giurgescu et al. 2015; Drukker and van Os 2003; Kruger, Reischl, and Gee 2007; Curry, Latkin, and Davey-Rothwell 2008; Tonorezos et al. 2008; Wilson-Genderson and Pruchno 2013; Blair et al. 2014).

To date, the biological mechanisms through which the neighborhood environment influences health are poorly understood (Steptoe and Marmot 2002). Prior studies linking individual-level socioeconomic stressors to decreased immune response (Dhabhar 2014; Dowd and Aiello 2009) suggest that the immune system may be an important biological pathway for understanding how neighborhood-level economic stressors may affect health (Steptoe 2012). Nonetheless, few studies have incorporated salient immunological biomarkers into population-based research on the social determinants of health. This dearth of research has made it difficult to examine the role of the immune systems as a central biological barometer of exposure to stressors. Studies examining neighborhood-level social determinants and immune function are currently limited to downstream immune biomarkers, such as indicators of elevated levels of inflammation and antibodies to cytomegalovirus infection (Keita et al. 2014; Lantos et al. 2015; Ford and Browning 2015).

Evidence is accumulating that the process of thymic involution, or the shrinking of the thymus over the life course and the associated reduction in naïve T-cells, may be an important indicator of immunological health at the population level (Ferrando-Martínez et al. 2009; Feinstein et al. 2016). As the main organ for de novo naïve T-cell production, the thymus plays an essential and global role in the quality of immune response (Steptoe 2012), and animal studies have shown that exposure to stressors reduces thymic output of naïve T-cells (Gruver and Sempowski 2008). Although the thymus is thought to recover following exposure to stressful events, the immune system is left vulnerable during these periods of reduced thymic function, increasing susceptibility to foreign pathogens (Gruver and Sempowski 2008). Whether recurring or prolonged periods of stress-induced atrophy over the life course result in a cumulative health impact in the long term remains unknown. Thymic function has only recently been characterized in a community-based cohort (Feinstein et al. 2016), and no study we are aware of has examined the relation between neighborhood characteristics and the population distribution of thymic function. Further, the literature has yet to identify

**Figure 1.** Conceptual Model, Neighborhood Economic Stressors on Immune Function

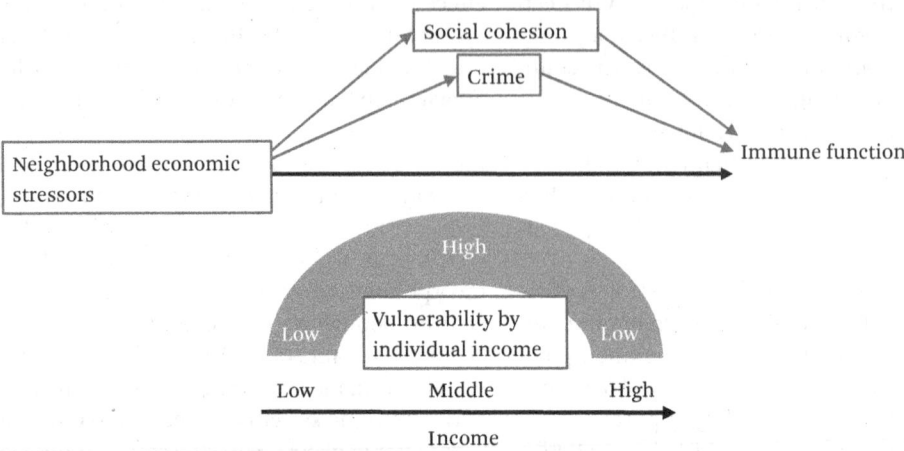

*Source:* Authors' calculations.

particular community-level characteristics through which the neighborhood physical environment may influence stress-related immunological alterations, or whether individual characteristics may buffer these area-level influences with regard to immune function.

The need and the opportunity to understand the mechanisms through which area-level economic stressors affect population health are pressing. We conducted the first analysis of this type using data from the Detroit Neighborhood Health Study (DNHS), a population-based cohort study of primarily African American adults that began data collection in 2008, near the very beginning of the economic downturn. The purpose of this study was to begin to develop hypotheses for the mechanisms through which the social environment affects health through the immune system. Figure 1 presents a conceptual model informed by the population health evidence and theory described, which suggests that immune function may be sensitive to acute and chronic neighborhood-level economic stress. Further, it shows two pathways through which these area-level stressors are embodied in diminished immune function—increased exposure to crime and decreased social cohesion. Finally, the literature indicates that individual socioeconomic status may buffer the negative impacts of area-level stressors on immune function, but none of the pathways shown has been assessed analytically. We hypothesized that living in a neighborhood with a higher prevalence of abandoned homes and home foreclosures would be associated with lower thymic function, in part due to increased exposure to neighborhood crime and loss of neighborhood social cohesion. Further, because evidence suggests that the Great Recession was particularly harmful to those with middle-class incomes (Ackerman, Fries, and Windle 2012), we additionally hypothesized that low- and high-income individuals would be less susceptible to effects of increases in foreclosures or abandoned homes, resulting in smaller decreases in thymic function, whereas middle-income individuals would experience the largest decrease in thymic function.

Motivated by our conceptual model, we first assessed the association between neighborhood-level environmental stressors associated with the Great Recession—including the prevalence of abandoned homes and home foreclosures—and thymic function; second, we characterized the roles of neighborhood crime and social cohesion as potential mediators of these associations; and third, we determined whether the effects of increases in foreclosures and abandoned homes on thymic function were modified by individual-level socioeconomic status.

## METHODS

The DNHS was conducted in five waves from 2008 to 2013. In the first study wave (2008–2009), 1,547 participants were recruited using a two-

**Figure 2.** Timeline for Relevant Measurements, Detroit Neighborhood Health Study

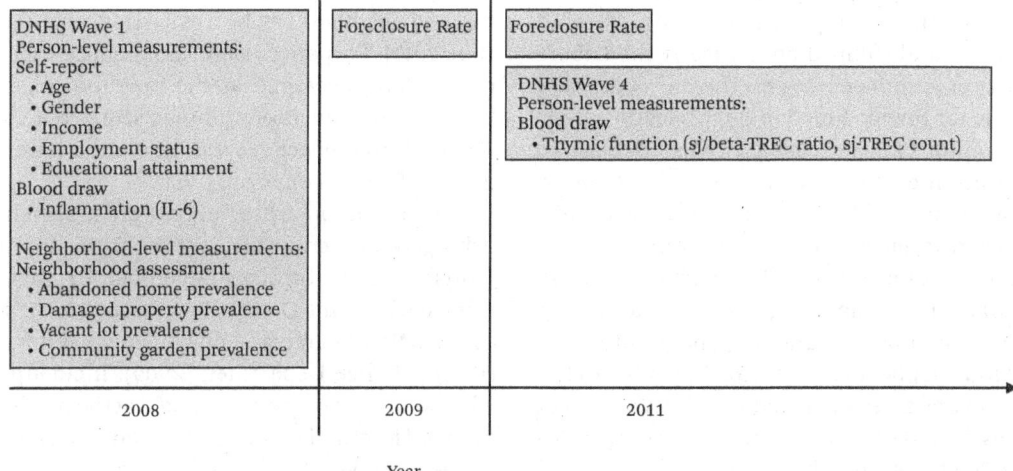

*Source:* Authors' calculations from the Detroit Neighborhood Health Study, 2008–2013.

stage area probability sample of households in the city limits (Goldmann et al. 2011). A telephone survey captured participants' demographic and socioeconomic information, health characteristics, social support, and exposure to trauma. In addition to the telephone survey, participants also had the option to provide a venous blood sample at their homes. Participants for whom thymic function was assessed and for whom complete residential location and covariate information was available were eligible for inclusion in the present analysis, resulting in a final sample size of 277. Figure 2 summarizes the DNHS study design and timing of each measurement described.

**Measures**

Of Detroit's fifty-four historically defined neighborhoods, fifty-two included DNHS study participants with available data for analysis (Hill and Gallagher 2002). We used these historically defined neighborhoods as the boundaries for neighborhood analyses. To capture characteristics of the neighborhood physical and social environment, a baseline neighborhood assessment was conducted by trained observers in 2008, many of whom were Detroit residents (Momper et al. 2012). Observers were assigned road sections for direct observation and assessed the presence of environmental factors, like abandoned homes (yes or no), on each street segment. Areas not directly assessed were assigned a value using spatial kriging of the directly assessed areas, as previously done in spatial analyses of urban environment (Auchincloss et al. 2007). The scores for each indicator were aggregated to the neighborhood level, with the prevalence measure representing the proportion of block segments in the neighborhood for which the answer to the abandoned homes question was yes (Momper et al. 2012). Other indicators of physical environmental quality—prevalence of damaged properties, vacant lots, and community gardens—were also measured as part of the neighborhood assessment. The score for each indicator was assessed independently and as a combined physical environmental quality score, all measured continuously at the neighborhood level for the present analysis. Community garden prevalence was reverse coded for the composite score.

The number of foreclosed properties in 2009 and 2011 by census tract were obtained from RealtyTrac, an authoritative source for historic United States real estate statistics and foreclosure trends (RealtyTrac 2011). Proportions were constructed as number of foreclosed properties divided by the number of total mortgages in each year within neighborhoods. The proportion for each year and the change in proportions between 2009 and 2011 was assessed in relation to thymic function.

## Outcome: Thymic Function

Participant DNA was extracted from venous whole blood samples, frozen and stored at −70°C, and shipped on dry ice to the Laboratory of Immunovirology at the University of Seville for thymic function quantification. T-cell receptor (TCR) excision circles (TRECs) are nonreplicated extrachromosomal DNA byproducts of alpha (signal joint) and beta chain TCR rearrangements that occur during the production of new T-cells (Lynch and Sempowski 2013). In this analysis, thymic function was measured by the ratio of signal joint to beta TRECs (sj/beta-TREC ratio). The sj/beta-TREC ratio was assessed in genomic DNA and analyses included a two-round quantitative PCR (qPCR) protocol, which is described in various studies (Ferrando-Martínez et al. 2010, 2013; Feinstein et al. 2016). The thymus is located near the heart, so direct measurement of its function is clinically contraindicated. The quantification of sjTREC is a more widely used indirect measurement of thymic function than the sj/beta-TREC ratio (Douek et al. 1998; Dion et al. 2007). However, sjTREC may be diluted by proliferation of naïve T-cells in peripheral blood, which can result in a reduction in number of sjTREC without a reduction in thymic function (Dion et al. 2004). The sj/beta-TREC ratio measure, used in this analysis, was developed to address the issue because it enables more direct estimation of intrathymic proliferation of T-cells, with regard to peripheral activity (Dion et al. 2004; Ferrando-Martínez et al. 2010). Thymic function was assessed in blood collected during the fourth study wave (2011) and is treated here as a continuous outcome, natural log-transformed to approximate a normal distribution.

## Covariates

Neighborhood levels of social cohesion and crime were examined as potential mediators of the association between the prevalence of abandoned homes and thymic function. Social cohesion was assessed in the first study wave by asking respondents whether they agreed on a 5-point Likert scale (1 = strongly disagree, 5 = strongly agree) with a series of statements related to whether their neighborhood is unified, residents are willing to help each other, neighbors get along, neighbors share common values, and neighbors can be trusted (McLaughlin et al. 2012). Responses were summed for each respondent, averaged at the neighborhood level, and treated as continuous scores out of 100, such that lower scores represent a lower degree of social cohesion.

Neighborhood crime levels were assessed using geocoded crime incidents occurring from January 1, 2009, through December 31, 2009, extracted from the Detroit Police Department's CrisNet/NetRMS records management system (Detroit Police Department 2009). Incidents with valid geocodes were summed at the neighborhood level and modeled in the present analysis as number of incidents per square mile, weighted for neighborhood population density.

Age, gender (male or female), baseline immunological status, and socioeconomic status were identified a priori as potential confounders via a directed acyclic graph (Greenland, Pearl, and Robins 1999) and included as covariates in adjusted models. Because thymic function was available only in wave 4, we quantified and controlled for a proxy for immunological status which was measured at the time of the baseline survey, serum levels of Interleukin-6 (IL-6), a marker of inflammation (DelaRosa et al. 2006; Hunter and Jones 2015) that has been shown to strongly predict thymic function in the DNHS population (Feinstein et al. 2016). Employment status at the time of the baseline survey was included as a marker of socioeconomic status and categorized into three levels: employed, unemployed, and other (such as retired, homemaker, student, on maternity or paternity leave, sick leave, and on disability). Additional indicators of socioeconomic status collected at baseline included education, dichotomized as high school or less versus beyond high school, and an ordinal indicator of household income (less than $25,000, $25,000 to less than $50,000, or $50,000 or more per year).

## Statistical Analyses

Standard descriptive statistics were used to characterize the study population. Medians and interquartile ranges (IQRs) were calculated for continuous variables. Counts and percentages were assessed for categorical variables. We used descriptive spatial analyses to generate maps displaying the unadjusted foreclosure prevalences, prevalence of abandoned homes, social cohesion scores, and population-density weighted crime incidents per square mile by neighborhood.

Two-level random intercept linear regression models, with participants nested within neighborhoods, were used to estimate the association between neighborhood prevalence of abandoned homes and thymic function (Subramanian and O'Malley 2010). Next, analyses were conducted to assess whether changes in proportion of homes foreclosed during the Great Recession influence thymic function. Models were run to examine the association between thymic function and neighborhood foreclosure proportions in 2009, 2011, and the change in proportion between these two periods. To further untangle the specificity of the foreclosure effect, we examined three additional neighborhood physical quality measures in relation to thymic function—prevalence of damaged properties, vacant lots, and community gardens—as well as a composite measure derived as a sum of all four exposures, with the community gardens prevalence reverse coded. Models were first adjusted only for participant age and then additionally sex, baseline immunological status, and employment status. Age was modeled in all analyses using a four-node cubic spline to better fit any curvature in the age-thymic function relationship (Howe et al. 2011).

To assess whether neighborhood levels of social cohesion and crime mediated the associations of both 2009 prevalence of foreclosures and neighborhood prevalence of abandoned homes with thymic function, we first examined the extent to which these potentially mediating variables were independently associated with neighborhood foreclosures and abandoned homes, as well as with thymic function. We then examined whether the overall association of foreclosures and neighborhood prevalence of abandoned homes with thymic function was attenuated by additionally adjusting for social cohesion, then crime.

To assess effect modification by individual-level socioeconomic status, we then examined the associations between neighborhood abandoned home prevalence as well as neighborhood foreclosure measurement and participant thymic function in analyses stratified by annual household income level (less than $25,000, $25,000 to less than $50,000, or $50,000 or more per year). A separate model was run for each stratum, adjusting for age, sex, and baseline immunological status. Statistical significance of modification was tested with an interaction term in the full model between income and each exposure (abandoned home prevalence and neighborhood foreclosures).

Spatial analyses and aggregation were completed in ArcMaps 10.3.1 (Environmental Systems Research Institute, Redlands, CA). All other statistical analyses were conducted in SAS 9.4 (SAS Institute, Inc.).

### Sensitivity Analyses

We conducted a sensitivity analysis using the absolute number of sjTREC per million whole blood, rather than sj/beta-TREC ratio as the outcome. The sjTREC number remains the most commonly applied measure of thymic function in the literature (Douek et al. 1998; Dion et al. 2007). It may have logistical advantages for application in large-scale population-based studies compared to the sj/beta-TREC ratio, which requires a more extensive laboratory methodology for analysis (Lynch et al. 2009). We also tested associations using baseline IL-6 as the outcome.

To determine whether our overall models were sensitive to the marker of socioeconomic status included, we examined the association between neighborhood prevalence of abandoned homes and thymic function as measured by the sj/beta-TREC ratio adjusting for education and then household income instead of employment status.

### RESULTS

There were 277 participants included in the present analysis. Table 1 shows the distributions of sociodemographic characteristics of the study population, overall and stratified by neighborhood levels of abandoned homes.

**Table 1.** Sample Characteristics by Prevalence of Abandoned Homes, Detroit Neighborhood Health Study

| Measure | Full Sample (N = 277) | Prevalence < 15% (N = 125) | Prevalence > 15% (N = 152) |
|---|---|---|---|
| Age, median (IQR) | 56 (47–67) | 59 (53–71) | 56 (47–66) |
| Female, N (%) | 167 (61) | 74 (69) | 93 (61) |
| Employed, N (%) | 96 (35) | 11 (32) | 85 (35) |
| Unemployed, N (%) | 39 (14) | 1 (3) | 38 (16) |
| Other employment status, N (%)[a] | 142 (51) | 22 (65) | 120 (49) |
| Interleukin 6 (IL-6), median (IQR) | 3 (2–4) | 4 (2–5) | 3 (2–5) |
| Neighborhood prevalence of abandoned homes, median (IQR) | 34 (23–45) | 14 (9–14) | 35 (28–45) |
| Neighborhood prevalence of damaged properties, median (IQR) | 33 (25–42) | 14 (5–16) | 38 (29–43) |
| Neighborhood prevalence of vacant lots, median (IQR) | 30 (13–52) | 6 (2–13) | 33 (15–53) |
| Neighborhood prevalence of community gardens, median (IQR) | 0 (0–1) | 0 (0–0) | 0 (0–1) |
| Neighborhood foreclosure prevalence 2009, median (IQR) | 3 (2–4) | 2 (1–3) | 3 (2–5) |
| Neighborhood foreclosure prevalence 2011, median (IQR) | 2 (1–2) | 2 (1–2) | 2 (1–2) |
| Neighborhood foreclosure rate change 2009–2011, median (IQR) | −1 (−2–0) | −2 (−3–1) | 1 (−1–2) |
| Neighborhood social cohesion score, median (IQR) | 52 (40–60) | 60 (48–72) | 48 (36–60) |
| Crimes per square mile, median (IQR) | 436 (374–516) | 436 (369–492) | 587 (410–593) |
| sj/beta-TREC ratio, median (IQR) | 5 (1–19) | 5 (1–19) | 5 (1–18) |

*Source:* Authors' calculations from the Detroit Neighborhood Health Study, 2008, and Detroit Police Department 2009.
[a]Other includes retired, homemaker, student, maternity-paternity leave, illness = sick leave, and disability.

Overall, participants were a median of fifty-six years old (IQR: forty-seven to sixty-seven years), had a median IL-6 measure of 3 pg/mL (IQR: 2–4 pg/mL), 61 percent were female, 35 percent were currently employed, 14 percent were unemployed, and 51 percent were retired, students, homemakers, or other (employment status). The median neighborhood prevalence of abandoned homes was 34 percent (IQR: 23 to 45 percent), that of damaged properties was 33 percent (IQR: 25 to 42 percent), vacant lots was 30 percent (IQR: 13 to 52 percent), and community gardens was 0 percent (IQR: 0 to 1 percent). Median neighborhood foreclosure proportion was 3 percent (IQR: 2 to 4 percent) in 2009 and 2 percent (IQR: 1 to 2 percent) in 2011. The median change in foreclosure proportion between 2011 and 2009 was −1 (IQR: −2 to 0) percentage points. Participants living in areas with a higher prevalence of abandoned homes (more than 15 percent) were more likely to be unemployed than those living in a neighborhood with a lower prevalence of abandoned homes (16 percent versus 3 percent unemployed, respectively). Those living in areas with a higher prevalence of abandoned homes were also slightly younger and more likely to be male. Respondents living in

**Table 2.** Sample Characteristics Versus Wave 1 Population, Detroit Neighborhood Health Study

| Measure | Sample (N = 277) | DNHS Wave 1 Population (N = 1,547) |
|---|---|---|
| Age, median (IQR) | 56 (47–67) | 48 (35–56) |
| Female, N (%) | 167 (61) | 833 (54) |
| Employed, N (%) | 97 (35) | 738 (52) |
| **Income, N (%)** | | |
| Less than $25,000 | 141 (51) | 738 (48) |
| $25,000–$49,999 | 89 (32) | 452 (29) |
| $50,000 or more | 47 (17) | 357 (23) |

*Source:* Authors' calculations from the Detroit Neighborhood Health Study, 2008, and Detroit Police Department 2009.

neighborhoods with a lower prevalence of abandoned homes were more likely to live in areas with greater social cohesion (60 percent versus 48 percent) and less crime (436 versus 587 crimes per square mile), damaged properties (14 percent versus 38 percent), vacant lots (6 percent versus 33 percent), and foreclosures in 2009 (2 versus 3 percent) than respondents living in neighborhoods with more abandoned homes. Measured characteristics in our sample differed slightly from those in the entire study population at wave 1. Our study sample had an older median age and a larger proportion female, unemployed, and of low income (table 2).

## Main Findings

Thymic function, as measured by the sj/beta-TREC ratio, was at a statistically significant lower level among participants living in neighborhoods with more abandoned homes. A 10 percentage point increase in the prevalence of abandoned homes was associated with a –0.03 (95% CI: –0.05, –0.01) log-unit decrease in sj/beta-TREC ratio, after controlling for age, sex, baseline IL-6, and employment status. Similar to the association with abandoned homes, neighborhood foreclosure proportions in 2009 and 2011 were associated with thymic function such that a one-unit increase in foreclosure proportion was associated with a –0.06 (95% CI: –0.11, –0.01) log-unit decline in sj/beta-TREC ratio in 2009 and a –0.04 (95% CI: –0.09, 0.00), log-unit decline in 2011. The association by change in foreclosure proportion over this period was not significant, $\beta = -0.19$ (95% CI: –0.62, 0.24).

None of the three other neighborhood characteristics assessed were statistically significantly associated with thymic function: prevalence of damaged property, $\beta = -0.04$ (95% CI: –0.10, 0.09); prevalence of vacant lots, $\beta = -0.02$ (95% CI: –0.12, 0.08); and prevalence of community gardens, $\beta = 0.00$ (95% CI: –0.10, 0.10). In addition, we combined all of these measures into an aggregate neighborhood disorder score by summing them with community garden prevalence reverse coded. The aggregate score was associated with reduced thymic function, but was not statistically significant, $\beta = -0.02$ (95% CI: –0.11, 0.08) (table 3, table A1).

## Mediation Analyses

The median neighborhood social cohesion score was 52 (IQR: 40 to 60). A 10 percent higher neighborhood prevalence of abandoned homes was significantly associated with lower social cohesion scores, $\beta = -0.27$ (95% CI: –0.43, –0.11) as was 2009 foreclosure proportion $\beta = -0.09$ (95% CI: –0.14, –0.04). The neighborhood social cohesion score was positively associated with thymic output. A one-unit increase in the social cohesion variable was associated with a 0.05 (95% CI: 0.02, 0.07) log-unit increase in sj/beta-

**Table 3.** Regression Coefficient Estimates and 95 Percent Confidence Intervals, for the Associations of Neighborhood Prevalences

| Neighborhood Characteristic | β (95% CI) Adjusted for Age Only | β (95% CI) Fully Adjusted[a] |
|---|---|---|
| For each 10 percentage point increase in abandoned home prevalence | -0.02 (95% CI: -0.05, 0.00) | -0.03 (95% CI: -0.05, -0.01)* |
| For each 10 percentage point increase in damaged property prevalence | -0.03 (95% CI: -0.08, 0.06) | -0.04 (95% CI: -0.10, 0.09) |
| For each 10 percentage point increase in vacant lot prevalence | -0.02 (95% CI: -0.09, 0.07) | -0.02 (95% CI: -0.12, 0.08) |
| For each 1 percentage point increase in community garden prevalence | 0.01 (95% CI: -0.11, 0.07) | 0.00 (95% CI: -0.10, 0.10) |
| For each 10 percentage point increase in composite environment score | -0.02 (95% CI: -0.11, 0.08) | -0.02 (95% CI: -0.11, 0.08) |
| For each 1 percentage point increase in 2009 foreclosures | -0.07 (95% CI: -0.11, -0.02)* | -0.06 (95% CI: -0.11, -0.01)* |
| For each 1 percentage point increase in 2011 foreclosures | -0.03 (95% CI: -0.07, 0.01) | -0.04 (95% CI: -0.09, 0.00) |
| For each 1 percentage point increase in foreclosure change (2009-2011) | -0.11 (95% CI: -0.54, 0.17) | -0.19 (95% CI: -0.62, 0.24) |

*Source:* Authors' calculations from the Detroit Neighborhood Health Study, 2008, and Detroit Police Department 2009.

[a] Adjusted for age, sex, baseline IL-6, and employment status. Coefficient estimates represent the change in log sj/beta-TREC ratio associated with a 10 percentage point increase in prevalence of environmental characteristics and a one per 100 mortgage increase in foreclosure rates.

*significant at the $\alpha = .05$ level.

TREC ratio. Abandoned homes and foreclosure proportions were similarly distributed spatially, and some spatial consistency in distributions of neighborhood social cohesion was evident (figure 3). Inclusion of social cohesion in the main models estimating the association of neighborhood prevalence of abandoned homes and 2009 foreclosure proportions with thymic function resulted in attenuation of the effect estimates, $\beta = 0.00$ (95% CI: -0.36, 0.18) (figure 4) and $\beta = -0.03$ (-0.06, 0.00) (figure 5), respectively.

The median number of population-size adjusted violent crimes per square mile was 436 (IQR: 374 to 516). A 10 percentage point increase in neighborhood prevalence of abandoned homes was associated with a 0.06 (95% CI: 0.02, 0.10) unit increase in violent crimes per square mile, and a 1 percentage point increase in 2009 foreclosures was associated with a 0.08 (95% CI: 0.00, 0.14) unit increase. Our model findings did not support the theory that crime was associated with a decline in thymic function, $\beta = 0.00$ (95% CI: -0.03, 0.01) and therefore did not meet justification for exploring mediation by crime in further analyses.

### Stratified Analyses

In analyses stratified by household income level, associations between abandoned home prevalence and foreclosure proportions in 2009 and 2011 were strongest in the middle-income group, $\beta = -0.10$ (95% CI: -0.26, 0.06); $= \beta = -0.11$ (95% CI: -0.29, 0.07); and $\beta = -0.08$ (95% CI: -0.18, 0.02), respectively. Among the lowest income group, associations were weak but the association between change in foreclosure proportions and thymic function was strongest, $\beta$ $\beta = -0.21$ (95% CI: -0.50, 0.08). Associations were weakest among the highest income group and no estimates were statistically significant at the $\alpha = 0.05$ level (table 4). In the full model, including an interaction term did not improve fit, nor was the term (testing heterogeneity of effect across levels of individual-level income) statistically significant.

**Figure 3.** Spatial Distributions by Neighborhood (N = 52)

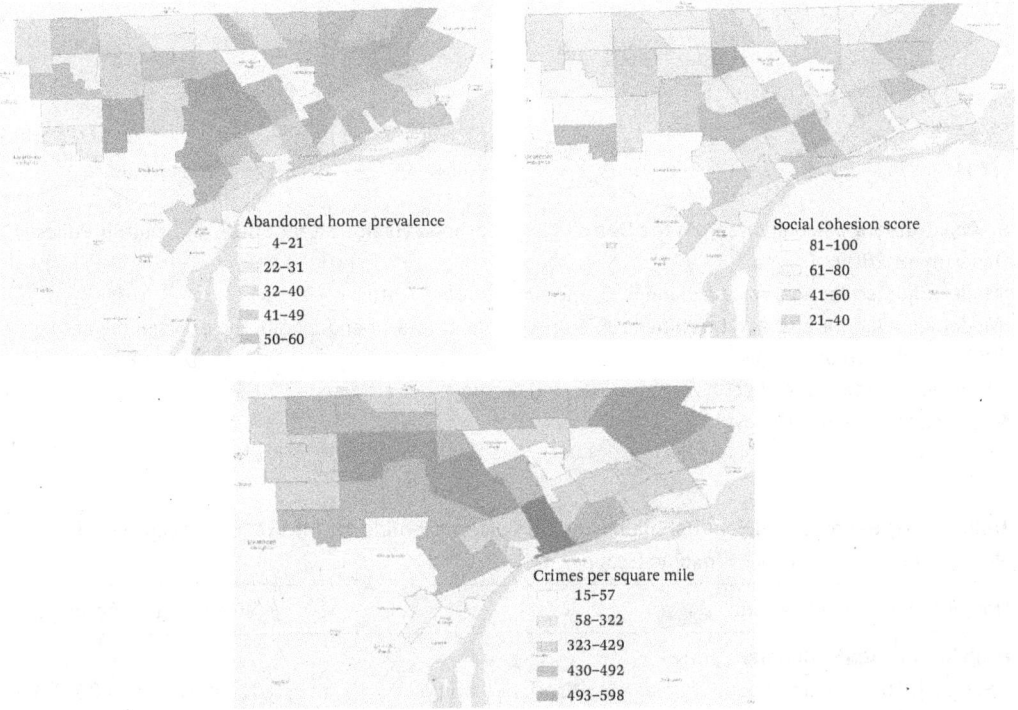

*Source:* Authors' calculations from the Detroit Neighborhood Health Study, 2008, and Detroit Police Department 2009.

**Figure 4.** Regression Coefficients and 95 Percent Confidence Intervals, Mediation Analysis, Abandoned Homes

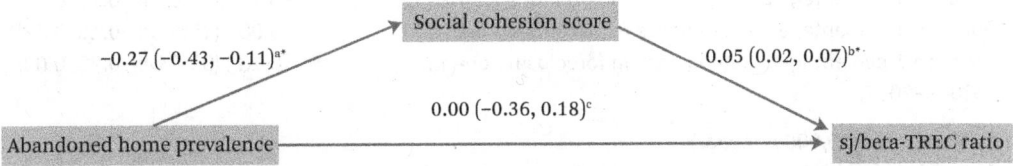

*Source:* Authors' calculations from the Detroit Neighborhood Health Study, 2008, and Detroit Police Department 2009.
[a]Model adjusted for age, sex, baseline IL-6, and employment status.
[b]Model adjusted for age, sex, baseline IL-6, employment status, abandoned home prevalence, and 2009 foreclosure prevalence.
[c]Model adjusted for social cohesion, age, sex, and employment status.
*significant at the $\alpha = .05$ level.

**Figure 5.** Regression Coefficients and 95 Percent Confidence Intervals, Mediation Analysis, Foreclosure Rate

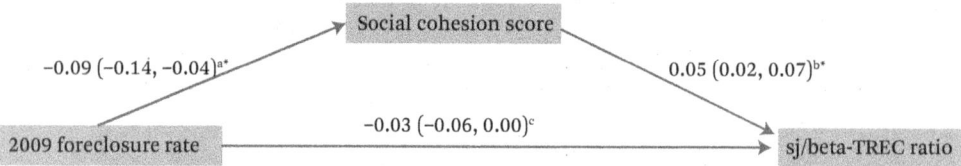

*Source:* Authors' calculations from the Detroit Neighborhood Health Study, 2008, and Detroit Police Department 2009.
[a]Model adjusted for age, sex, baseline IL-6, and employment status.
[b]Model adjusted for age, sex, baseline IL-6, employment status, abandoned home prevalence, and 2009 foreclosure prevalence.
[c]Model adjusted for social cohesion, age, sex, and employment status.
*significant at the $\alpha = .05$ level.

**Table 4.** Regression Coefficient Estimates and 95 Percent Confidence Intervals, Associations of Neighborhood Prevalence, by Income Group

| Neighborhood Characteristic | $\beta$ (95% CI) Fully Adjusted[a] |
|---|---|
| **High income (≥$50,000 per year)** | |
| For each 10 percentage point increase in abandoned home prevalence | 0.01   (95% CI: –0.05, 0.07) |
| For each 1 percentage point increase in 2009 foreclosures | 0.00   (95% CI: –0.10, 0.10) |
| For each 1 percentage point increase in 2011 foreclosures | –0.02   (95% CI: –0.10, 0.06) |
| For each 1 percentage point increase in foreclosure change (2009–2011) | –0.07   (95% CI: –0.15, 0.01) |
| **Middle income ($25,000 to <$50,000 per year)** | |
| For each 10 percentage point increase in abandoned home prevalence | –0.10   (95% CI: –0.26, 0.06) |
| For each 1 percentage point increase in 2009 foreclosures | –0.11   (95% CI: –0.29, 0.07) |
| For each 1 percentage point increase in 2011 foreclosures | –0.08   (95% CI: –0.18, 0.02) |
| For each 1 percentage point increase in foreclosure change (2009–2011) | –0.13   (95% CI: –0.29, 0.03) |
| **Low income (≤$25,000 per year)** | |
| For each 10 percentage point increase in abandoned home prevalence | –0.02   (95% CI: –0.08, 0.04) |
| For each 1 percentage point increase in 2009 foreclosures | –0.01   (95% CI: –0.03, 0.01) |
| For each 1 percentage point increase in 2011 foreclosures | 0.00   (95% CI: –0.12, 0.12) |
| For each 1 percentage point increase in foreclosure change (2009–2011) | –0.21   (95% CI: –0.50, 0.08) |

*Source:* Authors' calculations from the Detroit Neighborhood Health Study, 2008, and Detroit Police Department 2009.
[a]Adjusted for age, sex, baseline IL-6, and employment status. Coefficient estimates represent the change in log sj/beta-TREC ratio associated with a 10 percentage point increase in prevalence of environmental characteristics and a 1 percentage point increase in foreclosure prevalence.

## Sensitivity Analyses

We examined whether differing individual-level socioeconomic variables affected the association between abandoned homes and thymic function. The estimated association between abandoned homes and sj/beta-TREC ratio differed little when controlling for income instead of employment status in fully adjusted models for log sj/beta-TREC ratio, $\beta = -0.05$ (95% CI: −0.15, 0.05). We had similar findings when controlling for education rather than employment status, $\beta = -0.03$ (95% CI: −0.13, 0.07), suggesting that the influence of individual measures of socioeconomic status are similar and do not fully account for the influence of abandoned homes at the neighborhood level.

When assessing sensitivity to the thymic function measurement approach, neighborhood prevalence of abandoned homes was also associated with decline in thymic function as measured by the number of sjTREC per million whole blood cells, $\beta = -0.02$ (95% CI: −0.12, 0.08), but this estimate was not statistically significant at the $\alpha = 0.05$ level. Similarly, abandoned home prevalence was associated with higher baseline inflammation (as measured by IL-6 level), $\beta = 0.12$ (95% CI: −0.02, 0.17), as were neighborhood foreclosures $\beta = 0.08$ (95% CI: −0.05, 0.21).

## DISCUSSION

In this community-based study of adults living in Detroit in 2009, the height of the Great Recession impact on home prices and household wealth (U.S. Census Bureau 2013), we assessed the association between area-level indicators of the economic crisis—including neighborhood prevalence of abandoned homes, home foreclosure, and other measures of neighborhood disorder—and thymic function, a key measure of immunological well-being. We found that increased neighborhood prevalence of abandoned homes and home foreclosure during the recession were associated with decreased thymic function, particularly among middle-income individuals. Indeed, even after adjusting for covariates, a 10 percentage point increase in neighborhood prevalence of abandoned homes was roughly associated with the same decrease in thymic function as we observed for a 1.7-year increase in chronological age, and a 1 percentage point increase in 2009 home foreclosures was associated with the same decrease in thymic function as we observed for a 3.3-year increase in chronological age. Additionally, our findings support the hypothesis that social cohesion mediates the association between neighborhood environment and immune function. These findings strengthen the body of evidence supporting the significance of social context in influencing key biological health indicators over the life course, and, more specifically, stress-sensitive markers of immunity.

Given the economic climate and high home foreclosure rate in Detroit during the Great Recession, neighborhood prevalence of abandoned and foreclosed homes is an important source of chronic stress in the study population (Rooney 2008). We observed associations with reduced thymic function when assessing both prevalence of abandoned homes and foreclosure proportions. We also examined other measures of the physical environment (such as damaged property, gardens, and vacant lots) and found associations that, though not statistically significant, were consistent with our main findings that neighborhood quality affects health through immunological pathways. The robust and specific influence of abandoned homes and home foreclosures on our immune function measure underscore the importance of addressing structural factors influencing poor health outcomes and contributing to social health disparities in this population.

We are not aware of any other studies assessing the relationship between measures related to the Great Recession or neighborhood environment and thymic function. However, our findings complement the scant literature examining the association between neighborhood characteristics and general biological markers of health. Specifically, neighborhood affluence was found to be protective with respect to a measure of cumulative biological health (King, Morenoff, and House 2011) and type 2 diabetes (Piccolo et al. 2015). Several studies have also shown associations between foreclosure rates, mental health, and cardiovascular disease risk, suggesting that foreclosure stressors may ultimately influence health (Burgard, Ailshire, and Kalousova 2013; Catalano et al. 2011). Our work provides additional evidence in support for a potential biological mediator of these reported associations by examining a global measure of immune function, which is critical for fighting disease and promoting health.

The potential influence of stressors related to the Great Recession on thymic function is significant because it supports existing evidence that exposure to stressors negatively impacts the immune system (Dhabhar 2014). It may also influence overall health in adulthood, because the role of the thymus is important for production of naïve T-cells throughout the life course (Poulin et al. 1999). For example, decline in thymic function has been found to be associated with increased infection susceptibility as well as risk of autoimmune disease, cancer, and mortality (Ferrando-Martínez et al. 2013; Lynch et al. 2009). Further, our earlier research in the DNHS cohort suggests that reduced thymic function is associated with increased levels of pro-inflammatory biomarkers and other negative health outcomes, highlighting this measure as an important potential mechanism by which stressors may influence health at the population level (Feinstein et al. 2016).

Although we observed a significant association between foreclosures in 2009 and thymic function, our analyses did not identify a significant impact of changes in foreclosure prevalence from 2009 to 2011. Foreclosures were declining on average in that period. Indeed, 2009 showed the largest dip in home sale prices and loss of household wealth; in 2011, these measures began to bounce back (U.S. Census Bureau 2013). Therefore, 2011 represents a period of recovery, which may explain our findings. We also may not have captured the period of the most severe recession impacts for all neighborhoods. Moreover, Detroit experienced a history of industrial collapse, discriminatory residential lending, and racial segregation that had left many parts of the city vulnerable and under resourced decades before the Great Recession, which may have augmented the recession impacts in 2009 (Sugrue 2014).

Results of stratified analyses supported the hypothesis that socioeconomic status modifies the effect of abandoned homes and foreclosures on thymic function. Although the effects by income were not significantly different, the subgroup sample sizes did not provide adequate statistical power to detect heterogeneity. However, the differences in estimated effects by income group are of substantive interest. Individuals in the middle-income group showed the strongest association between increased abandoned home prevalence and prevalence of foreclosures and poorer immune function. This supports the theory that middle-income individuals were most sensitive to the impacts of area-level foreclosures and home vacancies. We observed that, among those in the lowest income group, changes in home foreclosure proportions from 2009 to 2011 (as opposed to prevalence of foreclosures in 2009, as observed for higher income groups) had the strongest impact on thymic function, suggesting that these individuals may have been particularly susceptible to ongoing changes in housing stability following the Great Recession. Previous work has found stronger impacts on physiological manifestations of major, recession-related financial stressors among low-income individuals (Boen and Yang 2016).

Our mediation analyses support the hypothesis that social cohesion may lie on the pathway between living in an adverse neighborhood environments and individual-level immune function. A higher prevalence of abandoned homes and foreclosure in the neighborhood were associated with lower social cohesion; higher social cohesion was associated with decreased thymic function. Further, adjustment for social cohesion attenuated the estimated effect of foreclosure and abandoned home prevalence on thymic function toward the null estimate. Our results support the growing literature suggesting that the level of social cohesion within neighborhoods is an important protective, mediating factor for mental health outcomes among African American women (Giurgescu et al. 2015) and the general U.S. population (Drukker and van Os 2003; Kruger, Reischl, and Gee 2007) as well as cardiovascular health in the United States (Diez Roux et al. 2001).

The number of population-adjusted crimes per square mile was associated with the prevalence of abandoned homes and foreclosure proportion, but was not associated with decreased thymic output. Given the administrative source of the crime data, we are aware that error is likely to be present in this measure (Black 1970; Biderman and Lynch 2012). Further work using more extensive crime data, such as crowd-sourced crime information, may help support a more robust analysis of this potential mediator (Shah et al. 2011). In addition to mechanistic insights, the roles of crime and social cohesion in the association between neighborhood environment and immune function also highlight the potential for community-level intervention opportunities for mitigating the deleterious effects of poor neighborhood physical environments.

Important strengths of this study include data from a predominantly African American, population-based sample and representation from neighborhoods with a wide variance in quality of the physical and social environments. The analyses were also strengthened by the use of a novel measure of immune health, which has been specifically characterized in the DNHS population (Feinstein et al. 2016). However, this study has some limitations. First, although the sj/beta-TREC ratio measure addresses peripheral blood dilution of sjTRECs (Dion et al. 2004), not all beta excision circles are captured, complicating interpretations of low function values (Ferrando-Martínez et al. 2010). Second, as in all nonexperimental studies of neighborhood characteristics and health, our study may suffer from issues related to selection into neighborhoods that may be related to the outcome (Oakes 2004). Therefore, the estimated effects may be an artifact of unmeasured factors both enabling some Detroit residents to move to neighborhoods with less foreclosure and causing them to have better immune function. However, the robustness of analyses to confounder adjustment, including a marker of immune health at baseline, provide enough confidence in the association to warrant further pursuit in a longitudinal or quasi-experimental setting in which a causal effect may be estimated. Third, our measure of abandoned homes was derived in 2008, only about a year into the Great Recession. We do not have data on duration of abandonment, and therefore some of the abandoned homes that were quantified may have been abandoned before the recession. Fourth, police department data are vulnerable to misclassification (approximated to fit available codes). Crime incident data are also biased by the absence of crimes not reported by citizens to the police and by police decisions not to record all crimes reported by citizens (Black 1970). Fifth, this analysis may be limited by the conceptualization of neighborhood. Historic administrative units defining neighborhoods in this study may not reflect the true function of the included area-level variables. Regardless, neighborhood definitions based on historically defined boundaries are likely a substantial improvement over measurements based on census tracts (Duncan et al. 2014). Sixth, the differences in the distribution of some sociodemographic characteristics of our study sample relative to the full DNHS study population may limit the generalizability of our results to the entire city of Detroit. We mitigated threats to internal validity by controlling for identified confounders distributed differently between the study sample and overall population. Finally, the analyses were limited by the small sample size of participants with available thymic function data, which may have under powered analyses to detect statistically significant effects in some instances, particularly those assessing heterogeneity of effect by individual income. However, the robust and consistent associations we did observe over multiple measures and despite our relatively small sample size suggest important immune health impacts of the Great Recession in part due to the profound proliferation of home foreclosures and subsequent neighborhood vacancy, which warrant further investigation.

This study, for the first time, suggests a population-level association between abandoned homes, home foreclosures, and a key global marker of immune function among Detroit residents. Although immune function is an objective and upstream measure that directly influences many health outcomes, it has not previously been assessed in relation to measures of the neighborhood environment. If the association that we observed here is causal, it may have far-reaching implications for addressing the health and well-being of individuals living in neighborhoods characterized by foreclosures and abandoned homes. Moreover, our results suggest that social cohesion may be an important buffering community-level factor that could reduce the detrimental impacts of living in neighborhoods during economic declines. The finding that social cohesion may mediate the association of abandoned homes and foreclosures with thymic function supports the hypothesis that neighborhoods may influence health through psychosocial mechanistic pathways. Future research is needed to identify the mechanisms through which neighborhood-level economic stressors impact health, particularly the role of historically determined area-level vulnerability in the context of a recession on biological pathways that influence health and well-being.

## APPENDIX

**Table A1.** Regression Coefficient Estimates and Confidence Intervals, Associations of Neighborhood Prevalence, by Age

| Neighborhood Characteristic | $\beta$ (95% CI) Fully Adjusted[a] | |
|---|---|---|
| **For each 10 percentage point increase in abandoned home prevalence** | −0.03 | (95% CI: −0.05, −0.01)[b] |
| Age node 1[b] | −0.15 | (95% CI: −0.25, −0.07)[b] |
| Age node 2[b] | −0.01 | (95% CI: −0.04, 0.00) |
| Age node 3[b] | 0.04 | (95% CI: −0.05, 0.11) |
| Age node 4[b] | 0.01 | (95% CI: −0.03, 0.04) |
| Female | −0.33 | (95% CI: −0.68, 0.02) |
| Baseline IL-6 | 0.02 | (95% CI: −0.02, 0.05) |
| Unemployed | −0.31 | (95% CI: −0.85, 0.23) |
| Other employment | 0.21 | (95% CI: −0.20, 0.62) |
| **For each 1 percentage point increase in 2009 foreclosures** | −0.06 | (95% CI: −0.11, −0.01)* |
| Age node 1[b] | −0.12 | (95% CI: −0.22, −0.04)[b] |
| Age node 2[b] | 0.00 | (95% CI: −0.04, 0.02) |
| Age node 3[b] | 0.04 | (95% CI: −0.03, 0.12) |
| Age node 4[b] | 0.02 | (95% CI: −0.01, 0.06) |
| Female | −0.31 | (95% CI: −0.61, 0.00) |
| Baseline IL-6 | 0.03 | (95% CI: −0.02, 0.06) |
| Unemployed | −0.28 | (95% CI: −0.81, 0.19) |
| Other employment | 0.18 | (95% CI: −0.17, 0.53) |
| **For each 1 percentage point increase in 2011 foreclosures** | −0.04 | (95% CI: −0.09, 0.00) |
| Age node 1[b] | −0.14 | (95% CI: −0.27, −0.06)[b] |
| Age node 2[b] | −0.03 | (95% CI: −0.08, 0.00) |
| Age node 3[b] | 0.01 | (95% CI: −0.06, 0.04) |
| Age node 4[b] | 0.04 | (95% CI: −0.03, 0.02) |
| Female | −0.33 | (95% CI: −0.61, 0.07) |
| Baseline IL-6 | 0.05 | (95% CI: 0.00, 0.11) |
| Unemployed | −0.30 | (95% CI: −0.83, 0.21) |
| Other employment | 0.18 | (95% CI: −0.21, 0.45) |
| **For each 1 percentage point increase in foreclosure change (2009–2011)** | −0.19 | (95% CI: −0.62, 0.24) |
| Age node 1[b] | −0.17 | (95% CI: −0.28, −0.07)[b] |
| Age node 2[b] | −0.06 | (95% CI: −0.12, 0.01) |
| Age node 3[b] | 0.01 | (95% CI: −0.07, 0.09) |
| Age node 4[b] | 0.05 | (95% CI: 0.01, 0.17)[b] |
| Female | −0.35 | (95% CI: −0.72, 0.18) |
| Baseline IL-6 | 0.05 | (95% CI: 0.00, 0.11) |
| Unemployed | −0.30 | (95% CI: −0.83, 0.18) |
| Other employment | 0.12 | (95% CI: −0.21, 0.43) |

*Source:* Authors' calculations from the Detroit Neighborhood Health Study, 2008, and Detroit Police Department 2009.

[a]Adjusted for age, sex, baseline IL-6, and employment status. Coefficient estimates represent the change in log sj/beta-TREC ratio associated with a 10 percentage point increase in prevalence of environmental characteristics and a 1 percentage point increase in foreclosure prevalence.
[b]Age was modeled as a 4-node cubic spline.
*Significant at the = .05 level.

## REFERENCES

Ackerman, Robert Argento, Gerhard Fries, and Richard A. Windle. 2012. "Changes in U.S. Family Finances from 2007 to 2010: Evidence from the Survey of Consumer Finances." *Federal Reserve Bulletin* 100(4): 1–80.

Auchincloss, Amy H., Ana V. Diez Roux, Daniel G. Brown, Trivellore E. Raghunathan, and Christine A. Erdmann. 2007. "Filling the Gaps: Spatial Interpolation of Residential Survey Data in the Estimation of Neighborhood Characteristics." *Epidemiology* 18(4): 469–78.

Bacigalupe, Amaia, and Antonio Escolar-Pujolar. 2014. "The Impact of Economic Crises on Social Inequalities in Health: What Do We Know So Far?" *International Journal for Equity in Health* 13: 52. DOI: 10.1186/1475-9276-13-52.

Biderman, Albert D., and James P. Lynch. 2012. *Understanding Crime Incidence Statistics: Why the UCR Diverges from the NCS*. New York: Springer.

Black, Donald J. 1970. "Production of Crime Rates." *American Sociological Review* 35(4): 733–48.

Blair, Alexandra, Nancy A. Ross, Geneviève Gariepy, and Norbert Schmitz. 2014. "How Do Neighborhoods Affect Depression Outcomes? A Realist Review and a Call for the Examination of Causal Pathways." *Social Psychiatry and Psychiatric Epidemiology* 49(6): 873–87.

Boen, Courtney, and Y. Claire Yang. 2016. "The Physiological Impacts of Wealth Shocks in Late Life: Evidence from the Great Recession." *Social Science & Medicine* 150 (February): 221–30. DOI: 10.1016/j.socscimed.2015.12.029.

Bureau of Labor Statistics. 2015. "Local Area Unemployment Statistics Map: Michigan; Unemployment Rates by State; Not Seasonally Adjusted, Annual." Washington: U.S. Department of Labor. Accessed August 12, 2017. https://www.bls.gov/lau/.

Burgard, Sarah A, Jennifer A. Ailshire, and Lucie Kalousova. 2013. "The Great Recession and Health: People, Populations, and Disparities." *Annals of the American Academy of Political and Social Science* 650(1): 194–213.

Burgard, Sarah A., K. S. Seefeldt, and S. Zelner. 2012. "Housing Instability and Health: Findings from the Michigan Recession and Recovery Study." *Social Science & Medicine* 75(12): 2215–24.

Cagney, K. A., C. R. Browning, J. Iveniuk, and N. English. 2014. "The Onset of Depression During the Great Recession: Foreclosure and Older Adult Mental Health." *American Journal of Public Health* 104(3): 498–505.

Catalano, Ralph, Sidra Goldman-Mellor, Katherine Saxton, Claire Margerison-Zilko, Meenakshi Subbaraman, Kaja LeWinn, and Elizabeth Anderson. 2011. "The Health Effects of Economic Decline." *Annual Review of Public Health* 32: 431–50. DOI: 10.1146/annurev-publhealth-031210-101146.

Curry, Aaron, Carl Latkin, and Melissa Davey-Rothwell. 2008. "Pathways to Depression: The Impact of Neighborhood Violent Crime on Inner-City Residents in Baltimore, Maryland, USA." *Social Science & Medicine* 67(1): 23–30.

DelaRosa, Olga, Graham Pawelec, Esther Peralbo, Anders Wikby, Erminia Mariani, Eugenio Mocchegiani, Raquel Tarazona, and Rafael Solana. 2006. "Immunological Biomarkers of Ageing in Man: Changes in Both Innate and Adaptive Immunity Are Associated with Health and Longevity." *Biogerontology* 7(5–6): 471–81.

Detroit Police Department. 2009. "CrisNet/NetRMS." Detroit Open Data. Accessed August 12, 2017. https://data.detroitmi.gov/.

Dhabhar, Firdaus S. 2014. "Effects of Stress on Immune Function: The Good, the Bad, and the Beautiful." *Immunological Research* 58(2–3): 193–210.

Diez Roux, Ana V., Sharon S. Merkin, Donna Arnett, Lloyd Chambless, Mark Massing, F. Javier Nieto, Paul Sorlie, Moyses Szklo, Herman A. Tyroler, and Robert L. Watson. 2001. "Neighborhood of Residence and Incidence of Coronary Heart Disease." *New England Journal of Medicine* 345(2): 99–106.

Dion, M. L., R. Bordi, J. Zeidan, R. Asaad, M. R. Boulassel, J. P. Routy, M. M. Lederman, R. P. Sékaly, and R. Cheynier. 2007. "Slow Disease Progression and Robust Therapy-Mediated CD4+ T-cell Recovery Are Associated with Efficient Thymopoiesis During HIV-1 Infection." *Blood* 109(7): 2912–20.

Dion, Marie-Lise, Jean-Françoise Poulin, Rebeka Bordi, Myriam Sylvestre, Rachel Corsini, Nadia Kettaf, Ali Dalloul, Mohamed-Rachid Boulassel, Patrice Debré, Jean-Pierre Routy, Zvi Grossman, Rafick-Pierre Sékaly, and Rémi Cheynier. 2004. "HIV Infection Rapidly Induces and Maintains a Substantial Suppression of Thymocyte Proliferation." *Immunity* 21(6): 757–68.

Douek, Daniel C., Richard D. McFarland, Philip H.

Keiser, Earl A. Gage, et al. 1998. "Changes in Thymic Function with Age and During the Treatment of HIV Infection." *Nature* 396(6712): 690–95.

Dowd, Jennifer B., and Allison E. Aiello. 2009. "Socioeconomic Differentials in Immune response." *Epidemiology* 20(6): 902–08.

Drukker, Marjan, and Jim van Os. 2003. "Mediators of Neighbourhood Socioeconomic Deprivation and Quality of Life." *Social Psychiatry and Psychiatric Epidemiology* 38(12): 698–706.

Duncan, Dustin T., Ichiro Kawachi, S. V. Subramanian, Jared Aldstadt, Steven J. Melly, and David R. Williams. 2014. "Examination of How Neighborhood Definition Influences Measurements of Youths' Access to Tobacco Retailers: A Methodological Note on Spatial Misclassification." *American Journal of Epidemiology* 179(3): 373–81.

Feinstein, Lydia, Sara Ferrando-Martínez, Manuel Leal, Xuan Zhou, Gregory D. Sempowski, Derek E. Wildman, Monica Uddin, and Allison E. Aiello. 2016. "Population Distributions of Thymic Function in Adults: Variation by Sociodemographic Characteristics and Health Status." *Biodemography and Social Biology* 62(2): 208–21.

Ferrando-Martínez, Sara, Jaime M. Franco, Ana Hernandez, Antonio Ordoñez, Encarna Gutierrez, Antonia Abad, and Manuel Leal. 2009. "Thymopoiesis in Elderly Human Is Associated with Systemic Inflammatory Status." *Age (Dordr)* 31(2): 87–97.

Ferrando-Martínez, Sara, Jaime M. Franco, Ezequiel Ruiz-Mateos, Anna Hernandez, Antonio Ordonez, Encarnacion Gutiérrez-Carretero, and Manuel Leal. 2010. "A Reliable and Simplified sj/beta-TREC Ratio Quantification Method for Human Thymic Output Measurement." *Journal of Immunological Methods* 352(1–2): 111–17.

Ferrando-Martínez, Sara, Maria C. Romero-Sanchez, Rafael Solana, Juan Delgado, Rafael de la Rosa, Ma Angeles Munoz-Fernandez, Ezequiel Ruiz-Mateos, and Manuel Leal. 2013. "Thymic Function Failure and C-Reactive Protein Levels Are Independent Predictors of All-Cause Mortality in Healthy Elderly Humans." *Age (Dordr)* 35(1): 251–59.

Flanagan, Christine, and Ellen Wilson. 2013. "Home Value and Homeownership Rates: Recession and Post-Recession Comparisons from 2007–2009 to 2010–2012." *American Community Survey Brief* 12-20. Washington: U.S. Census Bureau.

Ford, Jodi L., and Christopher R. Browning. 2015. "Exposure to Neighborhood Immigrant Concentration from Adolescence to Young Adulthood and Immune Function Among Latino Young Adults." *Health & Place* 32(1): 59–64.

Giurgescu, Carmen, Dawn P. Misra, Shawnita Sealy-Jefferson, Cleopatra H. Caldwell, Thomas N. Templin, Jaime C. Slaughter-Acey, and Theresa L. Osypuk. 2015. "The Impact of Neighborhood Quality, Perceived Stress, and Social Support on Depressive Symptoms During Pregnancy in African American Women." *Social Science & Medicine* 130 (April): 172–80.

Goldmann, Emily, Allison Aiello, Monica Uddin, Jorge Delva, Karestan Koenen, Larry M. Gant, and Sandro Galea. 2011. "Pervasive Exposure to Violence and Posttraumatic Stress Disorder in a Predominantly African American Urban Community: The Detroit Neighborhood Health Study." *Journal of Traumatic Stress* 24(6): 747–51.

Gould Ellen, Ingrid, and Samuel Dastrup. 2012. "Housing and the Great Recession." Stanford Center on Poverty and Inequality, October. Accessed August 12, 2017. http://furmancenter.org/files/publications/HousingandtheGreatRecession.pdf.

Greenland, Sander, Judea Pearl, and James M. Robins. 1999. "Causal Diagrams for Epidemiologic Research." *Epidemiology* 10(1): 37–48.

Gruver, Amanda L., and Gregory D. Sempowski. 2008. "Cytokines, Leptin, and Stress-Induced Thymic Atrophy." *Journal of Leukocyte Biology* 84(4): 915–23.

Hill, Eric J., and John Gallagher. 2002. *AIA Detroit: The American Institute of Architects Guide to Detroit Architecture*. Detroit, Mich.: Wayne State University Press.

Howe, Chanelle J., Stephen R. Cole, Daniel J. Westreich, Sander Greenland, Sonia Napravnik, and Joseph J. Eron Jr. 2011. "Splines for Trend Analysis and Continuous Confounder Control." *Epidemiology* 22(6): 874–45.

Hunter, Christopher A., and Simon A. Jones. 2015. "IL-6 as a Keystone Cytokine in Health and Disease." *Nature Immunology* 16(5): 448–57.

Kawachi, Ichiro, and Lisa F. Berkman. 2003. *Neighborhoods and Health*. Oxford: Oxford University Press.

Keita, Akilah Dulin, Suzanne E. Judd, Virginia J. Howard, April P. Carson, Jamy D. Ard, and Jose R. Fernandez. 2014. "Associations of Neighborhood

Area Level Deprivation with the Metabolic Syndrome and Inflammation Among Middle- and Older-Age Adults." *BMC Public Health* 14 (December): 1319.

King, Katherine E., Jeffrey D. Morenoff, and James S. House. 2011. "Neighborhood Context and Social Disparities in Cumulative Biological Risk Factors." *Psychosomatic Medicine* 73(7): 572-79.

Kruger, Daniel J, Thomas M. Reischl, and Gilbert C. Gee. 2007. "Neighborhood Social Conditions Mediate the Association Between Physical Deterioration and Mental Health." *American Journal of Community Psychology* 40(3-4): 261-71.

Lantos, Paul M, Sallie R. Permar, Kate Hoffman, and Geeta K. Swamy. 2015. "The Excess Burden of Cytomegalovirus in African American Communities: A Geospatial Analysis." *Open Forum Infectious Diseases* 2(4). DOI: 10.1093/ofid/ofv180.

Lichter, Daniel T., Domenico Parisi, and Michael C. Taquino. 2015. "Toward a New Macro-Segregation? Decomposing Segregation Within and Between Metropolitan Cities and Suburbs." *American Sociological Review* 80(4): 843-73.

Lynch, Heather E., Gabrielle L. Goldberg, Ann Chidgey, Marcel R. M. Van den Brink, Richard Boyd, and Gregory D. Sempowski. 2009. "Thymic Involution and Immune Reconstitution." *Trends in Immunology* 30(7): 366-73.

Lynch, Heather E., and G. D. Sempowski. 2013. "Molecular Measurement of T Cell Receptor Excision Circles." *Methods in Molecular Biology* 979: 147-59.

McLaughlin, Katie A., A. Nandi, Kyle M. Keyes, Monica Uddin, Allison E. Aiello, Sandro Galea, and Karestan C. Koenen. 2012. "Home Foreclosure and Risk of Psychiatric Morbidity During the Recent Financial Crisis." *Psychological Medicine* 42(7): 1441-48.

Michigan Foreclosure Task Force. 2016. "Michigan Historical Residential Foreclosure Data." Johnson Center at Grand Valley State University, October 20, 2016. Accessed August 12, 2017. http://cridata.org/michiganforeclosuretaskforce/.

Mishel, Lawrence, Josh Bivens, Elise Gould, and Heidi Shierholz. 2012. "Great Recession." In *The State of Working America*, 12th ed. Ithaca, N.Y.: Cornell University Press.

Momper, Sandra, Anne Nordberg, Leah James, and Jorge Delva. 2012. "Assessing Neighborhoods' Physical and Social Environments: Experiences from the Detroit Neighborhood Health Study." Paper presented at the Society for Social Work and Research Sixteenth Annual Conference "Research that Makes a Difference: Advancing Practice and Shaping Public Policy." Washington, D.C. (January 11-15, 2012).

Mulia, Nina, Sarah E. Zemore, Ryan Murphy, HiuGuo Liu, and Ralpj Catalano. 2014. "Economic Loss and Alcohol Consumption and Problems During the 2008 to 2009 U.S. Recession." *Alcoholism: Clinical and Experimental Research* 38(4): 1026-34.

Oakes, J. Michael. 2004. "The (Mis) Estimation of Neighborhood Effects: Causal Inference for a Practicable Social Epidemiology." *Social Science & Medicine* 58(10): 1929-52.

Piccolo, Rebecca S., Dustin T. Duncan, Neil Pearce, and John B. McKinlay. 2015. "The Role of Neighborhood Characteristics in Racial/Ethnic Disparities in Type 2 Diabetes: Results from the Boston Area Community Health (BACH) Survey." *Social Science & Medicine* 130 (April): 79-90.

Pollack, Craig E., Shanu K. Kurd, Alice Livshits, Mark G. Weiner, and Julia Lynch. 2011. "A Case-Control Study of Home Foreclosure, Health Conditions, and Health Care Utilization." *Journal of Urban Health* 88(3): 469-78.

Poulin, Jean-François, Mohan N. Viswanathan, Jeffrey M. Harris, Krishna V. Komanduri, Eric Wieder, Nancy Ringuette, Morgan Jenkins, Joseph M. McCune, and Rafick-Pierre Sékaly. 1999. "Direct Evidence for Thymic Function in Adult Humans." *Journal of Experimental Medicine* 190(4): 479-86.

RealtyTrac. 2011. "Michigan Foreclosures." RealtyTrac foreclosure activity. Accessed May 21, 2016. http://www.realtytrac.com/ContentManagement/.

Riumallo-Herl, Carlos, Sanjay Basu, David Stuckler, Emilie Courtin, and Maricio Avendano. 2014. "Job Loss, Wealth and Depression During the Great Recession in the USA and Europe." *International Journal of Epidemiology* 43(5): 1508-17.

Rooney, Ben. 2008. "Rust and Sun Belt Cities Lean '07 Foreclosures: Detroit, Stockton and Las Vegas Are Top Activity Centers for Troubled Homeowners, According to New Study." CNN Money, February 12. Accessed August 12, 2017. http://money.cnn.com/2008/02/12/real_estate/realtytrac/index.htm.

Shah, Sumit, Fenye Bao, Chang-Tien Lu, and Ing-Ray Chen. 2011. "Crowdsafe: Crowd Sourcing of Crime Incidents and Safe Routing on Mobile Devices." Paper presented at the 19th ACM SIGSPATIAL International Conference on Advances in Geographic Information Systems. Chicago (November 1–3, 2011).

Smith, George D., Carole Hart, Graham Watt, David Hole, and Victor Hawthorne. 1998. "Individual Social Class, Area-Based Deprivation, Cardiovascular Disease Risk Factors, and Mortality: The Renfrew and Paisley Study." *Journal of Epidemiology and Community Health* 52(6): 399–405.

Steptoe, Andrew. 2012. *Socioeconomic Status, Inflammation, and Immune Function*. New York: Oxford University Press.

Steptoe, Andrew, and Michael Marmot. 2002. "The Role of Psychobiological Pathways in Socio-Economic Inequalities in Cardiovascular Disease Risk." *European Heart Journal* 23(1): 13–25.

Subramanian, S. V., and A. James O'Malley. 2010. "Modeling Neighborhood Effects: The Futility of Comparing Mixed and Marginal Approaches." *Epidemiology* 21(4): 475–81.

Sugrue, Thomas J. 2014. *The Origins of the Urban Crisis: Race and Inequality in Postwar Detroit*. Princeton, N.J.: Princeton University Press.

Tonorezos, Emily S., Patrick N. Breysse, Elizabeth C. Matsui, Meredith C. McCormack, Jean Curtin-Brosnan, D'Ann Williams, Nadia N. Hansel, Peyton A. Eggleston, and Gregory B. Diette. 2008. "Does Neighborhood Violence Lead to Depression Among Caregivers of Children with Asthma?" *Social Science & Medicine* 67(1): 31–37.

Tsai, Alexander C. 2015. "Home Foreclosure, Health, and Mental Health: A Systematic Review of Individual, Aggregate, and Contextual Associations." *PLoS One* 10: e0123182.

U.S. Census Bureau. 2013. "Median and Average Sales Prices of New Homes Sold, Household Income in the United States." Accessed August 12, 2017. https://www.census.gov/construction/nrs/pdf/uspricemon.pdf.

Wilson-Genderson, Maureen, and Rachel Pruchno. 2013. "Effects of Neighborhood Violence and Perceptions of Neighborhood Safety on Depressive Symptoms of Older Adults." *Social Science & Medicine* 85 (May): 43–49.

# PART III
# Developmental and Intergenerational Processes

# A Biopsychosocial Approach to Examine Mexican American Adolescents' Academic Achievement and Substance Use

YANG QU, ADRIANA GALVÁN, ANDREW J. FULIGNI, AND EVA H. TELZER

*Taking a comprehensive biopsychosocial approach and using a two-wave longitudinal design, this study examines the relation between brain development and the social environment in Mexican American youth's (N = 41.56 percent female) academic achievement and substance use. We find that both Mexican American youth's structural brain development and social environment uniquely contribute to their adjustment. Specially, smaller hippocampal volume and parental cultural socialization each uniquely predict better academic achievement. Moreover, smaller nucleus accumbens volume and less affiliation with deviant peers each uniquely predict less substance use. These findings underscore the independent contributions of biological and psychosocial factors in youth's adjustment. The study provides a new biopsychosocial perspective on Mexican American youth's well-being.*

**Keywords:** academic achievement, cultural socialization, brain structure, substance use

Mexican Americans are the largest and fastest growing ethnic minority group in the United States, making up about 17 percent (fifty-six million people) of the U.S. population. Challenges associated with immigration, discrimination, and lower socioeconomic status place Mexican American youth at particularly high risk for poor adjustment, including school dropout and substance use. For example, Mexican American youth's school dropout rates are approximately double that of any other ethnic group (U.S. Department of Commerce 2006). Such disadvantage in K–12 schools results in negative long-term problems in school trajectories, such that Mexican American students have the lowest postsecondary enrollment rate (24 percent). In addition, relative to adolescents in other ethnic groups, Mexican American adolescents have higher rates of substance use, begin using drugs at an earlier age, and show greater risk for developing drug use disorders in adulthood due to early drug use on-

---

**Yang Qu** is a postdoctoral scholar at Stanford University. **Adriana Galván** is associate professor of psychology and faculty member of the Brain Research Institute at University of California, Los Angeles. **Andrew J. Fuligni** is professor in the Department of Psychology and faculty member of the Brain Research Institute and the Semel Institute for Neuroscience and Human Behavior at the University of California, Los Angeles. **Eva H. Telzer** is assistant professor in the Department of Psychology and Neuroscience at the University of North Carolina, Chapel Hill.

© 2018 Russell Sage Foundation. Qu, Yang, Adriana Galván, Andrew J. Fuligni, and Eva H. Telzer. 2018. "A Biopsychosocial Approach to Examine Mexican American Adolescents' Academic Achievement and Substance Use." *RSF: The Russell Sage Foundation Journal of the Social Sciences* 4(4): 84–97. DOI: 10.7758/RSF.2018.4.4.05. Direct correspondence to: Yang Qu at yangqu@stanford.edu, 450 Serra Mall, Stanford, CA 94305; Adriana Galván at agalvan@psych.ucla.edu; Andrew J. Fuligni at afuligni@ucla.edu; and Eva H. Telzer at ehtelzer@unc.edu, 235 E. Cameron Ave., Chapel Hill, NC 27599.

Open Access Policy: *RSF: The Russell Sage Foundation Journal of the Social Sciences* is an open access journal. This article is published under a Creative Commons Attribution-NonCommercial-NoDerivs 3.0 Unported License.

set (Eaton et al. 2006; Johnston et al. 2009; Marsiglia et al. 2005). It is therefore important to identify protective factors that are associated with better academic achievement and less substance use.

## A BIOPSYCHOSOCIAL APPROACH TO STUDY MEXICAN AMERICAN ADOLESCENTS

To address ethnic disparities in academic achievement and substance use, it is critical to systematically examine biological and psychosocial factors that influence Mexican American adolescents. Past research has taken either a biological or a psychosocial approach to understand adolescents' well-being, highlighting the importance of both biological (for example, brain structure) and psychosocial (for example, social environment) factors in adolescents' adjustment. For example, advances in neuroimaging techniques allow researchers to examine how social relationships get "under the skin" (Fuligni and Telzer 2013). In this endeavor, countless exciting findings have revealed how neural structure and function are related to adolescent adjustment. However, it is also acknowledged that examining brain structure and function alone cannot inform us how social environments are related to the neurobiology of the developing child.

Although both biological and psychosocial approaches provide valuable insights to our understanding of minority adolescents' well-being, few studies to date combine these two approaches to provide a more comprehensive perspective on adolescent development. In the absence of systematic investigation, it remains unclear whether biological and psychosocial factors play a unique role in minority adolescents' adjustment. This study therefore took an integrative biopsychosocial approach to systematically examine how biological (youth's brain development) and psychosocial (parents' cultural socialization and deviant peer association) factors are uniquely related to Mexican American youth's academic achievement and substance use. Findings will provide valuable insights into promoting Mexican American children's well-being during adolescence, an important period of brain development and socialization.

## Brain Structure and Adolescents' Well-being

Neuroimaging research has demonstrated dramatic brain development during adolescence. Prior research has characterized functional brain development in Mexican American adolescents, with attention to the role of family and peer contexts (Telzer et al. 2013a, 2013b; Telzer et al. 2015; Qu et al. 2015). However, no work to date has examined Mexican American adolescents' structural brain development and the potential unique effects of structural changes and social environment on adolescents' adjustment. This is a limitation because neural changes during adolescence not only involve changes in brain function, but also changes in brain structure. Although functional and structural changes often go hand in hand, they also uniquely predict adjustment outcomes. Thus, individual differences in brain structure may also predict individual differences in academic and psychological adjustment.

An interesting phenomenon during adolescence is the parallel between loss of cortical gray matter and improvement in cognitive abilities. Although the whole brain may reach its maximum size around the age of five years, grey and white matter subcomponents continue to undergo significant changes throughout adolescence (Giedd et al. 1999; Sowell et al. 2003; Gogtay et al. 2004). Specifically, cortical gray matter volume begins to decline in late childhood or early adolescence, and white matter shows a linear increase over the same period. For example, in a large-scale longitudinal neuroimaging study, a curvilinear change in grey matter was found, such that it increased from childhood to adolescence, and then decreased in adolescence and into adulthood (Giedd et al. 1999). The decline in gray matter is thought to be driven by synaptic pruning, a process through which unused synapses are eliminated to increase the efficiency of neuronal transmissions (Huttenlocher 1990). Therefore, lower gray matter volume may indicate greater pruning and more mature neural development.

A key neural region related to learning and memory is the hippocampus, a brain region in the medial temporal lobe (Cohen and Eichenbaum 1993; Maguire, Frackowiak, and Frith 1997; Maguire et al. 2000). Empirical studies have examined the association between hippocampal volume and adolescents' adjustment, which seem to yield inconsistent findings at first glance. Although some studies suggest that larger hippocampal volume is linked to better memory and learning (Erickson et al. 2011), others find the opposite pattern (Foster et al. 1999). A key factor overlooked in previous studies is the developmental stage. Indeed, a meta-analysis across development found age-related changes in such association (Van Petten 2004). Although hippocampal volume and memory have a weak positive relationship among adults (see Golomb et al. 1994; Raz et al. 1998), a negative relationship between hippocampal volume and memory was significant for studies with children and adolescents (see Riggins et al. 2012; Sowell et al. 2001). Similarly, this significant negative association between hippocampal volume and memory performance has been found in healthy young adults (Chantôme et al. 1999; Foster et al. 1999; Pruessner et al. 2007). Such association is thought to be explained by the degree of neural pruning that occurs during childhood and adolescence, with smaller gray matter volume indicating more pruning (that is, neural specialization). Thus, smaller hippocampus volume may indicate greater brain maturation and is related to educational advantages.

The nucleus accumbens plays a central role in reward seeking, risk taking, substance use, and addictive behaviors (Casey, Getz, and Galván 2008; Galván 2010; Knutson et al. 2001). Previous functional MRI studies have examined the association between nucleus accumbens activation and adolescents' adjustment, suggesting that greater activity in the nucleus accumbens is related to greater risk taking (for example, Galván et al. 2007; Qu et al. 2015). Only a few studies have used structural MRI to investigate the link between nucleus accumbens volume and risk taking. Accumulating evidence reveals a preliminary positive relationship between the two. For example, young adults who use cannabis showed larger nucleus accumbens volume than non–drug users (Gilman et al. 2014). Moreover, nucleus accumbens volume is positively associated with frequency of drinking among adolescents (Thayer et al. 2012). Interestingly, the developmental decline in reward sensitivity from late adolescence to young adulthood is accompanied by a decrease in nucleus accumbens volumes (Urošević et al. 2012). Thus, smaller nucleus accumbens volume may be associated with less reward-seeking behaviors such as substance use.

## SOCIAL ENVIRONMENT AND ADOLESCENTS' WELL-BEING

In a separate body of work, researchers have taken a psychosocial approach to identify factors in social environment that play a role in Mexican American adolescents' well-being. Based on findings from this line of research, parents and peers serve as two key socialization agents. Drawing on this literature, this study focuses on two important factors that may influence adolescents' academic achievement and substance use—parents' cultural socialization and adolescents' association with deviant peers.

In ethnic minority families, one socialization goal for parents is to help their children develop a strong connection to their ethnic heritage and understanding of cultural values (Hughes et al. 2006; Parke and Buriel 2006). Therefore, parents engage in related practices. Specifically, parents talk to their children about their country of origin, celebrate cultural holidays and historical events, and expose children to culturally relevant books, arts, and music (Hughes and Chen 1997; Knight et al. 1993). Because these practices are embedded in daily parent-child interactions, parents' cultural socialization is also a protective factor for minority adolescent well-being. Indeed, empirical studies suggest that parental cultural socialization practices are related to adolescents' development of ethnic pride and identification (Rivas-Drake, Hughes, and Way 2009), and ultimately lead to better academic and behavioral outcomes, such as more school engagement and less antisocial behavior (Hughes et al. 2009).

In addition, as children enter adolescence, they spend more time with their peers (Larson and Verma 1999). Their academic and psychological adjustment is thus also influenced by their peer groups. For example, exposure to delinquent peers may lead to increased involvement in substance abuse due to the processes of imitation, social learning, and peer pressure (Deater-Deckard 2001; Dishion, Patterson, and Griesler 1994; Moffitt 1993). Indeed, deviant peer association is one of the strongest predictors of substance use in adolescence (Barrera et al. 2002; Fergusson, Swain-Campbell, and Horwood 2002; Jenkins 1996). Importantly, among Mexican American adolescents, strong family values relate to less substance use because adolescents are less likely to associate with deviant peers (Telzer, Gonzales, and Fuligni 2014). Avoidance of deviant peers is thus an important protective factor in adolescents' substance use.

## CURRENT STUDY

Building on prior literature, the current research took an integrative biopsychosocial approach to systematically examine the role of biological (youth's brain development) and psychosocial (parents' cultural socialization and deviant peer association) factors on Mexican American youth's adjustment, focusing on their academic achievement and substance use. Given substantial variation among Mexican American adolescents, this study investigated how individual differences in structural brain development and social environment were predictive of individual differences in academic and psychological adjustment, rather than comparing Mexican American adolescents with their counterparts in other ethnic groups. Findings not only will provide insights into how biological and psychosocial factors are related to Mexican American youth's adjustment, but also have the potential to be generalized to other minority groups.

Our first goal was to examine the role of brain structure and social environment in Mexican American adolescents' academic achievement. Given that effective pruning leads to greater reduction in gray matter volume, we hypothesized that smaller volume in the hippocampus, a key region related to memory and learning, would predict better academic achievement. In addition, based on research on minority adolescents (Hughes et al. 2006), we hypothesized that parents' cultural socialization would contribute to youth's better academic achievement.

Our second goal was to investigate the mediating role through which brain structure and social environment play a role in Mexican American adolescents' academic achievement. Specifically, we focused on the adolescents' positive work habits. We hypothesized that smaller hippocampal volume and parents' cultural socialization would facilitate better work habits among adolescents, which ultimately promotes better academic achievement.

Our third goal was to examine the role of brain structure and social environment in Mexican American adolescents' substance use. We focused on the nucleus accumbens, a region consistently related to reward seeking and risk taking. Based on prior research, we predicted that smaller volume in the nucleus accumbens would be related to less substance use (Thayer et al. 2012). Given that deviant peer association consistently predicts adolescents' substance use across different studies, we further hypothesized that Mexican American adolescents' association with more deviant peers would be related to more severe substance use (Barrera et al. 2002; Telzer, Gonzales, and Fuligni 2014).

## METHODS

Forty-one Mexican American adolescents (mean age at T1 = 15.24 years, range = 14.02 to 16.25 years, SD = 0.54, 56 percent girls) participated in a two-wave longitudinal study. Most participants were from low-SES families with the majority of fathers (87 percent) and mothers (78 percent) receiving a high school diploma or less. At T1, adolescents reported on their parents' cultural socialization practices and their affiliation with deviant peers. To measure their brain structure, adolescents underwent a structural magnetic resonance imaging (sMRI) scan one year later (T2). Adolescents reported on their substance use at T2, and we obtained adolescents' grade point average (GPA) from school records and teachers report of adolescents' work habits. Participants completed written consent and assent in accordance with the Institutional Review Board.

### Measures

Youth reported on their parents' cultural socialization practices using the ethnic-racial socialization scale at T1 (Hughes and Chen 1997). This scale is a self-report scale designed to measure the amount of cultural socialization the adolescent has received from parents in the last year, and has been used in studies on Mexican

American parents' cultural socialization (for example, Hughes 2003). Using four items, adolescents reported how frequently (1 = never to 5 = six or more times) their parents engaged in cultural socialization in the past year (for example, "In the past year, how many times have your parents encouraged you to read books concerning the history or traditions of your ethnicity?"). Their responses were averaged, higher scores indicating greater cultural socialization ($\alpha = 0.74$).

For deviant peer association, at T1, youth indicated the number of their friends who engage in risky activities using a measure previously used among Mexican American youth (Barrera et al. 2002). This measure included fifteen deviant behaviors, such as got drunk or high, cheated on school tests, started a fight with someone, and stole something. For each behavior, adolescents reported on how many of their friends engaged in this risky activity in the last month on a five-point scale (1 = "none", 5 = "almost all"). Their responses were averaged, with higher scores indicating more deviant peers ($\alpha = 0.91$).

At the end of T2, teachers reported on adolescents' work habits based on criteria for marks for Los Angeles Unified School District. Work habits in four subjects, including math, English, science, and social science, were collected. Work habits capture a wide range of adolescent school behavior, such as effort, responsibility, and attendance. For each subject, students received an E (excellent; for example, "Makes explicit effort to examine work using both teacher-generated and self-generated criteria."), S (satisfactory; for example, "Makes effort to examine work using teacher-generated criteria."), or U (unsatisfactory; for example, "Makes use only of teacher-generated criteria to examine work on an inconsistent basis."), which was then converted to numbers (E = 2, S = 1, and U = 0). For each participant, work habits across four subjects were averaged, with higher scores indicating better work habits.

For adolescents' academic achievement, at the end of T2, adolescents' GPA was obtained from school records. Grades were originally in letters and converted to a four-point scale (0 = F to 4 = A).

At T2, adolescents reported on their use of substances on the Center for Disease Control and Prevention Youth Risk Behavior Survey Questionnaire, a common measure that has been shown to be valid and reliable for Mexican American youth (Kerr et al. 2003). This in-depth form asks about youth's lifetime use (for example, if you have ever tried marijuana, how old were you when you tried it for the first time?) for the following substances: cigarettes, alcohol (including beer, wine, wine coolers, and liquor that does not include sips of wine for religious purposes), marijuana (for example, pot, weed, grass, hash), cocaine (for example, powder, crack, or freebase), crystal meth (also called ice or glass), and other illegal drugs (for example, LSD, PCP, ecstasy, mushrooms, speed, or heroin). To examine substance use, an index was created that indicates the type of substance the adolescent had ever tried lifetime, where 0 = never tried any type of substance, 1 = tried legal substances (alcohol or cigarettes) at least once, 2 = tried marijuana at least once, and 3 = tried hard substances (cocaine, crystal meth, or other illegal drugs) at least once. Higher scores indicate more severe substance use.

Demographic information on adolescents' gender and parents' educational attainment were collected at T1. The primary caregiver indicated the highest educational attainment for each parent, which was assessed using a ten-point scale (1 = "some elementary school", 10 = "graduated from medical, law, or graduate school"). A composite score that averages father's and mother's highest educational attainment was calculated to represent parents' average educational attainment, with higher scores indicating higher educational attainment. Both adolescents' gender and parents' educational attainment were taken into account in all analyses.

*Structural MRI Data Acquisition*
Imaging data were collected using a 3.0 Tesla Siemens Trio MRI scanner. High resolution T1-weighted brain images were acquired using a 3D magnetization-prepared rapid-acquisition gradient echo (MPRAGE) scan with 160 contiguous axial slices, collected in ascending fashion parallel to the anterior and posterior commissures, echo time (TE) = 2.1 ms, repetition time (TR) = 2300 ms, field of view (FOV) = 256

mm, acquisition matrix 192 mm x 192 mm, sagittal plane, and slice thickness = 1 mm.

*Segmentation and Volumetric Analysis*
Segmentation and volumetric analysis of the hippocampus and nucleus accumbens were performed using FMRIB's (Oxford Center for Functional MRI of the Brain) Integrated Registration and Segmentation Tool (FIRST) in FMRIB's Software Library (FSL) version 4.1.9 (Patenaude et al. 2007a, 2007b). FIRST is a semi-automated, model-based subcortical tool using a Bayesian framework.

First, for each participant's MPRAGE, this method ran a two-stage affine registration to a standard space template (Montreal Neurological Institute space) with one millimeter resolution using twelve degrees of freedom and a subcortical mask to exclude voxels outside the subcortical regions. Second, the left and right hippocampus and nucleus accumbens were segmented with thirty, forty, and fifty modes of variation, respectively. To achieve accurate segmentation, the FIRST methodology models 317 manually segmented and labeled T1 brain images from normal children, adults, and pathological populations as a point distribution model with the geometry and variation of the shape of each structure submitted as priors. Volumetric labels are parameterized by a 3D deformation of a surface model based on multivariate Gaussian assumptions. FIRST searches through linear combinations of shape modes of variation for the most probable shape (that is, brain structure) given the intensity distribution in the T1-weighted image, and specific brain regions are extracted (for further description of the method, see Patenaude et al. 2007a, 2007b). Modes of variation are optimized based on leave-one-out cross-validation on the training set, and they increase the robustness and reliability of the results (Patenaude et al. 2007b). The segmentations were visually checked for errors. Finally, boundary correction was run, a process that classifies boundary voxels as belonging to the structure or not based on a statistical probability (z-score > 3.00; $p < .001$).

The volume of each participant's brain region was measured in millimeters cubed. Volumes were estimated separately for the left and right hemispheres. The left and right volumes for the hippocampus and nucleus accumbens were examined in the current analyses.

## RESULTS
Our analyses examined how brain structure and social environment relate to adolescents' academic achievement and substance use.

### Descriptive Statistics of Academic Achievement and Substance Use
We first examined youth's academic achievement. The average GPA was moderately low ($M = 2.20$; that is, C- average), with substantial variability within the group ($SD = 1.03$, range = .19 to 3.75). On average, girls tended to perform better in school ($M = 2.45$) compared with boys ($M = 1.88$), $t(39) = 1.78$, $p = .08$. Parents' educational attainment was not related to youth's academic achievement, $r = .06$, $p = .72$.

Next, we investigated youth's substance use. The frequency for lifetime substance use is presented in table 1. Nearly two-thirds of the sample engaged in substance use in their lifetime, the majority in marijuana. Males and females did not differ in their substance use, $t(39) = .50$, $p = .62$. Moreover, substance use did not vary across parents' educational attainment, $r = -.22$, $p = .16$.

Bivariate correlations between all study variables are presented in table 2. Hippocampal and nucleus accumbens volumes were not correlated to each other. Whereas hippocampal volume was correlated with work habits and GPA but not substance use, nucleus accumbens volume was associated with substance use but not GPA or work habits. Parents' cultural so-

**Table 1.** Current Stage of Substance Use in Mexican American Youth

| Stage | Male | Female | Total (%) |
|---|---|---|---|
| 0 | 9 | 6 | 15 (36.6) |
| 1 | 1 | 6 | 7 (17.1) |
| 2 | 4 | 8 | 12 (29.3) |
| 3 | 4 | 3 | 7 (17.1) |

*Source*: Authors' calculations.
*Note*: 0 = no substance use, 1 = substances that are legal for adults (such as tobacco and alcohol), 2 = marijuana, and 3 = other illicit substances (such as cocaine, crystal meth, heroin, and speed).

**Table 2.** Bivariate Correlations

|   | 1 | 2 | 3 | 4 | 5 | 6 | 7 | 8 | 9 |
|---|---|---|---|---|---|---|---|---|---|
| 1. Left hippocampal volume | — | | | | | | | | |
| 2. Right hippocampal volume | .51** | — | | | | | | | |
| 3. Left nucleus accumbens volume | .06 | .24 | — | | | | | | |
| 4. Right nucleus accumbens volume | .04 | .19 | .57*** | — | | | | | |
| 5. Cultural socialization | -.24 | .11 | -.10 | -.04 | — | | | | |
| 6. Deviant peer association | .02 | .17 | .16 | .07 | .37* | — | | | |
| 7. Work habits | -.41** | -.18 | -.08 | -.16 | .33* | .02 | — | | |
| 8. Academic achievement | -.44** | -.10 | -.09 | -.11 | .41** | .07 | .96*** | — | |
| 9. Substance use | .01 | .26 | .31* | .20 | .22 | .50** | -.16 | -.10 | — |

*Source:* Authors' calculations.
***$p < .001$, **$p < .01$, *$p < .05$

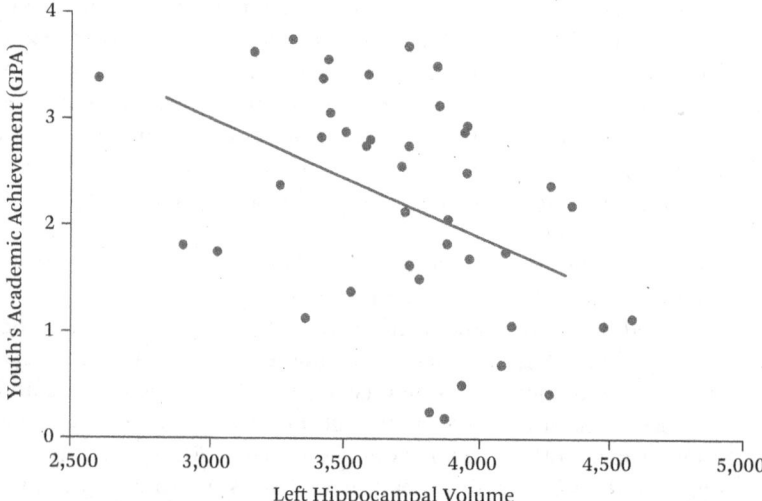

**Figure 1.** Left Hippocampal Volume and Youth's Academic Achievement

*Source:* Authors' calculations.

cialization and adolescents' deviant peer association were not related to hippocampal and nucleus accumbens volumes.

### The Role of Brain Structure and Social Environment in Academic Achievement

Our first analysis examined the role of biological and psychosocial factors in Mexican American youth's academic achievement. To this end, we conducted regression analyses with youth's brain structure, parents' cultural socialization, and deviant peer association predicting youth's GPA. Specifically, we focused on volume in the hippocampus, a region related to memory and learning. Consistent with previous research, our results indicated that smaller volume in the left hippocampus was associated with better academic achievement (that is, higher GPA), $p < .01$ (figure 1).

When parents' cultural socialization and adolescents' association with deviant peers were included in the regression model, results indicated that parents' cultural socialization was positively associated with youth's academic

**Table 3.** Regression Analysis for Academic Achievement

| Predictor | B | SE (B) | β | t |
|---|---|---|---|---|
| Gender | .09 | .16 | .09 | .55 |
| Parents' education | −.03 | .08 | −.05 | −.34 |
| Left hippocampal volume | −.001 | .00 | −.43 | −2.83** |
| Parents' cultural socialization | .50 | .17 | .44 | 2.92** |
| Deviant peer association | −.15 | .22 | −.10 | −.67 |

*Source:* Authors' calculations.
*Note:* For youth's gender, −1 = male and 1 = female.
**$p < .01$

**Figure 2.** Hippocampal Volume, Work Habits, and Academic Achievement

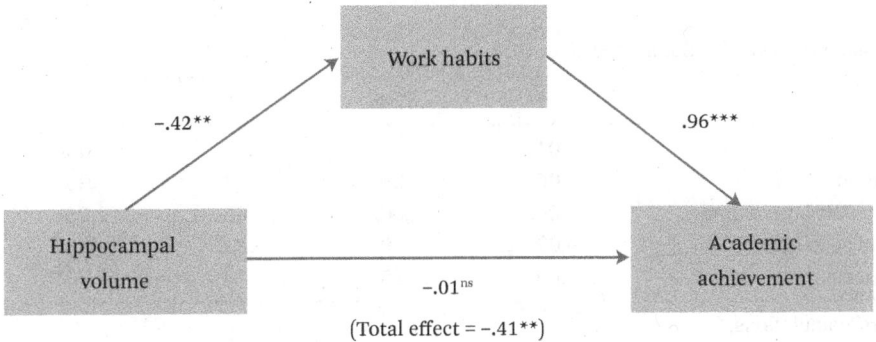

(Total effect = −.41**)

*Source:* Authors' calculations.
**$p < .01$; ***$p < .001$; ns = not significant

achievement (table 3). Importantly, both hippocampal volume and parents' cultural socialization had unique effects on youth's academic achievement. Affiliation with deviant peers was not related to academic achievement.

To understand how hippocampal volume and parents' cultural socialization are related to youth's academic achievement, we examined positive work habits. To test whether work habits mediate the link between hippocampal volume and academic achievement as well as that between parents' cultural socialization and academic achievement, we conducted two mediation analyses using bias-corrected bootstrapping resampling techniques (Preacher and Hayes 2008).

In the first set of mediation analyses, the independent variable was hippocampal volume, the dependent variable was youth's academic achievement, and the mediator was their work habits. Based on five thousand bootstrap resamples, the indirect path from hippocampal volume to academic achievement via work habits was significant: indirect effect = −.40, 95 percent CI: (−.74, −.11) (figure 2). The link between hippocampal volume and academic achievement was no longer significant after work habits were taken into account, which showed a 97 percent reduction in the total effect.

In the second set of analyses, the independent variable was parents' cultural socialization, the dependent variable was youth's academic achievement, and the mediator was their work habits. Based on five thousand bootstrap resamples, the indirect path from parents' cultural socialization to work habits to academic achievement was significant: indirect effect = .28, 95 percent CI: (.04, .54) (figure 3). The reduction in the total effect between cultural socialization and academic achievement was 72 percent, which remained significant after taking into account work habits.

**Figure 3.** Parents' Cultural Socialization, Work Habits, and Academic Achievement

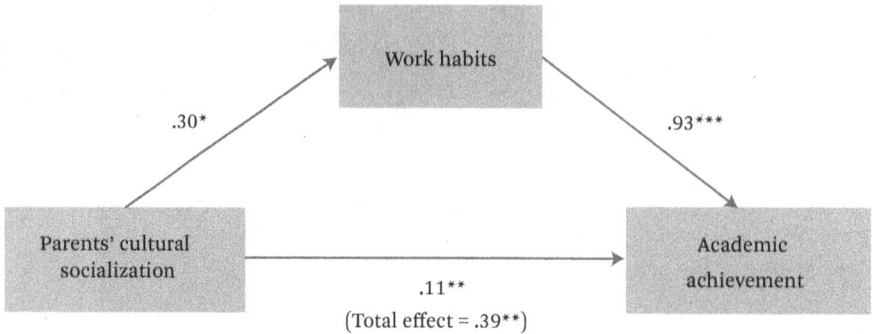

*Source:* Authors' calculations.
\*$p < .05$; \*\*$p < .01$; \*\*\*$p < .001$

**Table 4.** Regression Analysis for Substance Use

| Predictor | B | SE (B) | β | t |
| --- | --- | --- | --- | --- |
| Gender | .01 | .16 | .01 | .03 |
| Parents' education | −.09 | .09 | −.14 | −.95 |
| Left nucleus accumbens volume | .003 | .002 | .33 | 2.23* |
| Parents' cultural socialization | −.02 | .19 | −.02 | −.13 |
| Deviant peer association | .68 | .25 | .44 | 2.76** |

*Source:* Authors' calculations.
*Note:* For youth's gender, −1 = male and 1 = female.
\*$p < .05$; \*\*$p < .01$

### The Role of Brain Structure and Social Environment in Substance Use

Next, we examined the role of biological and psychosocial factors in Mexican American youth's substance use. Given prior research, we focused on the nucleus accumbens, a region involved in reward seeking and risk taking. Similar to analyses on academic achievement, we conducted regression analyses with youth's nucleus accumbens volume, parents' cultural socialization, and deviant peer association predicting youth's substance use. As shown in table 4, consistent with our hypotheses, smaller volume in the nucleus accumbens was associated with less substance use among Mexican American youth.

When parents' cultural socialization and deviant peer association were included in the regression model, results indicated that more deviant peers was positively associated with youth's substance use (table 4). Importantly, both nucleus accumbens volume and deviant peers had unique effects on Mexican American youth's substance use. Parents' cultural socialization was not related to substance use.

### DISCUSSION

With an increasing population, Mexican American adolescents' disadvantage in school and heightened substance use have drawn attention from researchers, educators, and policymakers. In this study, focusing on variation within a Mexican American sample, we took a biopsychosocial approach to examine how brain development and social environment are uniquely associated with adolescents' academic achievement and substance use. Adolescents who showed smaller hippocampal volume and whose parents provided greater cultural socialization showed better academic achievement. Moreover, smaller nucleus accumbens volume and less affiliation with deviant peers are related to less substance use. Taken together, our findings provide empirical evidence to demonstrate that both Mexican American youth's brain development and their social environment are uniquely associated with their academic achievement and substance use.

## The Role of Brain Structure and Social Environment in Academic Achievement

Smaller hippocampal volume was associated with better academic achievement. Despite evidence suggesting a negative correlation between hippocampal volume and memory during adolescence (Van Petten 2004), prior neuroimaging research has not examined the link between hippocampal volume and adolescents' actual performance in school, making it unclear whether hippocampal volume plays a role in academic achievement. We found a significant negative association between hippocampal volume and adolescents' GPA. Our findings thus underscore the important role of the hippocampus in adolescents' actual school performance. Consistent with synaptic pruning during adolescence, smaller hippocampal volume may indicate more effective pruning and greater brain maturation, which is linked to adolescents' better academic adjustment.

Previous studies have suggested the important role of parents' cultural socialization in promoting minority adolescents' performance in school. For example, greater cultural socialization is related to greater school engagement among minority adolescents (for example, Hughes et al. 2009). In line with these studies, adolescents who reported their parents providing more cultural socialization at T1 showed higher GPA at T2. Although it is possible that these parents provide more general support and guidance to their adolescents, research suggests that parents' cultural socialization, a unique parenting practice in ethnic minority families, may play a distinctive role in minority adolescents' adjustment over and above other family factors (for example, parental warmth) (Hughes et al. 2006). Parents' cultural socialization predicted adolescents' academic achievement above and beyond the effect of hippocampal volume. This finding contributes to the rich literature revealing that parents' transmission of cultural values in daily life benefits adolescents' academic adjustment, highlighting the unique role of parents' cultural socialization in shaping adolescents' learning. Such cultural transmission may be particularly important during adolescence, a time when adolescents actively seek to pursue their ethnic identity (for example, French et al. 2006). Interventions designed at promoting Mexican American adolescents' school performance can focus on encouraging parents to convey cultural values and heritages to their children.

The link between hippocampal volume and academic achievement and the link between parents' cultural socialization and academic achievement was mediated by adolescents' work habits. Specifically, adolescents who showed smaller hippocampal volume and who reported greater cultural socialization exhibited better work habits, as reported by their teachers. Moreover, better work habits were associated with higher GPA. In contrast, adolescents who showed larger hippocampal volume or who reported less cultural socialization exhibited worse work habits, which was associated with lower GPA. These findings suggest that smaller hippocampal volume and heightened parents' cultural socialization may facilitate adolescents' self-regulation in school. It is also possible that adolescents' self-regulation in school, such as their work habits, play a role in decreasing hippocampal volume. Moreover, these findings are in line with prior studies showing that greater self-regulation is related to better academic achievement (for a review, see Zimmerman 1990). In this study, adolescents' academic achievement and teacher-report work habits were highly correlated, highlighting that teachers largely incorporate judgments of work habits when assigning grades. Although our mediation analyses suggest that the link between hippocampal volume and academic achievement and the link between parents' cultural socialization and academic achievement might be due to better work habits, future studies also need more precise measurement of these habits and examine other mechanisms underlying these associations.

## The Role of Brain Structure and Social Environment in Substance Use

We also examined the role of brain development and social environment in Mexican American adolescents' substance use. Neuroimaging studies have paid considerable attention to how nucleus accumbens activation is related to adolescents' psychological adjustment. For example, previous fMRI research suggests that greater nucleus accumbens activation in the context of risk taking is related to adolescents' greater risk taking and substance use in real life (Galván et al. 2007). Structural MRI research has found that smaller nucleus accumbens volume, which may indicate less reward sensitivity, is associated with less cannabis (Gilman et al. 2014) and alcohol use (Thayer et al. 2012). Moreover, longitudinal declines in nucleus accumbens volume are related to declines in self-reported reward sensitivity from adolescence to young adulthood (Urošević et al. 2012). Consistent with these studies, we find that smaller nucleus accumbens volume predicts less substance use. Our finding, together with those from prior studies, suggest that smaller nucleus accumbens volume is related to adolescents' reward sensitivity and substance use.

Adolescents' social environment also played an important role in their substance use. Prior studies suggest that adolescents' risk taking may be largely influenced by their peer groups (Barrera et al. 2002; Fergusson, Swain-Campbell, and Horwood. 2002; Jenkins 1996). For example, minority adolescents whose peers use illegal drugs are more likely to do the same (Brook et al. 1998). Consistent with this line of research, we find that adolescents who have more deviant peers use more illicit drugs. This finding suggests that the characteristics of peer groups uniquely influence adolescents' risk-taking behavior and highlights the detrimental role of deviant peer association in adolescents' adjustment. Given emerging evidence that peers modulate neural activation in the reward-related regions (for example, Chein et al. 2011; Telzer et al. 2015), it is possible that adolescents' association with deviant peers may play a role in brain structure.

## LIMITATIONS AND FUTURE STUDIES

This study has several limitations, pointing to directions for future studies. First, given the small sample size, future studies are needed to examine this neurodevelopmental process in a larger sample of adolescents. Although forty-one participants is an acceptable sample size in neurobiological research, the number is considered relatively small in psychosocial research, which needs larger sample sizes to detect the association between psychosocial factors and adolescents' outcomes. However, our findings on the role of psychosocial factors in adolescents' adjustment are consistent with well-documented results based on survey studies with large samples (Barrera et al. 2002; Fergusson, Swain-Campbell, and Horwood 2002; Hughes et al. 2009; Jenkins 1996). Second, this study focuses on within-group variations among Mexican American adolescents, not across ethnic groups. These findings, then, may not necessarily be generalized to other ethnic groups. Moreover, although we took a biopsychosocial approach and examined adolescents' brain structure, parents' cultural socialization, and deviant peer association, we did not include other biological or psychosocial factors that may also influence Mexican American adolescents' academic achievement and substance use. For example, in earlier reports of the same sample, we examined the association between nucleus accumbens activation and adolescents' risk taking both concurrently and longitudinally (Telzer et al. 2013a, 2013b; Qu et al. 2015). Together, this study and our prior work suggest that structural brain development, functional brain development, and peer and family contexts play a key role in Mexican American adolescents' adjustment. Other psychosocial factors, such as parents' academic expectation, parental substance use, and adolescents' ethnic identity, may also play a role in adolescents' academic achievement and substance use. Therefore, future studies are needed to capture more aspects of psychosocial factors to better understand the causes of adolescents' problem behavior.

## CONCLUSIONS

Taken together, the current study builds on a significant body of literature highlighting the importance of biological and psychosocial factors in adolescents' well-being. Our findings provide a new contribution to the growing literature and suggest that Mexican American youth's brain development and their social environment are uniquely associated with their academic achievement and substance use. It is important to highlight that our findings are based on a multi-informant, multimethod, and multidimensional design. We used adolescents' self-reports (that is, cultural socialization and deviant peer association), along with neuroimaging assessment of their brain structure, to predict teacher reports of work habits and actual performance in school. Multiple dimensions of adolescents' adjustment, including academic achievement and substance use, were also assessed. This comprehensive design provides a new biopsychosocial perspective on understanding Mexican American youth's well-being, with the potential to be generalized to and have implications for other minority groups.

## REFERENCES

Barrera, Manuel Jr., Hazel M. Prelow, Larry E. Dumka, Nancy A. Gonzales, George P. Knight, Marcia L. Michaels, Mark W. Roosa, and JennYun Tein. 2002. "Pathways from Family Economic Conditions to Adolescents' Distress: Supportive Parenting, Stressors Outside the Family and Deviant Peers." *Journal of Community Psychology* 30(2): 135-52.

Brook, Judith S., David W. Brook, Mario Dela Rosa, Luis Fernan Doduque, Edgar Rodriguez, Ivan D. Montoya, and Martin Whiteman. 1998. "Pathways to Marijuana Use Among Adolescents: Culturual/Ecological, Family, Peer, and Personality Influences." *Journal of the American Academy of Child and Adolescent Psychiatry* 37(7): 759-66.

Casey, B. J., Sarah Getz, and Adriana Galván. 2008. "The Adolescent Brain." *Developmental Review* 28(1): 62-77.

Chantôme, Martine, Pierre Perruchet, Dominique Hasboun, Didier Dormont, Mokhran Sahel, Nader Sourour, Abderrezak Zouaoui, Claude Marsault, and Michel Duyme. 1999. "Is There a Negative Correlation Between Explicit Memory and Hippocampal Volume?" *NeuroImag* 10(5): 589-95.

Chein, Jason M., Dustin Albert, Lia O'Brien, Kaitlyn Uckert, and Laurence Steinberg. 2011. "Peers Increase Adolescent Risk Taking by Enhancing Activity in the Brain's Reward Circuitry." *Developmental Science* 14(2): F1-10.

Cohen, Neal J., and Howard Eichenbaum. 1993. *Memory, Amnesia, and the Hippocampal System.* Cambridge, Mass.: MIT Press.

Deater-Deckard, Kirby. 2001. "Annotation: Recent Research Examining the Role of Peer Relationships in the Development of Psychopathology." *Journal of Child Psychology and Psychiatry* 42(5): 565-79.

Dishion, Thomas J., Gerald R. Patterson, and Pamela C. Griesler. 1994. "Peer Adaptations in the Development of Antisocial Behavior: A Confluence Model." In *Aggressive Behavior: Current Perspectives*, edited by L. R. Huesmann. New York: Plenum.

Eaton, Danice K., Laura Kann, Steve Kinchen, James Ross, et al. 2006. "Youth Risk Behavior Surveillance Summaries—United States, 2005." *Morbidity and Mortality Weekly Report* 55 (SS-5): 1-108. http://www.cdc.gov/mmwr/preview/mmwrhtml/ss5505a1.htm.

Erickson, Kirby I., Michelle W. Voss, Ruchika S. Prakash, Chandramallika Basake, et al. 2011. "Exercise Training Increases Size of Hippocampus and Improves Memory." *Proceedings of the National Academy of Sciences* 108(7): 3017-22.

Fergusson, David M., Nicola R. Swain-Campbell, and L. John Horwood. 2002. "Deviant Peer Affiliations, Crime and Substance Use: A Fixed Effects Regression Analysis." *Journal of Abnormal Child Psychology* 30(4): 419-30.

Foster, Jonathan K., Andrew Meikle, Gregory Goodson, Andrew R. Mayes, Matthew Howard, and Sandra I. Sünram, Enis Cezayirli, and Neil Roberts. 1999. "The Hippocampus and Delayed Recall, Bigger Is Not Necessarily Better?" *Memory* 7(5-6): 715-32.

French, Sabine E., Edward Seidman, LaRue Allen, and J. Lawrence Aber. 2006. "The Development of Ethnic Identity During Adolescence." *Developmental Psychology* 42(1): 1-10.

Fuligni, Andrew J., and Eva H. Telzer. 2013. "Another Way Family Can Get in the Head and under the Skin: The Neurobiology of Helping the Family." *Child Development Perspectives* 7(3): 138-42.

Galván, Adriana. 2010. "Adolescent Development of the Reward System." *Frontiers in Human Neuroscience* 4: 6. DOI: 10.3389/neuro.09.006.2010.

Galván, Adriana, Todd Hare, Henning Voss, Gary Glover, and J. B. Casey. 2007. "Risk-Taking and the Adolescent Brain: Who Is at Risk?" *Developmental Science* 10(2): F8-14.

Giedd, Jay N., Jonathan Blumenthal, Neal O. Jeffries, F. X. Castellanos, Hong Liu, and Alex Zijdenbos, Tomás Paus, Alan C. Evans, and Judith L. Rapoport. 1999. "Brain Development During Childhood and Adolescence: A Longitudinal MRI Study." *Nature Neuroscience* 2(2): 861–63.

Gilman, Jodi M., John K. Kuster, Sang Lee, Myung Jung Lee, Byoung Wwoo Kim, Nikos Makris, Andre van der Kouwe, Anne J. Blood, and Hans C. Breiter. 2014. "Cannabis Use Is Quantitatively Associated with Nucleus Accumbens and Amygdala Abnormalities in Young Adult Recreational Users." *Journal of Neuroscience* 34(16): 5529–38.

Gogtay, Nitin, Jay N. Giedd, Leslie Lusk, Kiralee M. Hayashi, et al. 2004. "Dynamic Mapping of Human Cortical Development During Childhood Through Early Adulthood." *Proceedings of the National Academy of Sciences* 101(21): 8174–79.

Golomb, James, Alan Kluger, Mony J. de Leon, Steven H. Ferris, Antonio Convit, Mary S. Mittelman, Jacob Cohen, Henry Rusinek, Susan De Santi, and Ajax E. George. 1994. "Hippocampal Formation Size in Normal Human Aging: A Correlate of Delayed Secondary Memory Performance." *Learning and Memory* 1(1): 45–54.

Hughes, Diane. 2003. "Correlates of African American and Latino Parents' Messages to Children About Ethnicity and Race: A Comparative Study of Racial Socialization." *American Journal of Community Psychology* 31(1–2): 15–33.

Hughes, Diane, and Lisa Chen. 1997. "When and What Parents Tell Children About Race: An Examination of Race-Related Socialization Among African American Families." *Applied Developmental Science* 1(4): 200–14.

Hughes, Diane, James Rodriguez, Emilie P. Smith, Deborah J. Johnson, Howard C. Stevenson, and Paul Spicer. 2006. "Parents' Ethnic-Racial Socialization Practices: A Review of Research and Directions for Future Study." *Developmental Psychology* 42(5): 747–70.

Hughes, Diane, Dawn Witherspoon, Deborah Rivas-Drake, and Nia West-Bey. 2009. "Received Ethnic-Racial Socialization Messages and Youths' Academic and Behavioral Outcomes: Examining the Mediating Role of Ethnic Identity and Self-Esteem." *Cultural Diversity and Ethnic Minority Psychology* 15(2): 112–24.

Huttenlocher, Peter R. 1990. "Morphometric Study of Human Cerebral Cortex Development." *Neuropsychologia* 28(6): 517–27.

Jenkins, Jeanne E. 1996. "The Influence of Peer Affiliation and Student Activities on Adolescent Drug Involvement." *Adolescence* 31(122): 297–306.

Johnston, Lloyd D., Patrick M. O'Malley, Jerald G. Bachman, and John E. Schulenberg. 2009. *Monitoring the Future National Survey Results on Drug Use, 1975–2008*, vol. 1, *Secondary School Students*. NIH Publication No. 09-7402. Bethesda, Md.: National Institute on Drug Abuse.

Kerr, Melissa H., Kenneth Beck, Teresa Downs Shattuck, Candace Kattar, and Diego Uriburu. 2003. "Family Involvement, Problem and Prosocial Behavior Outcomes of Latino Youth." *American Journal of Health Behavior* 27(Suppl. 1): S55–65.

Knight, George P., Martha E. Bernal, Camile A. Garza, Marya K. Cota, and Katheryn A. Ocampo. 1993. "Family Socialization and the Ethnic Identity of Mexican American Children." *Journal of Cross-Cultural Psychology* 24(1): 99–114.

Knutson, Brian, Charles M. Adams, Grace W. Fong, and Daniel Hommer. 2001. "Anticipation of Increasing Monetary Reward Selectively Recruits Nucleus Accumbens." *Journal of Neuroscience* 21(16): 1–5.

Larson, Reed W., and Suman Verma. 1999. "How Children and Adolescents Spend Time Across the World: Work, Play, and Developmental Opportunities." *Psychological Bulletin* 125(6): 701–36.

Maguire, Eleanor A., Richard S. Frackowiak, and Christopher D. Frith. 1997. "Recalling Routes Around London: Activation of the Right Hippocampus in Taxi Drivers." *Journal of Neuroscience* 17(18): 7103–10.

Maguire, Eleanor A., David G. Gadian, Ingrid S. Johnsrude, Catriona D. Good, John Ashburner, Rrichard S. Frackowiak, and Christopher D. Frith. 2000. "Navigation-Related Structural Change in the Hippocampi of Taxi Drivers." *Proceedings of the National Academy of Sciences* 97(8): 4398–403.

Marsiglia, Flavio F., Stephen Kulis, David A. Wagstaff, Elvira Elek, and David Dran. 2005. "Acculturation Status and Substance Use Prevention with Mexican and Mexican American Youth." *Journal of Social Work Practice in the Addictions* 5(1–2): 85–111.

Moffitt, Terrie E. 1993. "Adolescence-Limited and Life-Course-Persistent Antisocial Behavior: A Developmental Taxonomy." *Psychological Review* 100(4): 674–701.

Parke, Ross D., and Raymond Buriel. 2006. "Socialization in the Family: Ethnic and Ecological Perspectives." In *Handbook of Child Psychology: So-*

cial, Emotional, and Personality Development, 6th ed., edited by Nancy Eisenberg, William Damon, and Richard M. Lerner. Hoboken, N.J.: John Wiley & Sons.

Patenaude, Brian, Stephen M. Smith, David Kennedy, and Mark Jenkinson. 2007a. "FIRST-FMRIB's Integrated Registration and Segmentation Tool." In *Human Brain Mapping Conference* (June): 420–28.

———. 2007b. "Bayesian Shape and Appearance Models." Technical report no. TR07BP1. Oxford: University of Oxford, FMRIB Center.

Preacher, Kristopher J., and Andrew F. Hayes. 2008. "Asymptotic and Resampling Strategies for Assessing and Comparing Indirect Effects in Multiple Mediator Models." *Behavior Research Methods* 40(3): 879–91.

Pruessner, Marita, J. C. Pruessner, Dirk H. Hellhammer, G. Bruce Pike, and Sonia J. Lupien. 2007. "The Associations Among Hippocampal Volume, Cortisol Reactivity, and Memory Performance in Healthy Young Men." *Psychiatry Research* 155(1): 1–10.

Qu, Yang, Adrdiana Galván, Andrew J. Fuligni, Matthew D. Lieberman, and Eva H. Telzer. 2015. "Longitudinal Changes in Prefrontal Cortex Activation Underlie Declines in Adolescent Risk Taking." *Journal of Neuroscience* 35(32): 11308–14.

Raz, Naftali, Faith M. Gunning-Dixon, Denise Head, James H. Dupuis, and James D. Acker. 1998. "Neuroanatomical Correlates of Cognitive Aging: Evidence from Structural Magnetic Resonance Imaging." *Neuropsychology* 12(1): 95–114.

Riggins, Tracy, Kelsey Cacic, Stacy Buckingham-Howes, Laura A. Scaletti, Betty Jo Salmeron, and Maureen M. Black. 2012. "Memory Ability and Hippocampal Volume in Adolescents with Prenatal Drug Exposure." *Neurotoxicology and Teratology* 34(4): 434–41.

Rivas-Drake, Deborah, Diane Hughes, and Niobe Way. 2009. "A Preliminary Analysis of Associations Among Ethnic Racial Socialization, Ethnic Discrimination, and Ethnic Identity Among Urban Sixth Graders." *Journal of Research on Adolescence* 19(3): 558–84.

Sowell, Elizabeth R., Dean Delis, Joan Stiles, and Terry L. Jernigan. 2001. "Improved Memory Functioning and Frontal Lobe Maturation Between Childhood and Adolescence: A Structural MRI Study." *Journal of the International Neuropsychological Society* 7(3): 312–22.

Sowell, Elizabeth R., Bradley S. Peterson, Paul M. Thompson, Suzanne E. Welcome, Amy L. Henkenius, and Arthur W. Toga. 2003. "Mapping Cortical Change Across the Human Life Span." *Nature Neuroscience* 6(3): 309–15.

Telzer, Eva H., Andrew J. Fuligni, Matthew D. Lieberman, and Adriana Galván. 2013a. "Meaningful Family Relationships: Neurocognitive Buffers of Adolescent Risk Taking." *Journal of Cognitive Neuroscience* 25(3): 374–87.

———. 2013b. "Ventral Striatum Activation to Prosocial Rewards Predicts Longitudinal Declines in Adolescent Risk Taking." *Developmental Cognitive Neuroscience* 3(1): 45–52.

———. 2015. "The Quality Of Adolescents' Peer Relationships Modulates Neural Sensitivity to Risk Taking." *Social Cognitive Affective Neuroscience* 10(3): 389–98.

Telzer, Eva H., Nancy Gonzales, and Andrew J. Fuligni. 2014. "Family Obligation Values and Family Assistance Behaviors: Protective and Risk Factors for Adolescent Substance Use." *Journal of Youth and Adolescence* 43(2): 270–83.

Thayer, Rachel E., Shirley M. Crotwell, Tiffany J. Callahan, Kent E. Hutchison, and Angela D. Bryan. 2012. "Nucleus Accumbens Volume Is Associated with Frequency of Alcohol Use Among Juvenile Justice-Involved Adolescents." *Brain Sciences* 2(4): 605–18.

Urošević, Snezana, Paul Collins, Ryan Muetzel, Kelvin Lim, and Monica Luciana. 2012. "Longitudinal Changes in Behavioral Approach System Sensitivity and Brain Structures Involved in Reward Processing During Adolescence." *Developmental Psychology* 48(5): 1488–500.

U.S. Department of Commerce. 2006. "Census Bureau, American Community Survey." Accessed November 10, 2016. http://nces.ed.gov/pubs 2008/nativetrends/tables/table_3_4a.asp.

Van Petten, Cyma. 2004. "Relationship Between Hippocampal Volume and Memory Ability in Healthy Individuals Across the Lifespan: Review and Meta-Analysis." *Neuropsychologia* 42(10): 1394–413.

Zimmerman, Barry J. 1990. "Self-Regulated Learning and Academic Achievement: An Overview." *Educational Psychologist* 25(1): 3–17.

# Gender Differences in Biological Function in Young Adulthood: An Intragenerational Perspective

MARGOT I. JACKSON AND SUSAN E. SHORT

*Sex-gender differences in health are a function of social and biological factors and their interplay over the life course. A large body of research documents sex-gender as a determinant of health behavior and outcomes. Far less scholarship examines how these differences are reflected in physiologic function in young adulthood. Using nationally representative, longitudinal data from the National Longitudinal Study of Adolescent to Adult Health, we examine the relationship between gender and biological function in young adulthood. We also examine the contribution of social and economic circumstances in childhood and early adulthood to gender differences in health. The findings reveal strong gender differences in inflammation and immune function, which are robust to the inclusion of many indicators of the social environment.*

**Keywords:** gender, biomarkers, life course

Sex and gender differences in health and longevity are well established (Read and Gorman 2010; Rieker, Bird, and Lang 2010). Female advantages in survival and life expectancy exist across time and place (Austad 2006). The factors that contribute to these patterns are multifaceted, but sex and gender differences in patterns of acute and chronic illnesses are pervasive (Crimmins et al. 2010). In the United States, for example, women report higher rates of chronic illness, and men report higher rates of acute illness. Further, men are more likely to die from cardiovascular disease and cancer at younger ages and to be more vulnerable to illness and death once gender-differentiated social and behavioral factors are taken into account (Case and Paxson 2005). Nonetheless, although these patterns provide a logic, the underlying mechanisms remain elusive.

Sex and gender differences in health and longevity are understood to be a function of social and biological factors, and their interplay over the life course (Bird and Rieker 2002; Institute of Medicine 2001; Yang and Kozloski 2011; Short, Yang, and Jenkins 2013). Notably, scholarship on sex and gender-differentiated aging tends to focus on middle and late adulthood, when ill health and death are more fre-

**Margot I. Jackson** is associate professor of sociology at Brown University. **Susan E. Short** is professor of sociology and director of the Population Studies and Training Center at Brown University.

© 2018 Russell Sage Foundation. Jackson, Margot I., and Susan E. Short. 2018. "Gender Differences in Biological Function in Young Adulthood: An Intragenerational Perspective." *RSF: The Russell Sage Foundation Journal of the Social Sciences* 4(4): 98–119. DOI: 10.7758/RSF.2018.4.4.06. We are grateful to the Population Studies and Training Center at Brown University, which receives funding from the NIH (P2C HD041020), for general support. In addition, we thank Kristen McNeill and Kiera Peltz for research assistance. Direct correspondence to: Margot I. Jackson at margotj@brown.edu, Brown University, Department of Sociology, Box 1916, Providence, RI 02912; and Susan E. Short at seshort@brown.edu, Population Studies and Training Center, Box 1836, 68 Waterman St., Providence, RI 02912.

Open Access Policy: *RSF: The Russell Sage Foundation Journal of the Social Sciences* is an open access journal. This article is published under a Creative Commons Attribution-NonCommercial-NoDerivs 3.0 Unported License.

quent, rather than on the early adulthood period, a time that is formative in shaping long-term health trajectories (Harris 2010). Moreover, although a large body of research documents the importance of sex and gender as a determinant of health behavior and health outcomes, far less scholarship examines how these differences are reflected in physiologic function, especially in young adulthood. Yet, physiologic function is an important mediator through which social experiences, such as health behaviors, may "get under the skin" with consequence for later life health.

A life course perspective leads us to expect that physiologic function in young adulthood is shaped by circumstances during childhood (Hayward and Gorman 2004; Heckman 2006; Jackson 2010; McDade et al. 2014). The adoption of behaviors begins early in life, when morbidity risk is low but youth decide whether to initiate behaviors that "track" into adulthood, such as smoking, exercise, and health-seeking behavior (for example, Chen and Kandel 1995). Research on socioeconomic status and health has long adopted a life course perspective, but research on gender and health has less systematically incorporated early life experiences, even though many health behaviors and social circumstances are shaped by gender. One result is that we know little about whether we should attribute differences in health between men and women to experiences during adulthood, to the cumulative and persistent effect of earlier behaviors and circumstances, or to other factors.

Using nationally representative, longitudinal data from the National Longitudinal Study of Adolescent to Adult Health (Add Health), we have two goals. First, we examine the relationship between gender and biological function in young adulthood, considering biomarkers of inflammation and immunosuppression, two markers associated with later life morbidities. Second, we examine the contribution of social and economic circumstances in childhood and early adulthood to the size of any gender differences in health, as indicated by levels of Epstein-Barr virus (EBV) and C-reactive protein (CRP). Examining health within a cohort of young men and women in early adulthood will reveal the emergence of gender differences in both biological and clinical markers of health, as well as differences both within and across women and men according to profiles of childhood and adulthood environments. Understanding the intragenerational process by which gender-specific variation in health is produced will inform our broader understanding of the emergence of gender differences in health over the life course.

## BACKGROUND

Sex and gender differences in health vary across contexts and change over time. On average, for example, U.S. women live 4.8 years longer than men, down from a peak gap of 7.8 years in the late 1970s (Arias 2014). Explanations for the gender gap as well as changes the gap over time have focused on health behaviors among adults, revealed variation in the size of gender differences across educational groups, and documented differences in the social and economic pressures both men and women face, underscoring the role of social experiences in shaping sex and gender patterns of health (Arias 2014; Berkman 2012; Meara, Richards, and Cutler 2008; Montez and Zajacova 2013; Pampel 2001).

At the same time, sex-specific variation in biology has promoted biologically anchored explanations for differences in health and survival (Bird and Rieker 2002; Short, Yang, and Jenkins 2013). These include differences tied to immune competence, which is related to reproductive biology and possibly shaped by hormones; differences in insulin-like growth factor 1, signaling, and oxidative stress production; and differences in genomes that stem from the presence of X and Y chromosomes, and processes such as a cell mosaicism (Fish 2008).

Previous research indicates that disease exposure and susceptibility, immune response, and markers of inflammation vary with sex and gender (Lleo et al. 2008; Markle and Fish 2014; Ordaz and Luna 2012). The prevalence, onset, and severity of autoimmune diseases and allergic diseases are one example. Generally, women are two to three times as likely to develop an autoimmune disease as men, but disease severity can be worse in men (Shames 2002). Research points to a role for "sex" steroids and hypothalamic-pituitary hormones in immune system development and immune response, but the associated mechanisms and models are not well specified (Fish 2008; Shames 2002). Evidence that puberty, pregnancy, and hormonal contraceptive use are associated with variation in immune system response is well documented (Shames 2002). For example, asthma severity is affected by menstruation, pregnancy, and menopause (Shames 2002). Likewise, inflammation varies by sex and gender, with patterns indicating differences in prevalence, severity, and onset that are not well understood (Fish 2008). Overall, data from the National Health and Nutrition Survey (NHANES) indicates that inflammation is higher among women than men, the difference diminishing with age, and especially so in late adulthood (Yang and Kozloski 2011). Notably, numerous exposures shape levels, and sometimes in gender-differentiated ways. Existing research, based on clinic and population samples, claims adiposity, smoking, and sleep is related to inflammation levels differently in women and men (Cartier et al. 2009; Le-Ha et al. 2014; Miller et al. 2009).

## A Life Course Perspective

Despite a robust body of research documenting the association between gender and health among adults, limited scholarship to date examines gender differences in physiologic function at a relatively young age. Evidence is clear that young women are more likely than young men to demonstrate high levels of CRP (Ishii et al. 2012; Shanahan, Freeman, and Bauldry 2014), and that gender-specific HPA-axis reactivity is observed in adolescence (Oldehinkel and Bouma 2011). We know less, however, about the extent of gender differences in young adults' biologic function across the full distribution of risk, or about the intragenerational process by which these patterns are produced. The behaviors and health outcomes we observe among adult men and women are generated from behaviors and exposures occurring earlier in life, given ample evidence that health behaviors, as well as biomarkers of health, track from adolescence into adulthood (for example, Chen and Kandel 1995; McDade, Williams, and Snodgrass 2007).

Studying biomarkers of health is particularly useful among young adults because these measures offer insight into future disease risk among a population in which clinically defined disease is low, but predictive power for future disease prevalence is high. Life course theory emphasizes the possibility that circumstances across ages may have differing and combined effects on childhood and adulthood outcomes, pointing to the importance of the timing, duration and stability of a circumstance (Ben-Schlomo and Kuh 2002; Ferraro and Shippee 2009; Schoon et al. 2002). This perspective enables consideration of whether we should attribute differences between men and women to experiences during adulthood, to the cumulative and persistent effect of earlier behaviors and circumstances, or to something else.

### Circumstances During Adulthood

Ample evidence documents a strong relationship between individuals' social and economic environments and health, whether health is self-reported or defined by particular acute, chronic or disabling conditions. A growing literature also documents the ways in which health affects social and economic processes over the life course (Kitagawa and Hauser 1973; Jackson 2015; Lynch 2003; Marmot 2001; Moore and Hayward 1990; Morenoff 2003; Palloni 2006). The gender gap in life expectancy is particularly pronounced among women with less education; relatedly, some dimensions of socioeconomic status (SES), such as education and employment, are increasing across historical time in their predictive power for health, suggesting that circumstances during adulthood remain strongly linked to health (Kunst et al. 2005; Lynch 2003; Meara, Richards and Cutler 2008; Montez and Zajacova 2013; Smith et al. 2000). Studies that bridge two literatures—those on the socioeconomic determinants of health and on links among biological markers and morbidity-mortality—have also yielded important findings about the role of the social environment in predicting physiologic functioning among adults (see, for example, McDade et al. 2014). Poverty is associated with elevated levels of C-reactive protein, an inflammatory marker related to cardiovascular disease (Alley et al. 2006; Kanjilal et al. 2006), as well as elevated blood pressure and cholesterol (Karlamangla et al. 2005). In addition, data from national health surveys, such as NHANES, or disease-specific surveys, such as CARDIA (Coronary Artery Risk Development in Young Adults), show how biological measures of health are unequally distributed by race-ethnicity and socioeconomic indices.

*Circumstances During Childhood and Adolescence*
Considering adulthood circumstances exclusively, however, only partly accounts for the environments that may result in gender differences in health. Circumstances during childhood have far-reaching effects and are key to understanding outcomes during adulthood (Hayward and Gorman 2004; Heckman 2006; Jackson 2010). Evidence is compelling that the socioeconomic "gradient" in health has origins in childhood—education is strongly related to health even before birth, and that relationship grows with age (Case, Lubotsky, and Paxson 2002; Finch 2003). Similarly, behavior and mortality during adulthood are strongly predicted by childhood socioeconomic status (Duncan, Ziol-Guest, and Kalil 2010; Hayward and Gorman 2004). Evidence is accumulating that childhood socioeconomic status leads to differences in physiologic functioning, such as EBV and CRP, before adulthood (Dowd et al. 2014; McDade, Stallings, and Worthman 2000). Whether youth decide to adopt particular behaviors also depends in part on their family socioeconomic circumstances (Duncan, Ziol-Guest, and Kalil 2010). Youth in low-resource families are more likely to be exposed to unhealthy behaviors and living circumstances, less likely to pursue higher education, and more likely to experience financial instability and unemployment (Duncan, Ziol-Guest, and Kalil 2010; Wagmiller et al. 2006).

*Socioeconomic Pathways Linking Gender to Biological Function*
Given evidence that socioeconomic circumstances during childhood, adolescence and adulthood are strongly related to health and biological function, biological risk should be greater among both men and women who experience low-resource environments during childhood and the transition to adulthood. To the extent that socioeconomic circumstances, or the meaning of such differences, at different points in the early life course are gender differentiated, gender differences in biological function may be explained in part by differential exposures and experiences. If women are especially likely to experience persistently low or declining SES environments through early adulthood, greater or cumulative exposure to stressful and unhealthy circumstances might contribute to gender differences in biological function.

Evidence of gender differences in exposures and socioeconomic circumstances that are plausibly linked to health is stronger among adults than among children and adolescents. For example, in the United States, adult women on average earn lower wages than men and have lower incomes (Jacobson 2016). Occupational segregation leads women and men to experience different workplace environments (Read and Gorman 2010). Social integration and behaviors such as smoking and exercising vary by gender (Pampel 2001; Umberson, Crosnoe, and Reczek 2010; Yang et al. 2013). Men and women experience differences in family responsibilities and different forms of gender-specific harassment, both of which also shape health (Bianchi, Robinson, and Milke 2006; Rieker, Bird, and Lang 2010). Many of these patterns implicate social structures that shape health through constraining choices in gender-differentiated ways (Rieker, Bird, and Lang 2010).

Although evidence to date is scant, youth circumstances can also differ by gender, and such differences may well vary with family resources (Williams 2002). A growing literature, for example, demonstrates a more favorable environment for girls with respect to the development and sanctioning of social and behavioral skills. Girls are less likely than boys to exhibit aggressive behavior, as indicated by externalizing behaviors, and some evidence suggests that they are less likely than boys to be penalized in school for the same problematic behaviors (DiPrete and Jennings 2012; Entwisle et al. 2007; Farkas 1990). At the same time, increasing social pressure to conform to gender expectations may reduce girls' perceived or real opportunities as they enter adolescence, and may contribute to higher levels of depression among girls (Nolen-Hoeksema 2001; Pomeranz et al. 2002). In sum, experiences vary in gendered ways over the life course and may reasonably be related to health and aging (Short, Yang, and Jenkins 2013). Our goal in this article is to investigate whether gender differences in physiological function are evident among young adults, and to describe the social and demographic correlates over the life course associated with these patterns.

## DATA

Our analyses are based on data from waves one through four of the National Longitudinal Study of Adolescent to Adult Health, a longitudinal study of adolescents' health and its determinants. The first wave of this nationally representative, school-based sample of about twenty thousand adolescents was conducted in 1994 and 1995, when students were in grades seven through twelve, ranging in age from eleven to twenty-one; mean age at the first wave is sixteen. Information was gathered from schools, adolescents, and parents. Data collection has resulted in three subsequent waves to date: one to two years after baseline (1996), seven years after baseline (2001), and fourteen years after baseline (2008). In line with the survey's goal of understanding the transition into adulthood, information is collected from respondents about their health, relationships, educational experiences, and labor market participation. At wave one, information about family background was also collected from parents. Add Health data are useful for this research in that they offer detailed information on socioeconomic background, behaviors, health, and social and economic transitions during the period of the life course when behaviors are initiated and key transitions are made.

## MEASURES

Biomarkers are key to this analysis—measures of inflammatory and immune functioning, available at wave four. We examine high-sensitivity C-reactive protein (hsCRP) and EBV antibodies. CRP is a commonly used indicator of inflammation that is highly correlated with cardiovascular disease, type 2 diabetes, and mortality (Fahdi et al. 2003; Ridker et al. 1998).

EBV is a commonly used measure of immune function. Although EBV is extremely common, with approximately 90 percent of the human population estimated to be infected (Dowd, Palermo, Brite, et al. 2013), the virus is usually latent unless reactivated. Higher levels of EBV antibodies indicate greater difficulty in the immune system's ability to regulate the virus, and have been linked to diseases such as cancer, lupus, and multiple sclerosis (Esen et al. 2012; Hsu and Glaser 2000; James and Robertson 2012; Levin et al. 2010; Thompson and Kurzrock 2004). EBV antibody levels indicate reduced cell-mediated immune function and are associated with social stressors (McDade, Stallings, and Worthman 2000).

In the Add Health, both CRP and EBV were measured via dried blood spot samples, and results are reported as milligrams per liter for CRP, and as arbitrary units per milliliter for EBV. Both measures have been used in previous research with Add Health data (for example, Everett et al. 2014; McDade et al. 2014). We represent CRP and EBV using logged measures in final analyses. We considered representing CRP and EBV using sex-standardized measures, but did not find sufficient rationale in the existing literature for adopting this approach. In particular, CRP and EBV are not uniformly patterned by sex across populations. Further, a given level of CRP or EBV does not translate consistently into a clear level of risk across populations. Explanations for sex and gender differences in both patterns and risks note the complicated interaction of social, behavioral, and biological factors in producing patterns. Taken together, our overall approach is guided by a desire to impose as few assumptions as possible on the measurement of CRP and EBV. Thus, in our analyses, rather than computing risk thresholds that may impose arbitrary cutoffs between individuals, or constructing sex-specific measures, we examine variation across the full distribution of each measure, without sex-specific standardization, using quantile regression techniques.

We measure several sociodemographic variables, some of which are of primary interest and all of which are potentially correlated with both gender and biologic function. *Gender* is a dichotomous variable based on respondents' identification as either male or female (reference category). *Race-ethnicity* distinguishes among those who identify as non-Hispanic and white (reference category), non-Hispanic and black, Hispanic, Asian, and other (including Native Americans). Respondents who identify within multiple racial-ethnic categories are represented by the one that they report to best reflect their identity. *Nativity status* distinguishes among first-generation (immigrant, reference), second-generation (one or both immigrant parents), and third-generation (both parents U.S.-born) youth.

*Parental education* is measured categorically at wave 1 through responding parents' reports: less than high school (reference), high school completion, some college, and college diploma or higher. In the vast majority of cases (94 percent) the responding parent is the mother. We take the natural log of *family income* at wave 1; income coefficients can therefore be interpreted as a percentage change. *Parental marital status* is also measured at wave 1 and separates those whose parents are currently married from all other union statuses (reference). We use these three measures as our focal indicators of socioeconomic circumstances in childhood and adolescence.

We also control for measures of *parental obesity* and respondent *birthweight*. Parental obesity captures both genetic and environmental sources of weight and height. We combine mothers' and fathers' reports at wave one into a measure indicating whether either parent has ever been told by a doctor that he or she is obese. Birthweight is a continuous measure indicating respondents' weight (in pounds) at birth. Finally, we include a continuous measure of *age*.

At waves three and four, we measure several important indicators of respondents' social and economic environments. To capture socioeconomic status in early adulthood, we measure respondents' *educational attainment* by wave four, differentiating some college and college-plus relative to those with a high school education or less. We measure *household income* at wave four with a continuous measure that uses the midpoint of each income band. A binary measure indicates whether respondents have *ever been married* at wave four. We measure current *employment status,* as well as a measure indicating how often respondents have had to reduce work hours in the past year because of *family responsibilities*. Finally, we measure the *number of live births* resulting from pregnancies up to and including wave four.

We also control for several *health behaviors,* including an indicator of daily smoking (yes-no) and physical activity (yes-no) at wave four. We control for obesity (yes-no) at wave four—results are not sensitive to using a three-category measure of normal weight, overweight or obesity, or to measuring BMI-overweight at wave three. Finally, we control for *pregnancy status* at wave 4, and test the sensitivity of the results to excluding women who are currently pregnant; we include all women because the results do not change.

In all analyses, we examine the sensitivity of our results to the inclusion of measures of morbidity to understand the extent to which our biomarkers are affected by preexisting and contemporaneous health. These include several wave three and four measures of health: self-rated health (on a five-point scale ranging from excellent to poor) at wave three, and self-reports of a physician diagnosis of high blood pressure (waves three and four), high cholesterol (wave three), and asthma (wave three). We control for recent acute illness and infection, for whether respondents have an inflammatory disease, and for respondents' anti-inflammatory and immune-suppression medication use at wave four. Finally, we control for women's use of hormonal contraception at wave four.

## ANALYSIS

We use quantile regression to consider variation in the effects of gender across the observed distributions of CRP/EBV. Typical regression approaches identify group differences in the mean of the dependent variable. Although this approach is often a sensible one, it assumes that the determinants of the center of a distribution are the same as those at the extremes. This assumption may lead researchers to obscure important variation among respondents, or to unnecessarily exclude cases in an effort to avoid undue influence from extreme observations. In the case of CRP levels, for example, respondents with very high levels of CRP (typically considered to be above 10 mg/L) are often excluded from analyses because of the possibility that these levels reflect acute (rather than chronic or systemic) inflammation (O'Connor et al. 2009). At the same time, however, some evidence indicates both that high CRP levels not only are a proxy for recent illness, but also more strongly predict future cardiovascular and mortality risk than low levels, and that women are more likely to have very high CRP levels (for example, Shanahan, Freeman, and Bauldry 2014). These findings suggest that understanding variation in biological function across the distribution is equally important to understanding average variation. Quantile regression estimates conditional differences in the median and other quantiles (10th, 25th, 50th, 75th, and 90th percentile) using least-absolute-value estimation. Differences between men and women are estimated at each percentile, given their other characteristics. For models with covariates other than gender, the gender coefficient can be interpreted as differences in CRP and EBV levels between men and women, for those with otherwise identical characteristics on observed covariates. We consider differences among women across the distribution, and between men and women at and across percentiles.

We begin with a baseline model that only includes gender, and successively incorporate childhood or adolescent and then early adulthood characteristics. In addition to identifying gender differences in inflammation and immune function, this strategy allows us to examine the contribution of social and economic environments at different points of the early life course to gender differences observed in adulthood. We compare quantile regression estimates to those from ordinary least squares (OLS) regression models that incorporate the same childhood or adolescent and early adulthood factors.

## RESULTS

We begin by describing gender differences in biological function in bivariate and multivariate perspective. Next, we examine variation across the distribution and describe several sensitivity analyses.

### Establishing Differences in Biological Function

Table 1 presents weighted characteristics of the analytic sample by gender. Male and female respondents have highly equivalent sociodemographic characteristics during childhood or adolescence. About two-thirds of each group identify as non-Hispanic white, and about 15 percent of respondents are from immigrant families, either immigrants themselves or the child of an immigrant parent (16 percent of men, 15 percent of women). Almost 25 percent of respondents lived in families with a college-educated parent (23 percent of males, 22 percent of females). By early adulthood, women are more likely to have received a college degree (34 percent of women versus 28 percent of men). Women are also more likely to have ever been married by wave 4 (55 percent of women versus 45 percent of men).

Male and female respondents also have generally similar early health environments, with almost 25 percent of respondents having an obese parent at baseline, and with mean birthweight about 7.5 pounds (7.75 for men, 7.47 for women). By wave 3, young women are slightly more likely to have been diagnosed by a doctor with high blood pressure and asthma. By wave 4, men and women are equally likely to be obese (37 percent and 36 percent), and women are slightly less likely to be regular smokers than men (22 percent versus 28 percent). Despite their shared environments with respect to parental circumstances and sociodemographic characteristics, women have higher measured CRP and EBV levels at wave 4. Mean CRP is 3.3 for men and 6.3 for women, and mean EBV is 138.4 for men and 164.2 for women. These descriptive patterns suggest that, by early adulthood (approximately age thirty), women in Add Health demonstrate more inflammation and lower immune function than their male peers.

Table 2 presents the results from an OLS regression of logged CRP and EBV (respectively) on gender and the other covariates. Net of respondents' childhood or adolescent and early adulthood social, economic, and health environments, men and women have significantly different levels of inflammation and immune function in young adulthood. Levels of CRP in

**Table 1.** Weighted Characteristics of Sample by Gender, Add Health

|  | Male (49%) | Female (51%) |
|---|---|---|
| **Race-ethnicity** | | |
| Non-Hispanic white (reference) | 69 | 69 |
| Hispanic | 12 | 11 |
| Black | 14 | 16 |
| Asian | 4 | 3 |
| Other | 1 | 1 |
| **Nativity** | | |
| First generation (reference) | 6 | 5 |
| Second generation | 10 | 10 |
| Third-plus generation | 84 | 85 |
| **Parental education, wave 1** | | |
| Less than high school (ref.) | 16 | 17 |
| High school | 32 | 33 |
| Some college | 29 | 28 |
| College or more | 23 | 22 |
| Logged family income, wave 1 | 3.16 | 3.12 |
| Parents married, wave 1 | 73 | 73 |
| Age (years) | 30 | 29.8 |
| **Education, wave 4** | | |
| High school or less | 40 | 31 |
| Some college | 32 | 35 |
| College or more | 28 | 34 |
| Ever married, wave 4 | 45 | 55 |
| Employed part or full-time, wave 4 | 86 | 67 |
| **Work hours affected by family duties, wave 4** | | |
| Frequently | 3 | 9 |
| Sometimes | 15 | 20 |
| Rarely | 23 | 19 |
| Never | 60 | 52 |
| **Health** | | |
| CRP (mg/L) | 3.3 | 6.2 |
| EBV (AU/L) | 138.4 | 164.2 |
| Parent obese, wave 1 | 23 | 24 |
| Birthweight | 7.75 | 7.47 |
| Smoke daily, wave 4 | 28 | 22 |
| Exercise daily, wave 4 | 13 | 17 |
| Obese, wave 4 | 37 | 36 |
| Self-rated health, wave 3 | 1.9 | 2.1 |
| Asthma, wave 3 | 15 | 18 |
| High blood pressure, wave 3 | 5 | 7 |
| High cholesterol, wave 3 | 4 | 4 |
| N | 6,451 | 6,715 |

*Source:* Authors' compilation based on Add Health, Waves 1–4.

**Table 2.** OLS Regression of Logged CRP (mg/L) and EBV (AU/L), Add Health

|  | Log CRP | Log EBV |
|---|---|---|
| Male | −0.524*** | −0.190*** |
|  | (−21.58) | (−14.52) |
| **Race-ethnicity** | | |
| Hispanic | 0.131** | 0.0786*** |
|  | (3.25) | (3.62) |
| Black | −0.00982 | 0.200*** |
|  | (−0.31) | (11.61) |
| Asian | −0.313*** | 0.0448 |
|  | (−5.69) | (1.52) |
| Other race | −0.129 | 0.133 |
|  | (−1.01) | (1.93) |
| **Nativity** | | |
| Second generation | 0.00164 | 0.0504 |
|  | (0.03) | (1.74) |
| Third-plus generation | 0.0520 | 0.0525 |
|  | (0.96) | (1.80) |
| **Parental education** | | |
| High school | −0.0591 | −0.0190 |
|  | (−1.60) | (−0.95) |
| Some college | −0.115** | −0.0266 |
|  | (−3.03) | (−1.30) |
| College or more | −0.139*** | −0.0718** |
|  | (−3.34) | (−3.21) |
| Logged family income | −0.00104 | 0.0109*** |
|  | (−0.18) | (3.48) |
| Parent obese | 0.137*** | 0.0228 |
|  | (4.90) | (1.51) |
| Birth weight | −0.0328*** | 0.00212 |
|  | (−4.00) | (0.48) |
| Parents married | −0.0116 | −0.0192 |
|  | (−0.43) | (−1.31) |
| Age (wave 1) | −0.000455 | 0.0118** |
|  | (−0.07) | (3.16) |
| Obese, wave 4 | 0.157*** | 0 |
|  | (21.63) | (0.03) |
| Smoke daily, wave 4 | −0.0325 | 0.0569*** |
|  | (−1.10) | (3.56) |
| Exercise daily, wave 4 | 0.182*** | −0.0111 |
|  | (5.66) | (−0.64) |
| Ever married, wave 4 | 0.0772** | 0.0450*** |
|  | (3.15) | (3.41) |
| Some college, wave 4 | −0.0583* | −0.0321* |
|  | (−2.03) | (−2.07) |
| College or more, wave 4 | −0.133*** | −0.0159 |
|  | (−4.38) | (−0.98) |
| Household income, wave 4 | 8.81e-08 | 2.89e-08 |
|  | (1.73) | (1.05) |
| Employed part or full time | −0.0828* | −0.0204 |
|  | (−2.09) | (−0.98) |
| Work or family conflict | −0.00185 | −0.0045 |
|  | (−0.11) | (−0.49) |
| Constant | 0.908*** | 4.569*** |
|  | (6.24) | (58.38) |
| N | 13,166 | 13,238 |

*Source:* Authors' compilation based on Add Health, Waves 1–4.
*Note:* Models also control for pregnancy status at wave 4, and parity at wave 4.
*p < .05; **p < .01; ***p < .001

men are more than 50 percent lower than among women, and levels of EBV 19 percent lower. Higher levels of CRP in women is consistent with other examinations at of the Add Health, as well as Multiethnic Study of Atherosclerosis and NHANES (Lakoski et al. 2006; Yang and Kozloski 2011), but this pattern is not universal across populations (Oksuzyan et al. 2015). Similarly, EBV is higher in women than men in analyses of the NHANES (ages six through nineteen), and a national population-based sample in Taiwan (Chen et al. 2015; Dowd, Palermo, Chyu, et al. 2013), and in heterosexual respondents in the Add Health. However, analyses of gay and bisexual respondents in the Add Health find little evidence of difference between and men and women (Everett et al. 2014).

Consistent with previous research, the findings also reveal higher CRP levels among Hispanic respondents. Compared with non-Hispanic whites, CRP levels are 13 percent higher among Hispanics; EBV levels are 8 percent higher among Hispanics and 20 percent higher among blacks. Asian respondents have CRP levels that are 31 percent lower than among non-Hispanic whites, on average, but no difference is observed for EBV levels. After controlling for socioeconomic factors, no nativity-based differences in CRP and EBV are significant. Education shows an educational gradient in CRP and EBV, whereby respondents with college-educated parents have 13 percent lower CRP levels and 7 percent lower EBV levels, on average, than their peers from the most poorly educated families. By early adulthood, respondents who attain a college education experience a similarly lower risk of inflammation, with a 13 percent difference between college-educated respondents than their peers with a high school education or less. There is also a higher risk associated with marriage, on average, whereby respondents who have ever been married by wave four have 7 percent higher CRP levels and 5 percent higher EBV levels than their peers.

Finally, respondents' family health environments and early health characteristics are associated with inflammation—respondents with an obese parent have 13 percent higher CRP levels and 3 percent higher EBV levels, on average; each additional pound at birth is associated with a 3 percent decrease in CRP in adulthood. In general, the covariates are more consistently and strongly associated with inflammation than with immune function, though there is certainly evidence of meaningful gender differences in immune function.

## Gender Differences in Biological Function Across the Distribution

The results from OLS analyses establish gender differences in biological function at the center of the distribution. This approach establishes a useful benchmark against which to examine variation across the distribution of CRP and EBV. Given evidence that young adult women are more likely than men to have very high levels of CRP, and that it is common to exclude such cases from analyses despite their strong relationship with future morbidity and mortality, it is important to understand the degree of risk at extreme values of the distribution.

Table 3 presents the results from the quantile regression of CRP on gender and the other covariates. The results show that, for those with identical observed characteristics, the size of gender differences in inflammation increases significantly across the distribution. Model 1, which shows the bivariate relationship between gender and CRP, shows that men at the 10th percentile have CRP levels that are approximately 17 percent lower than women, and that this difference rises to 36 percent at the 25th percentile, 60 percent at the median, 66 percent at the 75th percentile, and 69 percent at the 90th percentile. Coefficient equality tests across percentiles show that these differences are significant at the 0.01 level. Results for EBV, presented in table 4, are somewhat different. There is no evidence of a monotonic gradient—instead, gender differences are most pronounced in the middle of the distribution, with women at the median having EBV levels about 21 percent lower than their similar male peers. The size of the gender difference is 16 percent at the 10th percentile, and 16 percent at the 95th percentile.

Exploring the contribution of childhood or adolescent and early adulthood factors in explaining gender differences in CRP and EBV reveals robust differences. After controlling for

**Table 3.** Quantile Regression of Logged CRP (mg/L) on Gender, Add Health

| | Percentile | | | | | |
|---|---|---|---|---|---|---|
| | 0.1 | | | 0.25 | | |
| | (1) | (2) | (3) | (1) | (2) | (3) |
| Male | -0.190*** | -0.173*** | -0.214*** | -0.358*** | -0.354*** | -0.444*** |
| | (-6.95) | (-4.14) | (-4.27) | (-16.39) | (-11.25) | (-11.28) |
| **Race or ethnicity** | | | | | | |
| Hispanic | | 0.201*** | 0.133* | | 0.269*** | 0.127* |
| | | (3.53) | (1.99) | | (3.87) | (2.31) |
| Black | | -0.0725 | -0.137** | | 0.00530 | -0.0627 |
| | | (-1.74) | (-2.68) | | (0.13) | (-1.18) |
| Asian | | -0.329*** | -0.303*** | | -0.319*** | -0.338*** |
| | | (-3.71) | (-4.72) | | (-4.44) | (-3.94) |
| Other race | | 0.118 | 0.123 | | 0.379* | 0.0509 |
| | | (0.94) | (0.57) | | (2.03) | (0.31) |
| **Nativity** | | | | | | |
| Second generation | | -0.0190 | -0.0468 | | 0.179** | 0.0335 |
| | | (-0.31) | (-0.60) | | (2.89) | (0.40) |
| Third-plus generation | | 0.0620 | 0.0199 | | 0.223*** | 0.0706 |
| | | (1.20) | (0.26) | | (3.29) | (0.93) |
| **Parental education** | | | | | | |
| High school | | -0.104* | -0.0800 | | -0.189*** | -0.0904 |
| | | (-2.09) | (-1.15) | | (-5.29) | (-1.59) |
| Some college | | -0.148** | -0.143* | | -0.284*** | -0.152** |
| | | (-2.97) | (-2.07) | | (-4.26) | (-3.02) |
| College or more | | -0.263*** | -0.147* | | -0.387*** | -0.136 |
| | | (-4.98) | (-1.99) | | (-7.94) | (-1.84) |
| Logged family income | | -0.00207 | -0.00780 | | 0.000830 | -0.00465 |
| | | (-0.34) | (-0.96) | | (0.15) | (-0.47) |
| Parents married | | -0.0485 | -0.0127 | | -0.0246 | -0.0483 |
| | | (-1.38) | (-0.29) | | (-0.74) | (-1.29) |
| Ever married, wave 4 | | | 0.0520 | | | 0.0658* |
| | | | (1.55) | | | (2.02) |
| Some college, wave 4 | | | 0.0478 | | | -0.0243 |
| | | | (0.98) | | | (-0.54) |
| College or more, wave 4 | | | -0.162** | | | -0.204*** |
| | | | (-3.17) | | | (-4.93) |
| Household income, wave 4 | | | 7.88e-08 | | | 6.70e-08 |
| | | | (0.85) | | | (0.67) |
| Employed part or full time | | | -0.0421 | | | -0.172* |
| | | | (-0.69) | | | (-2.19) |
| Work or family conflict | | | -0.0229 | | | 0.0212 |
| | | | (-0.60) | | | -0.8 |
| Constant | -0.949*** | 1.174*** | -0.778*** | -0.0471* | -0.413 | 0.0558 |
| | (-45.07) | (-5.17) | (-3.53) | (-2.07) | (-1.94) | (0.25) |
| N | 13,600 | 13,600 | 11,359 | | | |

*Source:* Authors' compilation based on Add Health, Waves 1–4.
*Note:* Models also control for measures listed in table 1, pregnancy status at wave 4, and parity at wave 4. T statistics in parentheses.
*$p < .05$; **$p < .01$; ***$p < .001$

|  | Percentile | | | | | | | | |
|---|---|---|---|---|---|---|---|---|---|
|  | 0.5 | | | 0.75 | | | 0.9 | | |
|  | (1) | (2) | (3) | (1) | (2) | (3) | (1) | (2) | (3) |
|  | -0.616*** | -0.573*** | -0.606*** | -0.674*** | -0.645*** | -0.663*** | -0.695*** | -0.694*** | -0.695*** |
|  | (-27.20) | (-20.27) | (-17.44) | (-21.08) | (-21.10) | (-19.12) | (-24.94) | (-21.75) | (-12.49) |
|  |  | 0.247*** | 0.131* |  | 0.215*** | 0.162*** |  | 0.193*** | 0.159* |
|  |  | (5.00) | (2.17) |  | (4.58) | (3.52) |  | (3.68) | (2.07) |
|  |  | 0.110** | 0.0177 |  | 0.154*** | 0.0430 |  | 0.192*** | 0.0865 |
|  |  | (2.60) | (0.50) |  | (3.75) | (0.79) |  | (6.26) | (1.81) |
|  |  | -0.272*** | -0.304*** |  | -0.182** | -0.266** |  | -0.204 | -0.334*** |
|  |  | (-4.95) | (-3.86) |  | (-2.76) | (-3.02) |  | (-1.82) | (-4.63) |
|  |  | 0.402* | 0.268 |  | 0.505*** | 0.532*** |  | 0.605*** | 0.369* |
|  |  | (2.40) | (1.82) |  | (5.81) | (4.53) |  | (4.71) | (2.04) |
|  |  | 0.159* | -0.0163 |  | 0.145** | -0.0121 |  | 0.0648 | -0.0670 |
|  |  | (2.46) | (-0.23) |  | (2.65) | (-0.17) |  | (1.01) | (-0.77) |
|  |  | 0.213*** | -0.0289 |  | 0.244*** | 0.101 |  | 0.184* | 0.0166 |
|  |  | (4.06) | (-0.49) |  | (5.99) | (1.25) |  | (2.02) | (0.17) |
|  |  | -0.148*** | -0.0573 |  | -0.119** | -0.0583 |  | -0.0812 | -0.0142 |
|  |  | (-3.67) | (-1.28) |  | (-2.76) | (-1.48) |  | (-1.59) | (-0.29) |
|  |  | -0.271*** | -0.151** |  | -0.240*** | -0.128** |  | -0.133 | -0.0215 |
|  |  | (-5.29) | (-3.14) |  | (-4.35) | (-2.77) |  | (-1.87) | (-0.31) |
|  |  | -0.403*** | -0.149* |  | -0.332*** | -0.144*** |  | -0.229*** | -0.0558 |
|  |  | (-11.04) | (-2.56) |  | (-6.40) | (-3.60) |  | (-3.44) | (-0.75) |
|  |  | -0.000617 | 0.00101 |  | -0.00670 | -0.000577 |  | 0.00247 | 0.0112 |
|  |  | (-0.08) | (0.13) |  | (-0.93) | (-0.06) |  | (0.33) | (1.24) |
|  |  | -0.0345 | -0.0129 |  | -0.00435 | 0.00748 |  | -0.00452 | 0.0116 |
|  |  | (-1.19) | (-0.46) |  | (-0.12) | (0.31) |  | (-0.13) | (0.35) |
|  |  |  | 0.103** |  |  | 0.0706* |  |  | 0.0614* |
|  |  |  | (2.87) |  |  | (2.12) |  |  | (1.98) |
|  |  |  | -0.0583 |  |  | -0.0819* |  |  | -0.112 |
|  |  |  | (-1.83) |  |  | (-2.36) |  |  | (-1.86) |
|  |  |  | -0.157*** |  |  | -0.0931** |  |  | -0.0954 |
|  |  |  | (-4.01) |  |  | (-2.62) |  |  | (-1.74) |
|  |  |  | 0.000000141* |  |  | 0.000000172** |  |  | 1.78e-08 |
|  |  |  | (2.16) |  |  | (2.89) |  |  | (0.30) |
|  |  |  | -0.0859 |  |  | -0.117 |  |  | -0.0190 |
|  |  |  | (-1.36) |  |  | (-1.84) |  |  | (-0.25) |
|  |  |  | 0.00342 |  |  | -0.017 |  |  | -0.0198 |
|  |  |  | -0.12 |  |  | (-0.64) |  |  | (-0.62) |
|  | 1.066*** | 0.762*** | 0.903*** | 2.003*** | 1.650*** | 2.051*** | 2.729*** | 2.428*** | 2.615*** |
|  | (45.27) | (5.32) | (4.73) | (105.83) | (7.21) | (10.17) | (116.94) | (8.47) | (10.81) |

**Table 4.** Quantile Regression of Logged EBV (AU/L) on Gender, Add Health

| | Percentile | | | | | |
|---|---|---|---|---|---|---|
| | 0.1 | | | 0.25 | | |
| | (1) | (2) | (3) | (1) | (2) | (3) |
| Male | -0.164*** | -0.176*** | -0.180*** | -0.209*** | -0.199*** | -0.197*** |
| | (-5.26) | (-7.54) | (-6.17) | (-7.58) | (-12.01) | (-11.45) |
| **Race-ethnicity** | | | | | | |
| Hispanic | | 0.161*** | 0.197*** | | 0.0929*** | 0.124*** |
| | | (4.22) | (6.67) | | (4.73) | (4.38) |
| Black | | 0.219*** | 0.248*** | | 0.244*** | 0.254*** |
| | | (8.04) | (7.38) | | (9.74) | (10.93) |
| Asian | | 0.145* | 0.203*** | | 0.0229 | 0.0688 |
| | | (2.51) | (4.38) | | (0.79) | (1.84) |
| Other race | | 0.0994 | 0.0997 | | -0.000739 | -0.0895 |
| | | (1.46) | (1.64) | | (-0.01) | (-1.01) |
| **Nativity** | | | | | | |
| Second generation | | 0.0152 | 0.0563 | | 0.0819 | 0.0792 |
| | | (0.26) | (1.31) | | (1.89) | (1.91) |
| Third-plus generation | | 0.0534 | 0.105* | | 0.0879* | 0.113* |
| | | (1.09) | (2.34) | | (2.47) | (2.50) |
| **Parental education** | | | | | | |
| High school | | 0.0127 | -0.00129 | | -0.0333 | -0.0156 |
| | | (0.40) | (-0.03) | | (-1.14) | (-0.52) |
| Some college | | 0.0268 | 0.0269 | | -0.0351 | -0.0153 |
| | | (0.86) | (0.65) | | (-1.25) | (-0.46) |
| College or more | | -0.0867** | -0.0795 | | -0.104** | -0.0832* |
| | | (-2.85) | (-1.93) | | (-3.27) | (-2.00) |
| Logged family income | | 0.0133* | 0.0170 | | 0.0148*** | 0.0149** |
| | | (2.00) | (1.77) | | (4.44) | (2.63) |
| Parents married | | -0.0134 | 0.00155 | | -0.0172 | -0.0165 |
| | | (-0.51) | (0.05) | | (-0.75) | (-0.69) |
| Ever married, wave 4 | | | 0.127*** | | | 0.0781*** |
| | | | (4.20) | | | (3.31) |
| Some college, wave 4 | | | 0.00445 | | | -0.0113 |
| | | | (0.19) | | | (-0.74) |
| College or more, wave 4 | | | -0.0451* | | | -0.00775 |
| | | | (-1.96) | | | (-0.33) |
| Household income, wave 4 | | | 9.29e-08 | | | 8.82e-08* |
| | | | (1.83) | | | (2.10) |
| Employed part or full time | | | -0.0139 | | | 0.0185 |
| | | | (-0.33) | | | (0.64) |
| Work or family conflict | | | -0.0128 | | | 0.0129 |
| | | | (-0.78) | | | (0.60) |
| Constant | 3.970*** | 3.302*** | 3.217*** | 4.443*** | 3.916*** | 3.935*** |
| | (169.27) | (24.46) | (24.21) | (237.19) | (34.20) | (38.71) |
| N | 13,679 | 13,679 | 11,428 | | | |

*Source:* Authors' compilation based on Add Health, Waves 1–4.
*Note:* Models also control for measures listed in table 1, pregnancy status at wave 4, and parity at wave 4. T statistics in parentheses.
*p < .05; **p < .01; ***p < .001

|  | Percentile | | | | | | | | |
|---|---|---|---|---|---|---|---|---|---|
|  | 0.5 | | | 0.75 | | | 0.9 | | |
| (1) | (2) | (3) | (1) | (2) | (3) | (1) | (2) | (3) |
| -0.211*** | -0.207*** | -0.218*** | -0.169*** | -0.172*** | -0.184*** | -0.158*** | -0.135*** | -0.157*** |
| (-9.06) | (-11.80) | (-11.45) | (-8.36) | (-12.30) | (-15.31) | (-9.32) | (-7.65) | (-12.13) |
|  | 0.0361 | 0.0620 |  | 0.0736* | 0.0576* |  | 0.0220 | 0.00382 |
|  | (1.25) | (1.87) |  | (2.17) | (1.98) |  | (0.68) | (0.11) |
|  | 0.213*** | 0.198*** |  | 0.182*** | 0.156*** |  | 0.197*** | 0.175*** |
|  | (15.19) | (9.77) |  | (11.09) | (6.92) |  | (9.86) | (5.09) |
|  | -0.0264 | 0.00500 |  | 0.0205 | 0.0110 |  | 0.0536 | 0.0350 |
|  | (-0.59) | (0.09) |  | (0.59) | (0.24) |  | (1.40) | (1.27) |
|  | 0.0798 | 0.0536 |  | -0.0190 | 0.00478 |  | -0.0655 | -0.0160 |
|  | (1.03) | (0.73) |  | (-0.48) | (0.07) |  | (-0.90) | (-0.26) |
|  | 0.0531 | 0.0792 |  | 0.0644 | 0.0607 |  | 0.0142 | -0.0315 |
|  | (1.31) | (1.53) |  | (1.80) | (1.23) |  | (0.48) | (-0.65) |
|  | 0.0445 | 0.0922 |  | 0.0417 | 0.0306 |  | -0.00744 | -0.0520 |
|  | (1.45) | (1.71) |  | (1.46) | (0.75) |  | (-0.25) | (-1.03) |
|  | -0.0370 | -0.0287 |  | 0.0133 | 0.00392 |  | -0.0263 | -0.0255 |
|  | (-1.48) | (-0.92) |  | (0.66) | (0.23) |  | (-1.26) | (-0.88) |
|  | -0.0379 | -0.0367 |  | -0.00181 | -0.00905 |  | -0.0567* | -0.0499* |
|  | (-1.82) | (-1.22) |  | (-0.10) | (-0.42) |  | (-2.17) | (-1.97) |
|  | -0.0978*** | -0.0899** |  | -0.0593* | -0.0589* |  | -0.102** | -0.0869*** |
|  | (-4.25) | (-2.79) |  | (-2.42) | (-2.26) |  | (-2.79) | (-3.57) |
|  | 0.00607 | 0.00755 |  | 0.00133 | 0.00530 |  | 0.00659* | 0.00852 |
|  | (1.46) | (1.50) |  | (0.26) | (0.86) |  | (2.55) | (1.95) |
|  | 0.00113 | -0.00721 |  | -0.00540 | -0.0361* |  | -0.0266 | -0.0433* |
|  | (0.06) | (-0.31) |  | (-0.25) | (-2.25) |  | (-1.26) | (-2.24) |
|  |  | 0.0317 |  |  | 0.0189 |  |  | 0.00252 |
|  |  | (1.79) |  |  | (0.95) |  |  | (0.15) |
|  |  | -0.0437 |  |  | -0.0492* |  |  | -0.0388 |
|  |  | (-1.62) |  |  | (-2.27) |  |  | (-1.70) |
|  |  | 0.0123 |  |  | -0.00428 |  |  | -0.0151 |
|  |  | (0.63) |  |  | (-0.20) |  |  | (-0.74) |
|  |  | 2.73e-08 |  |  | 1.74e-08 |  |  | 1.96e-08 |
|  |  | (0.98) |  |  | (0.50) |  |  | (-0.48) |
|  |  | 0.0067 |  |  | -0.052* |  |  | -0.0486 |
|  |  | (0.34) |  |  | (-2.27) |  |  | (-1.40) |
|  |  | -0.0017 |  |  | -0.0245* |  |  | -0.0036 |
|  |  | (-.20) |  |  | (-2.50) |  |  | (-0.27) |
| 4.956*** | 4.593*** | 4.526*** | 5.389*** | 5.080*** | 5.167*** | 5.753*** | 5.615*** | 5.736*** |
| (520.53) | (41.91) | (37.75) | (482.49) | (49.22) | (56.21) | (443.19) | (48.30) | (49.86) |

demographic factors and for variation in earlier-life circumstances such as parental education, family income, and family structure, the magnitude and significance of gender differences in both biomarkers are essentially identical. Similarly, controlling for variation in early adulthood characteristics—health behaviors, educational attainment, and family formation—does not reduce, and in some cases slightly increases, gender differences. This pattern is similar across both outcomes and across the distribution, suggesting that variation in the socioeconomic environments of young adult men and women is not large enough—at least among the overall population—to contribute meaningfully to pronounced differences in biological function.

Tables 3 and 4 also show the extent to which the relationship between other social categories and biomarkers is explained by different circumstances over the early life course, and whether patterns vary across the distribution. Although differences between Hispanic and non-Hispanic white respondents, and between Asians and non-Hispanic whites, are similarly robust to the inclusion of socioeconomic and health measures, black-white differences in CRP (but not EBV) are more substantially reduced by the inclusion of early adulthood circumstances, especially at higher points in the distribution. Early adulthood characteristics also go further in explaining the relationship between high parental education (college or more) and inflammation than for immune function. Finally, differences are pronounced in inflammation according to respondents' education, college-educated respondents having lower levels of inflammation (but not immune function), especially at lower levels of the distribution.

Figures 1 and 2 visualize gender differences in CRP and EBV, respectively. The x-axis on each graph is the percentile and the y-axis is the coefficient size. Each graph, therefore, shows the degree of gender differences in CRP or EBV at different percentiles. The line with shading around it is the gender coefficient from the quantile regression (from the full model, model 3) at a particular percentile and the gray shading graphs the 90 percent confidence interval. The dark horizontal line shows the OLS regression coefficient from the CRP or EBV regression, respectively. The figures confirm the findings displayed in tables 3 and 4, and show that gender differences at the extremes of the distribution vary from those at the mean. This variation is especially pronounced for the case of inflammation. That these differences are so large at a young age is striking, given evidence that those with high levels of CRP have significantly higher risk for cardiovascular disease and premature mortality.

### Sensitivity Analyses

We conduct several additional analyses to test the sensitivity of our results to sample restrictions. First, we limit CRP analyses to those with levels at or below 10 mg/L. Because results are nearly identical, we retain these observations in final models. Second, we limit EBV analyses to those who are seropositive, in order to prevent seronegative respondents from biasing coefficients, given evidence that seropositivity is predicted by sociodemographic factors. We use a method established by Jennifer Dowd, Tai Palermo, Laura Chyu, and their colleagues of establishing seronegativity as the bottom 10 percent of continuous EBV antibody values (2013). Coefficients are nearly identical, so we retain seronegative respondents. Finally, we estimate sibling fixed effects models to better control for childhood family environments among siblings. These models, which are identified from siblings who differ in gender, also show a significant gender gap in inflammation and immune function. These results suggest that results from quantile regression analyses are not unduly biased by unmeasured childhood circumstances that are shared by siblings.

### DISCUSSION

We use nationally representative, longitudinal data from the National Longitudinal Study of Adolescent Health to better understand the relationship between gender and biological function in young adulthood, and to begin to consider the extent to which social and economic circumstances in childhood, adolescence and young adulthood contribute to differences between men and women. We focus on biologic function—specifically, inflammation and immune function—because their pre-

**Figure 1.** Gender Coefficient for CRP Across Distribution

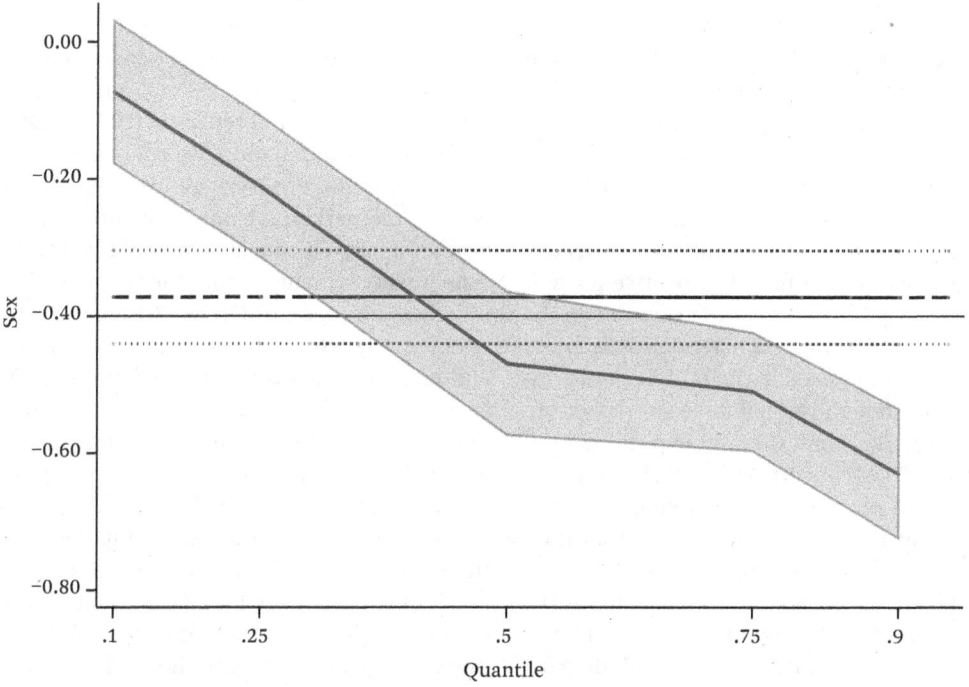

*Source:* Authors' compilation based on Add Health, Waves 1-4.

**Figure 2.** Gender Coefficient for EBV Across Distribution

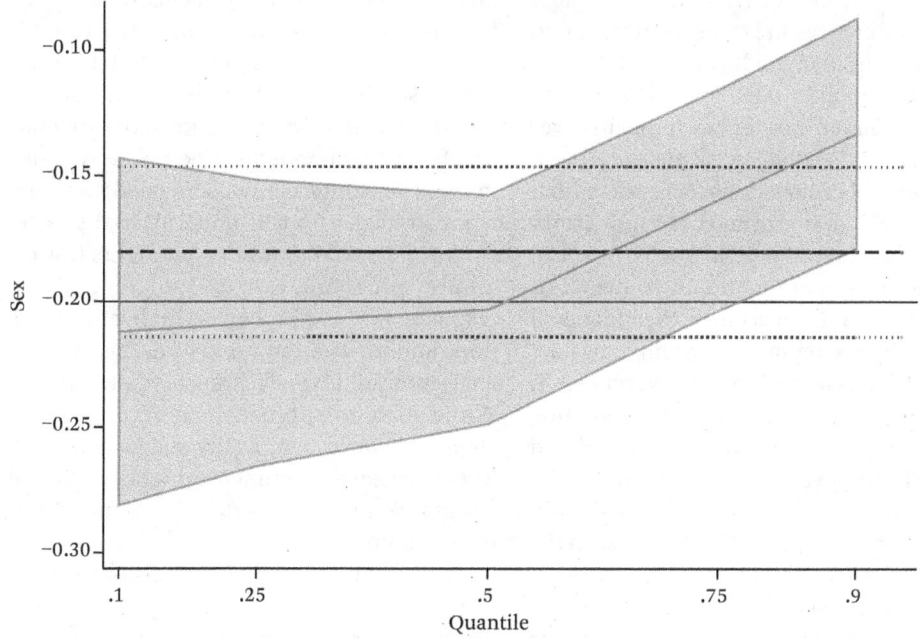

*Source:* Authors' compilation based on Add Health, Waves 1-4.

dictive power for future disease risk is high, and because research on gender differences in physiologic risk at young ages is scant.

Results from OLS and quantile regression reveal strong gender differences in both inflammation and immune function among this sample of young adults. Although OLS results offer a useful benchmark, examining variation across the distribution reveals that women have disproportionately higher inflammation and lower immune function relative to their male peers at the top of the distribution. In the case of immune function, gender differences are most pronounced in the middle of the distribution, though women have also lower immune function than their male peers at both extremes. These results suggest that gender differences in physiologic function appear relatively early in the life course, and that substantial differences exist in the early part of individuals' adult trajectories. Considering the contribution of childhood or adolescent and early adulthood circumstances—including demographic factors, family socioeconomic background, health behaviors, and respondents' family formation and socioeconomic attainment—to the magnitude and significance of gender differences yields little evidence of a strong explanatory role for these factors.

Our findings, particularly for the robustness of gender differences in biological function to the inclusion of many indicators of the social environment in our model, inform the debate about how gender differences in health over the life course reflect biological and social variation. Biological explanations for gender differences in health and mortality are well established, as is evidence for variation in the social and economic environments of young adult men and women. By measuring the individual and family-level circumstances and behaviors that may give rise to gender differences in health, our analysis provides a more comprehensive test of the importance of social and economic factors over the life course in explaining gender differences observed in early adulthood. The stability of gender differences in the presence of these factors suggests, at minimum, that variation in the social and economic environments of young men and women in the United States—at least among the overall population—is not large enough to produce the observed pronounced differences in biological function by early adulthood.

Although we do not find evidence for a primary role of early life social environments in explaining gender differences in CRP and EBV in the overall population, we caution against concluding that observed gender differences in these biomarkers are only a function of biology. First, such a conclusion would be inconsistent with evidence from other settings that indicates no mean difference CRP or EBV by sex or gender. Second, our measures of social and economic environments are limited. For example, we are not able to measure cumulative environments as comprehensively as we would like, given that parent-reported data are only available during the first wave. Add Health data do permit us to test a more comprehensive life course model than has been the case in previous research, but it is possible that a more cumulative measure of socioeconomic status—one that captures early-childhood SES in addition to adolescent and young adulthood SES, for example—would yield a larger contribution of the social environment to gender differences in young adulthood. For this to be the case, however, girls and boys would need to experience significantly different childhood environments, and we find little evidence of meaningful variation with our available data (see table 1). Moreover, the results are robust to the inclusion of sibling fixed effects, which capture unobserved, shared family circumstances of male and female respondents. The results are also insensitive to alternative coding and measurement strategies for CRP and EBV, to the exclusion of potential outlier respondents (for example, pregnant women and recently ill respondents), and to controls for health conditions and medication use. Third, this analysis focuses on additive effects and not interactions. While such an approach is a necessary first step, real-world complexity suggests that effects of social environments might be masked if biomarker levels are a function of interactive relationships.

Further, although higher levels of CRP and EBV are associated with risk of chronic disease, including cancer, cardiovascular and metabolic disease, whether a given level in these biomarkers translates into similar risk for men and women is difficult to discern from current studies. Existing research is based on different samples and populations, investigates different health outcomes, and produces results that show both equivalent and different risks (Cushman et al. 2005; Han et al 2002; Pai et al. 2004; Yamada et al. 2001). Further, existing practice guidelines do not offer guidance. For example, in 2003, a statement from the Centers for Disease Control and Prevention and the American Heart Association identified over 3 mg/L of CRP as high risk for cardiovascular disease for both men and women, but also noted the need for additional high-quality evidence (Pearson et al. 2003). In short, we emphasize that though we document difference in physiologic function by gender, and patterns and correlates of such difference, the implications for differences in risk are unclear. In future research it will be useful to examine a more comprehensive life course model that includes the critical and sensitive early childhood years. In addition, it will be useful to consider gender variation in the effects of social and economic circumstances during adulthood on biological function. Variation in patterns of family formation between men and women, such as the high prevalence of single motherhood in the United States, mean that adult men and women experience different social stressors that may condition the influence of gender on biological function. Conversely, contemporary patterns of higher educational attainment among women may offset some of the physiologic and health disadvantages associated with low socioeconomic status. Further, additional work on the implications of differences in physiologic function for risk is needed. Examining health within a cohort of young men and women in early adulthood advances our understanding of the intragenerational predictors of pronounced gender differences in biological function, highlights the robustness of those differences, and describes patterns that can be further explored.

## REFERENCES

Alley, Dawn E., Teresa E. Seeman, Jung Ki Kim, Arun Karlamangla, Peifeng Hu, and Eileen M. Crimmins. 2006. "Socioeconomic Status and C-Reactive Protein Levels in the U.S. Population: NHANES IV." *Brain, Behavior, and Immunity* 20(5): 498–504.

Arias, Elizabeth. 2014. "United States Life Tables, 2010." *National Vital Statistics Reports* 63(7): 1–62.

Austad, Steven N. 2006. "Why Women Live Longer than Men: Sex Differences in Longevity." *Gender Medicine* 3(2): 79–92.

Ben-Schlomo, Yoav, and Diana Kuh. 2002. "A Life Course Approach to Chronic Disease Epidemiology: Conceptual Models, Empirical Challenges, and Interdisciplinary Perspectives." *International Journal of Epidemiology* 31(2): 285–93.

Berkman, Lisa. 2012. "United States: Challenges of Economic and Demographic Trends." *Social Science and Medicine* 74(5): 656–57.

Bianchi, Suzanne M., John P. Robinson, and Melissa Milke. 2006. *The Changing Rhythms of American Family Life.* New York: Russell Sage Foundation.

Bird, Chloe E., and Patricia P. Rieker. 2002. "Integrating Social and Biological Research to Improve Men's and Women's Health." *Women's Health Issues* 12(3): 113–15.

Cartier, Amélie, Mélanie Côté, Isabelle Lemieux, Louis Pérusse, Angelo Tremblay, Claude Bouchard, and Jean-Pierre Després. 2009. "Sex Differences in Inflammatory Markers: What Is the Contribution of Visceral Adiposity?" *American Journal of Clinical Nutrition* 89(5): 1307–14.

Case, Anne, Darren Lubotsky, and Christina Paxson. 2002. "Economic Status and Health in Childhood: The Origins of the Gradient." *American Economic Review* 92(5): 1308–34.

Case, Anne, and Christina Paxson. 2005. "Sex Differences in Morbidity and Mortality." *Demography* 42(2): 189–214.

Chen, Kevin, and Denise B. Kandel. 1995. "The Natural History of Drug Use from Adolescence to the Mid-Thirties in a General Population Sample." *American Journal of Public Health* 85(1): 41–47.

Chen, Chao-Yu, Kuan-Ying A. Huang, Jen-Hsiang Shen, Kuo-Chien Tsao, and Yhu-Chering Huang. 2015. "A Large-Scale Seroprevalence of Epstein-Barr Virus in Taiwan." *PLoS One.*

Crimmins, Eileen, Jung Ki Him, and Aida Solé-Auró. 2010. "Gender Differences in Health: Results from SHARE, ELSA and HRS." *European Journal of Public Health* 21(1): 81–91.

Cushman, Mary, Alice M. Arnold, Bruce M. Psaty, Teri A. Manolio, Lewis H. Kuller, Gregory L. Burke, Joseph F. Polak, and Russell P. Tracy.

2005. "C-Reactive Protein and the 10-Year Incidence of Coronary Heart Disease in Older Men and Women: The Cardiovascular Health Study." *Circulation* 112(1): 25–31.

DiPrete, Thomas A., and Jennifer L. Jennings. 2012. "Social and Behavioral Skills and the Gender Gap in Early Educational Achievement." *Social Science Research* 41(1): 1–15.

Dowd, Jennifer Beam, Tia Palermo, Jennifer Brite, Thomas W. McDade, and Allison Aiello. 2013. "Seroprevalence of Epstein-Barr Virus Infection in U.S. Children Ages 6–19, 2003–2010." *PLoS One* 8(5): e64921.

Dowd, Jennifer Beam, Tia Palermo, Laura Chyu, Emma Adam, and Thomas W. McDade. 2013. "Re: Childhood Adversity and Cell-Mediated Immunity in Young Adulthood." *Brain Behavior and Immunity* 34 (November): 176.

Dowd, Jennifer B., Tia Palermo, Laura Chyu, Emma Adam, and Thomas W. McDade. 2014. "Race/Ethnic and Socioeconomic Differences in Stress and Immune Function in the National Longitudinal Study of Adolescent Health." *Social Science and Medicine* 115 (August): 49–55.

Duncan, Greg J., Kathleen M. Ziol-Guest, and Ariel Kalil. 2010. "Early-Childhood Poverty and Adult Attainment, Behavior, and Health." *Child Development* 81(1): 306–25.

Entwisle, Doris R., Karl L. Alexander, and Linda Steffle Olson. 2007. "Early Schooling: The Handicap of Being Poor and Male." *Sociology of Education* 80(2): 114–38.

Esen, Bahar Artim, Guldin Yilmaz, Sami Uzun, Melda Ozdamar, et al. 2012. "Serologic Response to Epstein-Barr Virus Antigens in Patients with Systemic Lupus Erythematosus: A Controlled Study." *Rheumatology International* 32(1): 79–83.

Everett, Bethany G., Margaret Rosario, Katie A. McLaughlin, and S. Bryn Austin. 2014. "Sexual Orientation and Gender Differences in Markers of Inflammation and Immune Functioning." *Annals of Behavioral Medicine* 47(1): 57–70.

Fahdi, Ibrahim E., Venkat Gaddam, Luis Garza, Francesco Romeo, and Jawahar L. Mehta. 2003. "Inflammation, Infection, and Atherosclerosis." *Brain, Behavior, and Immunity* 17(4): 238–44.

Farkas, George, Robert Grobe, David Sheehan, and Yuan Shuan. 1990. "Cultural Resources and School Success: Gender, Ethnicity and Poverty Groups Within an Urban School District." *American Sociological Review* 55(1): 127–42.

Ferraro, Kenneth F., and Tetyana Pylypiv Shippee. 2009. "Aging and Cumulative Inequality: How Does Inequality Get Under the Skin?" *The Gerontologist* 49(3): 333–43.

Finch, Brian K. 2003. "Early Origins of the Gradient: The Relationship Between Socioeconomic Status and Infant Mortality in the United States." *Demography* 40(4): 675–99.

Fish, Eleanor N. 2008. "The X-Files in Immunity: Sex-Based Differences Predispose Immune Responses." *Nature Reviews Immunology* 8(9): 737–44.

Han, Thang S., Naveed Sattar, Ken Williams, Clicerio Gonzalez-Villalpando, Michael E. J. Lean, and Steven M. Haffner. 2002. "Prospective Study of C-Reactive Protein in Relation to the Development of Diabetes and Metabolic Syndrome in the Mexico City Diabetes Study." *Diabetes Care* 25(11): 2016–21.

Harris, Kathleen M. 2010. "An Integrative Approach to Health." *Demography* 47(1): 1–22.

Hayward, Mark D., and Bridget K. Gorman. 2004. "The Long Arm of Childhood: The Influence of Early-Life Social Conditions on Men's Mortality." *Demography* 41(1): 87–107.

Heckman, James J. 2006. "Skill Formation and the Economics of Investing in Young Children." *Science* 312(5782): 1900–902.

Hsu, Joe L., and Sally L. Glaser. 2000. "Epstein-Barr Virus-Associated Malignancies: Epidemiologic Patterns and Etiologic Implications." *Critical Reviews in Oncology/Hematology* 34(1): 27–53.

Institute of Medicine. 2001. *Exploring the Biological Contributions to Human Health: Does Sex Matter?* Washington, D.C.: National Academies Press.

Ishii, Shinya, Arun S. Karlamangla, Marcos Bote, Michael R. Irwin, David R. Jacobs Jr., Hyong Jin Cho, and Teresa E. Seeman. 2012. "Gender, Obesity and Repeated Elevation of C-Reactive Protein: Data from the CARDIA Cohort." *PLoS One* 7(4): e36062.

Jackson, Margot I. 2010. "A Life Course Perspective on Child Health, Cognition and Occupational Skill Qualifications in Adulthood: Evidence from a British Cohort." *Social Forces* 89(1): 89–116.

———. 2015. "Cumulative Inequality in Child Health and Academic Achievement." *Journal of Health and Social Behavior* 56(2): 262–80.

Jacobsen, Joyce. 2016. "Gender Wage Gap." In *The Wiley Blackwell Encyclopedia of Gender and Sexuality Studies* edited by Nancy Naples, Renee C.

Hoogland, Maithree Wickramasinghe, and Wai Ching Angela Wong. New York: Wiley Blackwell.

James, Judith A., and Julie M. Robertson. 2012. "Lupus and Epstein-Barr." *Current Opinion in Rheumatology* 24(4): 383–88.

Kanjilal, Sanjat, Edward W. Gregg, Yiling J. Cheng, Ping Zhang, David E. Nelson, George Mensah, and Gloria L. A. Beckles. 2006. "Socioeconomic Status and Trends in Disparities in Four Major Risk Factors for Cardiovascular Disease Among U.S. Adults, 1971–2002." *Archives of Internal Medicine* 166(2): 2348–55.

Karlamangla, Arun S., Burton H. Singer, David R. Williams, Joseph E. Schwartz, Karen A. Matthews, Catarina I. Kiefe, and Teresa E. Seeman. 2005. "Impact of Socioeconomic Status on Longitudinal Accumulation of Cardiovascular Risk in Young Adults: The CARDIA Study (USA)." *Social Science and Medicine* 60(5): 999–1015.

Kitagawa, Evelyn M., and Philip M. Hauser. 1973. *Differential Mortality in the United States: A Study in Socioeconomic Epidemiology*. Cambridge, Mass.: Harvard University Press.

Kunst, Anton E., Vivian Bos, Eero Lahelma, Mel Bartley, et al. 2005. "Trends in Socioeconomic Inequalities in Self-Assessed Health in 10 European Countries." *International Journal of Epidemiology* 34(2): 295–305.

Lakoski, Susan G., Mary Cushman, Michael Criqui, Tatjana Rundek, Roger S. Blumenthal, Ralph B. D'Agostino, and David M. Herrington. 2006. "Gender and C-Reactive Protein: Data from the Multiethnic Study of Atherosclerosis (MESA) Cohort." *American Heart Journal* 152(3): 593–98.

Le-Ha, Chi, Lawrence J. Beilin, Sally Burrows, Wendy H. Oddy, Beth Hands, and Trevor A. Mori. 2014. "Gender and the Active Smoking and High-Sensitivity C-Reactive Protein Relation in Late Adolescence." *Journal of Lipid Research* 55(4): 758–64.

Levin, Lynn I., Kassandra L. Munger, Eilis J. O'Reilly, Kerstin I. Falk, and Alberto Ascherio. 2010. "Primary Infection with the Epstein-Barr Virus and Risk of Multiple Sclerosis." *Annals of Neurology* 67(6): 824–30.

Lleo, Ana, Pier Maria Battezzati, Carlo Selmi, M. Eric Gershwin, and Mauro Podda. 2008. "Is Autoimmunity a Matter of Sex?" *Autoimmunity Reviews* 7(8): 626–30.

Lynch, Scott M. 2003. "Cohort and Life-Course Patterns in the Relationship Between Education and Health: A Hierarchical Approach." *Demography* 40(2): 309–31.

Markle, J. G., and Eleanor N. Fish. 2014. "SeXX Matters in Immunity." *Trends in Immunology* 35(3): 97–104.

Marmot, Michael G. 2001. "Inequalities in Health." *New England Journal of Medicine* 345(2): 134–35.

McDade, Thomas W., Molly W. Metzger, Laura Chyu, Greg J. Duncan, Craig Garfield, and Emma K. Adam. 2014. "Long-Term Effects of Birth Weight and Breastfeeding Duration on Inflammation in Early Adulthood." *Proceedings of the Royal Society of London B: Biological Sciences* 281(784): 20133116.

McDade, Thomas W., Joy F. Stallings, and Carol M. Worthman. 2000. "Culture Change and Stress in Western Samoan Youth: Methodological Issues in the Cross-Cultural Study of Stress and Immune Function." *American Journal of Human Biology* 12(6): 792–802.

McDade, Thomas W., Sharon Williams, and J. J. Snodgrass. 2007. "What a Drop Can Do: Dried Blood Spots as a Minimally Invasive Method for Integrating Biomarkers into Population-Based Research." *Demography* 44(4): 899–925.

Meara, Ellen R., Seth Richards, and David M. Cutler. 2008. "The Gap Gets Bigger: Changes in Mortality and Life Expectancy, by Education: 1981–2000." *Health Affairs* 27(2): 350–60.

Miller, Michelle A., Ngianga-Bakwin Kandala, Mika Kivimaki, Meena Kumari, Eric J. Brunner, G. D. Lowe, Michael G. Marmot, and Francesco P. Cappuccio. 2009. "Gender Differences in the Cross-Sectional Relationships Between Sleep Duration and Markers of Inflammation: Whitehall II Study." *Sleep* 32(7): 857–64.

Montez, Jennifer K., and Anna Zajacova. 2013. "Explaining the Widening Education Gap in Mortality Among U.S. White Women." *Journal of Health and Social Behavior* 54(2): 166–82.

Moore, David E., and Mark D. Hayward. 1990. "Occupational Careers and Mortality of Elderly Men." *Demography* 27(1): 31–53.

Morenoff, Jeffrey D. 2003. "Neighborhood Mechanisms and the Spatial Dynamics of Birth Weight." *American Journal of Sociology* 108(5): 976–1017.

Nolen-Hoeksema, Susan. 2001. "Gender Differences in Depression." *Current Directions in Psychological Science* 10(5): 173–76.

Ockene, Ira S., Charles E. Matthews, Nader Rifai,

Paul M. Ridker, George Reed, Edward Stanek. 2001. "Variability and Classification Accuracy of Serial High-Sensitivity C-Reactive Protein Measurements in Healthy Adults." *Clinical Chemistry* 47(3): 444–50.

O'Connor, Mary-Frances, Julie E. Bower, Hyong Jin Cho, J. David Creswell, et al. 2009. "To Assess, to Control, to Exclude: Effects of Biobehavioral Factors on Circulating Inflammatory Markers." *Brain, Behavior, and Immunity* 23(7): 887–97.

Oksuzyan, Anna, Maria Shkolnikova, James W. Vaupel, Kaare Christensen, and Vladimir M. Shkolnikov. 2015. "Sex Differences in Biological Markers of Health in the Study of Stress, Aging and Health in Russia." *PLoS One* 10(6): e0131691.

Oldehinkel, Albertine J., and Esther M. Bouma. 2011. "Sensitivity to the Depressogenic Effect of Stress and HPA-Axis Reactivity in Adolescence: A Review of Gender Differences." *Neuroscience & Biobehavioral Reviews* 35(8): 1757–70.

Ordaz, Sarah, and Beatriz Luna. 2012. "Sex Differences in Physiological Reactivity to Acute Psychosocial Stress in Adolescence." *Psychoneuroendocrinology* 37(8): 1135–57.

Pai, Jennifer K., Tobias Pischon, Jing Ma, JoAnn E. Manson, et al. 2004. "Inflammatory Markers and the Risk of Coronary Heart Disease in Men and Women." *New England Journal of Medicine* 351(25): 2599–610.

Palloni, Alberto. 2006. "Reproducing Inequalities: Luck, Wallets, and the Enduring Effects of Childhood Health." *Demography* 43(4): 587–615.

Pampel, Fred C. 2001. "Cigarette Diffusion and Sex Differences in Smoking." *Journal of Health and Social Behavior* 32(4): 388–404.

Pearson, Thomas A., George A. Mensah, R. Wayne Alexander, Jeffrey L. Anderson, et al. 2003. "Markers of Inflammation and Cardiovascular Disease: Application to Clinical and Public Health Practice." *Circulation* 107(3): 499–511.

Pomerantz, Eva M., Ellen R. Altermatt, Ellen Rydell, and Jill L. Saxson. 2002. "Making the Grade but Feeling Distressed: Gender Differences in Academic Performance and Internal Distress." *Journal of Educational Psychology* 94(2): 396–404.

Read, Jen'nan Ghazal, and Bridget K. Gorman. 2010. "Gender and Health Inequality." *Annual Review of Sociology* 36(1): 371–86.

Ridker, Paul M., Julie E. Buring, Jessie Shih, Mathew Matias, and Charles H. Hennekens. 1998. "Prospective Study of C-Reactive Protein and the Risk of Future Cardiovascular Events Among Apparently Healthy Women." *Circulation* 98(8): 731–33.

Rieker, Patricia P., Chloe E. Bird, and Martha E. Lang. 2010. "Understanding Gender and Health." In *Handbook of Medical Sociology*, 6th ed., edited by Chloe E. Bird, Peter Conrad, Allen M. Freemont, and S. Timmermans. Nashville, Tenn.: Vanderbilt University Press.

Schoon, Ingrid, John Bynner, Heather Joshi, Samantha Parsons, Richard D. Wiggins, and Amanda Sacker. 2002. "The Influence of Context, Timing, and Duration of Risk Experiences for the Passage from Childhood to Midadulthood." *Child Development* 73(5): 1486–504.

Shames, Richard S. 2002. "Gender Differences in the Development and Function of the Immune System." *Journal of Adolescent Health* 30(4): 59–70.

Shanahan, Lilly, Jason Freeman, and Shawn Bauldry. 2014. "Is Very High C-Reactive Protein in Young Adults Associated with Indicators of Chronic Disease Risk?" *Psychoneuroendocrinology* 40(1): 76–85.

Short, Susan E., Y. Claire Yang, and Tania M. Jenkins. 2013. "Sex, Gender, Genetics, and Health." *American Journal of Public Health* 103(S1): S93–101.

Smith, G. Davey, Martin J. Shipley, Michael Marmot, and George Davey Smith. 2000. "Physical Activity and Cause-Specific Mortality in the Whitehall Study." *Public Health* 114(5): 308–15.

Thompson, Matthew P., and Razelle Kurzrock. 2004. "Epstein-Barr Virus and Cancer." *Clinical Cancer Research* 10(3): 803–21.

Umberson, Debra, Robert Crosnoe, and Corinne Reczek. 2010. "Social Relationships and Health Behavior Across Life Course." *Annual Review of Sociology* 36(1): 139–57.

Wagmiller, Robert L., Mary Clare Lennon, Li Kuang, Philip M. Alberti, J. Lawrence Aber. 2006. "The Dynamics of Economic Disadvantage and Children's Life Chances." *American Sociological Review* 71(5): 847–66.

Williams, L. Susan. 2002. "Trying on Gender, Gender Regimes, and the Process of Becoming Women." *Gender & Society* 16(1): 29–52.

Yamada, Seishi, Tadao Gotoh, Yoshiyki Nakashima, Kazunori Kayaba, Shizukiyo Ishikawa, Naoki Nago, Yosikazu Nakamura, Yoshihisa Itoh, and

Eiji Kajii. 2001. "Distribution of Serum C-Reactive Protein and Its Association with Atherosclerotic Risk Factors in a Japanese Population." *American Journal of Epidemiology* 153(12): 1183–90.

Yang, Yang, and Michael Kozloski. 2011. "Sex Differences in Age Trajectories of Physiological Dysregulation: Inflammation, Metabolic Syndrome, and Allostatic Load." *Journals of Gerontology Series A: Biological Sciences and Medical Sciences* 66(5): 493–500.

Yang, Yang Claire, Martha K. McClintock, Michael Kozloski, and Ting Li. 2013. "Social Isolation and Adult Mortality: The Role of Chronic Inflammation and Sex Differences." *Journal of Health and Social Behavior* 54(2): 183–203.

# PART IV

# Genes and Environments over the Life Course

# The Sociogenomics of Polygenic Scores of Reproductive Behavior and Their Relationship to Other Fertility Traits

MELINDA C. MILLS, NICOLA BARBAN, AND FELIX C. TROPF

*Human reproductive behavior until relatively recently has been explained exclusively via individual and social characteristics. This article applies results from a recent Genome-Wide Association Study that combined sixty-two data sources to isolate twelve genetic loci associated with reproductive behavior. We create polygenic scores that allow us to include a summary variable of genetic factors into our statistical models. We use four datasets: the U.S. Health and Retirement Study, Dutch LifeLines, TwinsUK and the Swedish Twin register. First, we provide a brief overview of the dominant explanations of reproductive behavior. Second, we test the predictive power of polygenic scores. Third, we interrogate the robustness of our models using a series of sensitivity analyses to take into account possible confounders due to population stratification and selection.*

**Keywords:** human reproduction, polygenic scores, genetics, educational attainment, age at first birth, number of children ever born, fertility

Human reproductive behavior—measured by age at first birth (AFB) and number of children ever born (NEB)—is a central topic of study within the social, medical, and biological sciences. AFB and NEB are complex behaviors not only related to biological fecundity, but also have a strong behavioral element in that they are driven by the reproductive choice of individuals and their partners. They are likewise influenced by the environment and social in-

**Melinda C. Mills** is Nuffield Professor of Sociology at the University of Oxford and Nuffield College and leads the Sociogenome project. **Nicola Barban** is senior research associate in the Department of Sociology at the University of Oxford and Nuffield College. **Felix C. Tropf** is a postdoctoral researcher in the Department of Sociology at the University of Oxford and Nuffield College.

© 2018 Russell Sage Foundation. Mills, Melinda C., Nicola Barban, and Felix C. Tropf. 2018. "The Sociogenomics of Polygenic Scores of Reproductive Behavior and Their Relationship to Other Fertility Traits." *RSF: The Russell Sage Foundation Journal of the Social Sciences* 4(4): 122–36. DOI: 10.7758/RSF.2018.4.4.07. The research leading to these results has received funding from the following awards to PI M.C. Mills, European Research Council (ERC) Consolidator Grant SOCIOGENOME (615603, www.sociogenome.com), and Economic and Social Research Council (ESRC) UK, National Centre for Research Methods (NCRM) grant SOCGEN, European Union's FP7 FamiliesAndSocieties project (no.320116) and the Wellcome Trust ISSF and John Fell Fund. Direct correspondence to: Melinda C. Mills at melinda.mills@nuffield.ox.ac.uk, Department of Sociology, Nuffield College, University of Oxford, OX1 3UQ United Kingdom; Nicola Barban at nicola.barban@sociology.ox.ac.uk; and Felix C. Tropf at felix.tropf@sociology.ox.ac.uk.

Open Access Policy: *RSF: The Russell Sage Foundation Journal of the Social Sciences* is an open access journal. This article is published under a Creative Commons Attribution-NonCommercial-NoDerivs 3.0 Unported License.

stitutions, including multiple factors such as contraceptive legislation and availability, educational expansion, and social norms (Balbo, Billari, and Mills 2013). The past four decades have brought a rapid postponement of AFB by around four to five years in many advanced societies and a growth in childlessness (Mills et al. 2011). The biological ability to conceive starts to steeply decline for some women as early as age twenty-five, and almost 50 percent of women are sterile by the age of forty (Leridon 2008). This delay has been linked to an unprecedented growth in infertility (involuntary childlessness), which now affects around 10 to 15 percent of couples in Western societies, and forty-eight million couples worldwide are estimated as infertile (Boivin et al. 2007).

Relatively little is known about the specific genetic architecture of human reproductive behavior of AFB and NEB and the genetic relationship to other fertility traits that mark the reproductive window such as menarche and menopause or behaviorally relevant traits such as educational attainment (Okbay, Beauchamp, et al. 2016). The current study uses polygenic scores constructed from a recent large meta-GWAS (Genome-Wide Association Study) of AFB and NEB, which used data from sixty-two sources to isolate twelve loci linked to these traits (Barban et al. 2016). Some of the results reported here are briefly reported in the supplementary material of this study, but without detailed discussion, clarification or reflection.

## CENTRAL EXPLANATIONS OF REPRODUCTIVE BEHAVIOR

Reproductive behavior has been largely explained by social scientists by focusing on individual and couple characteristics and social structural or institutional factors (Balbo, Billari, and Mills 2013). Core explanations, bolstered by a large body of empirical evidence, has related the timing and number of children to educational systems and the educational level of individuals (particularly women) (Bhrolcháin and Beaujouan 2012; Rindfuss, Morgan, and Offutt 1996; Tropf and Mandemakers 2017), gender equity (McDonald 2002; Mills et al. 2011), normative changes in preferences for children (de Kaa 1987), effective contraception (Murphy 1993), availability of childcare (Brewster and Rindfuss 2000), women's employment and occupation (Begall and Mills 2013; Brewster and Rindfuss 2000), social interactions (Balbo and Barban 2014) and economic uncertainty (Mills, Blossfeld, and Klijzing 2005).

The genetic basis of human reproduction has often been ignored or even actively resisted by social scientists. As a recent review of the biodemographic approach to fertility highlighted, the avoidance is largely attributed to the dark history related to eugenic policies, lack of proper interdisciplinary training, and appropriate genetic data that also contains social science behavioral measures (Mills and Tropf 2016). As noted by pioneers in this field (Kohler, Rodgers, and Christensen 1999; Rodgers et al. 2001), another reason this connection has been avoided is often attributed to an erroneously interpreted version of Ronald Fisher's (1930) Fundamental Theorem of Natural Selection. Some interpreted Fisher's theory to mean that since fertility is a fitness trait, this should theoretically entail that a genetic basis (referred to as *heritability*[1]), should be zero. Fisher actually argued that fitness is moderately heritable in human populations. A naïve interpretation has been that genes that reduce fitness should have been less frequently passed on, leading to the elimination of genetic variability in traits such as fertility (Courtiol, Tropf, and Mills 2016). Nevertheless, we find that fitness traits such as NEB and AFB have what is known as significant narrow-sense heritabilities.[2] It may be that new mutations restore any genetic variance lost to selection, that there are sexual an-

---

1. Heritability ($H^2$) is a statistical term used to denote the proportion of phenotypic (trait) variance due to variance in genotypes. It is important to note that it is specific to the population and environment of analysis and that it is a population and not an individual estimate. It is not a simple measure of the degree to which a trait or phenotype is genetic but rather the proportion of phenotypic variance that is the result of genetic factors.

2. Both broad- and narrow-sense heritability can be estimated. Broad-sense heritability is the ratio of the total genetic variance to total phenotypic (trait) variance or: $H^2 = V_G/V_P$. Narrow-sense heritability refers to ratio of the additive genetic component in contrast to the total (nonadditive) phenotypic variance or: $h^2 = V_A/V_P$.

tagonistic genetic effects (genes have opposite effects for the fertility of men and women), nonadditive genetic effects, environment and gene-environment interaction (Tropf et al. 2017; Verweij et al. 2017).

At least some genetic underpinnings of fertility behavior are plausible. In fact, a growing number of twin and family studies have shown a genetic component underlying AFB and NEB (Briley, Tropf, and Mills 2017; Tropf, Barban, et al. 2015; Zietsch et al. 2014). A recent meta-analysis of all twin studies conducted until 2012 shows average heritability of 0.45 (SE = 0.027, N = 50,265) among sixty-four reproductive disease traits of women and of 0.36 (SE= 0.054, N = 9,376) among twenty-five reproductive disease traits of men (Polderman et al. 2015). The advent of molecular genetic data and complementary analytical tools means that we are now able to go beyond twin models to examine for the first time the genetic relatedness of unrelated individuals (Mills and Tropf 2016; Yang et al. 2010). A recent study using whole-genome data of unrelated individuals shows that 10 percent of the variance in NEB and 15 percent in AFB are associated with common additive genetic variance (Tropf, Stulp, et al. 2015). These previous studies, however, were merely able to state that genetics contributed to fertility behavior only a certain proportion or amount. Until recently, we did not isolate any specific genes related to this behavior or whether they had a biological function. Our recent study isolated twelve genetic loci associated with AFB and NEB (Barban et al. 2016), which allows us for the first time to include a genetic variable or predictor of this behavior in our social science research. Given that human reproduction is a complex behavioral outcome, it is not simply one candidate gene that can be used to predict outcomes. Rather, the myriad of genetic loci are compiled into a comprehensive polygenic score (PGS). It is the relevance of these scores for AFB and NEB for research in the area of fertility and reproduction in the social sciences and beyond which that we explore in this article.

## DATA

To examine these questions and avoid false positives from examining the associations in one limited dataset, we test our results using four datasets: the Health and Retirement Study (HRS), LifeLines, TwinsUK, and Swedish Twin Registry (STR).

### HRS

The Health and Retirement Study is an ongoing cohort study of Americans, with interview data collected biennially on demographics, health behavior, health status, employment, income and wealth, and insurance status. The first cohort was interviewed in 1992 and subsequently every two years; five additional cohorts were added between 1994 and 2010. Between 2006 and 2008, the HRS genotyped 12,507 respondents who provided DNA samples and signed consent. DNA samples were genotyped using the Illumina Human Omni-2.5 Quad BeadChip, with coverage of approximately 2.5 million single nucleotide polymorphisms (SNPs). The full details of the study are described in (Juster and Suzman 1995).

### LifeLines Cohort Study

The LifeLines Cohort Study is a multidisciplinary prospective population-based cohort study from the Netherlands, examining in a unique three-generation design the health and health-related behaviors of 167,729 persons living in the north of the Netherlands, including genotype information from more than thirteen thousand unrelated individuals (Klijs, Scholtens, and Mandemakers 2015). It employs a broad range of investigative procedures in assessing the biomedical, socio-demographic, behavioral, physical, and psychological factors that contribute to the health and disease of the general population; its special focus is on multimorbidity and complex genetics.

### TwinsUK

For the UK, we use data from TwinsUK, the largest adult twin registry in the country with more than twelve thousand respondents (Moayyeri et al. 2013). The TwinsUK Study recruited white monozygotic (MZ) and dizygotic (DZ) twin pairs from the TwinsUK adult twin registry, a group designed to study the heritability and genetics of age-related diseases. These twins were recruited from the general population through national media campaigns in the United Kingdom and shown to be comparable to age-matched population singletons in terms of clinical phenotype and lifestyle characteristics.

## STR

The Swedish Twin Registry was first established in the late 1950s to study the importance of smoking and alcohol consumption on cancer and cardiovascular diseases while controlling for genetic propensity to disease. Between 1998 and 2002, the STR conducted telephone interview screening of all twins born in 1958 or earlier regardless of gender composition or vital status of the pair. This effort is known as Screening Across the Lifespan Twin study (SALT). A subsample of SALT (≈10,000) was genotyped as part of the TwinGene project (Lichtenstein et al. 2006) and we use this information in the current study.

## CONSTRUCTING LINEAR POLYGENIC SCORES OF REPRODUCTION

Because we have direct access to genotypic data, we first performed out-of-sample prediction using cohorts for the four data sources. GWAS results are generally performed by a meta-analysis of the results from multiple datasets, which in our case was the combined results from sixty-two sources. Out-of-sample prediction refers to the fact that when we construct the PGS to use with a particular dataset, we first need to remove the contribution of the results from that dataset to avoid overfitting the model. In other words, the descriptive results from all of the four datasets were in the original meta-analysis that included sixty-two datasets, which we used to discover the genetic loci associated with AFB and NEB (Barban et al. 2016). To properly construct the PGS for use in the HRS, for example, we need to remove HRS from the results and re-run the meta-analysis without the HRS results to produce a new bespoke or tailored PGS, which can used for that dataset. We therefore calculated polygenic scores for AFB and NEB, based on GWA meta-analysis results and used regression models to predict the same phenotypes in each independent data source.

A polygenic score is a linear combination of the effects of genetic variants present in the entire genome and can be interpreted as a single quantitative measure of genetic predisposition. Just as a battery of multiple questions on personality types or attitudes toward immigration can make up a scale that is measured by one index, a PGS assumes that individuals fall somewhere on a continuum of genetic predisposition resulting from small contributions from many genetic variants. This is particularly relevant when single genetic variants have too small of an effect in explaining complex phenotypes, a common case for complex behavioral traits such as educational attainment (Okbay, Beauchamp, et al. 2016), well-being, neuroticism, depression (Okbay, Baselmans, et al. 2016), or fertility. A PGS for individual $i$ can be calculated as the sum of the allele counts $a_{ij}$ (0,1 or 2) from each SNP $j = 1,..M$, multiplied by a weight $w_j$:

$$PGS_i = \sum_{j=1}^{m} w_j a_{ij},$$

using as a choice of weights the association coefficients derived from our recent GWAS on fertility traits. To be clear, it is not the summary of the top genetic loci that were previously isolated, but a sum of the allele counts from all SNPs.

A pivotal question for social scientists is how relevant these PGSs are for applied research and for inclusion in our statistical models. In other words, do the genetic scores that we produce actually predict those observed outcomes? If so, what percentage of the variance do they explain? To determine this, we ran ordinary least-squares (OLS) regression models and report the R-squared as a measure of goodness-of-fit of the model. In addition, we tested how well our polygenic scores for NEB could predict childlessness at the end of the reproductive period (using age forty-five for women and fifty-five for men) and estimated a Cox model examining the impact of the PGS of AFB on observed AFB.

We then reran meta-analyses of the pooled AFB and NEB phenotypes, excluding each of the four independent cohorts. Using these summary statistics, we constructed linear polygenic scores using the effect sizes from the original meta-analysis. We constructed all scores using the software PLINK (Purcell et al. 2007) and PRSice (Euesden, Lewis, and O'Reilly 2014) based on best call genotypes imputed to Hap-Map reference 3 panel. For each phenotype, we calculated nine scores using different *p*-value thresholds: 5e-08, 5e-07, 5e-06, 5e-05, 5e-04, 5e-03, 0.05, 0.5 and 1. Results are clumped using the genotypic data as a reference panel for linkage disequilibrium structure.

To control for cohort effects, we first regressed each phenotype on birth year, its square and cubic to control for nonlinear trends in fertility, and the first ten principal components. If the cohort included both men and women, we included sex as a covariate in the regression models. Next, we regressed the residuals from the previous regression on the polygenic score.

## AFB and NEB

We now examine whether the polygenic scores predict AFB and NEB.

*OLS and Goodness-of-Fit*

To test the variance explained or statistical power of our PGS on predicting the actual observed AFB and NEB, we adopt two models. First, we performed a set of OLS regressions where we calculated the R-squared as an indicator of goodness-of-fit of the regression model. For the twin studies (STR and Twins-UK), we included only one MZ twin in the analysis and used clustered standard errors at the family level. Because MZ twins share the same genetics, their PGS is identical. At the same time, DZ twins share on average 50 percent of their genetic variants, leading to correlated PGSs in the sample. Removing a random MZ twin for each family from the sample and using robust clustered errors in the analysis allow us to control for correlated observations in the analysis. To obtain 95 percent confidence intervals around the incremental R-squareds, bootstrapping was performed with one thousand repetitions.

The results of the polygenic score analyses are depicted in figure 1. The sample-size-weighted mean predictive power of the AFB score constructed with all SNPs is 0.9 percent, and the NEB is 0.2 percent. On average, one standard deviation (SD) variation on the polygenic score for AFB is associated with 0.48 years (175 days) AFB for women and 0.33 years (120 days) for men. In other words, those who score higher on the genetic continuum are more prone to having their first child later and have an observed delay in first birth of almost six months for women and four months for men. The variation of one SD in the polygenic score for NEB is associated with an increase of 0.04 children on average. Although it is hard to think in terms of a "fraction" of a child for individuals, our results do indicate that those genetically prone to have more children indeed have more.

*Cox Model of Age at First Birth*

The previous OLS regression results for AFB include only those in the analysis who have a reported AFB. Logically, AFB is assessed only for men and women who ever became parents and does not take into account that a proportion of respondents are still at risk of having a child (that is, did not have a child yet by the date of the interview) or will remain childless. This problem is commonly referred to in the statistical literature as *right censoring* because the outcome is not observed for all respondents, even though some respondents may still experience the birth of their first child (Mills 2011).

As touched on previously, to model age at first birth more appropriately, it is important to account for right-censored data. The previous OLS models included information for only those who had actually experienced a first birth. Many individuals, however, either did not have a first child by the time of the interview due to their age or are childless. These are referred to as right-censored cases. In an event history framework such as a Cox model, it is possible to include these cases by including the information about these individuals up to the date of the last observation (Mills 2011). For this reason, we estimated a second model in the form of a semi-parametric Cox regression model (Cox 1972) for the effect of the polygenic score on increasing the hazard of having a child conditional on age. This class of models takes into account censoring and is widely used to study fertility timing. Our results show that the calculated PGS for AFB based on all SNPs is associated with an increased risk of childbearing at any age (see tables 1 and 2). The median AFB

**Figure 1.** Variance Explained by AFB and NEB Polygenic Scores

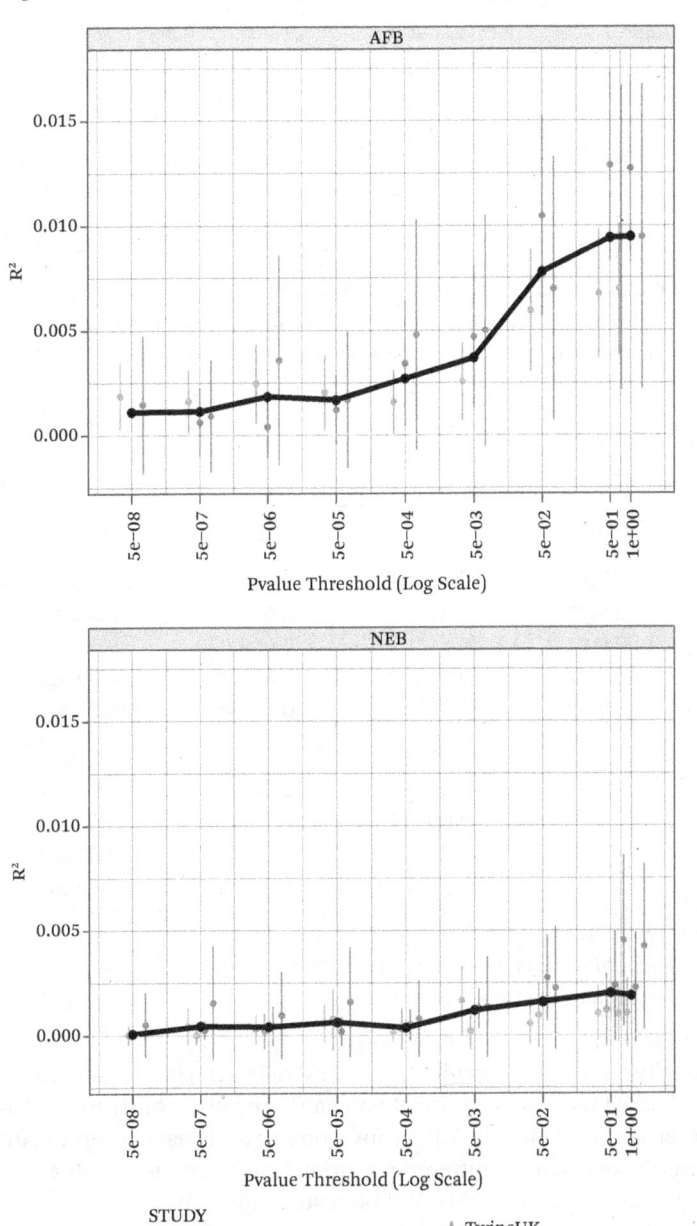

*Source:* Authors' calculations from the Health and Retirement Survey, LifeLines Cohort Study, TwinsUK, and STR.
*Note:* Calculated with the inclusion of SNPs at different levels of significance. Polygenic scores were calculated from the meta-analysis results excluding the validation cohort. The y-axis is the variance explained (R-squared from OLS regression with polygenic score as sole predictor). The x-axis represents the p-value inclusion threshold used in the construction of the polygenic score. The black line is the sample-size-weighted mean R-squared. Cohort-specific estimates and 95 percent confidence intervals obtained with one thousand bootstrap samples. Results are adjusted for birth cohort, first ten principal components, and sex. Clustered standard errors have been used for family-based studies.

**Table 1.** Logit Regression of Childlessness on NEB Polygenic Score

|  | Pooled Sample | | LifeLines | | STR | | TwinsUK |
|---|---|---|---|---|---|---|---|
|  | Women | Men | Women | Men | Women | Men | Women |
| Childless | | | | | | | |
| PGS NEB (all SNPs) | 0.911*** | 0.979 | 0.904* | 0.988 | 0.913 | 0.945 | 0.909* |
| SE | (0.022) | (0.037) | (0.038) | (0.043) | (0.043) | (0.081) | (0.037) |
| N | 17,465 | 10,126 | 5,411 | 4,536 | 7,795 | 5,590 | 4,259 |

*Source:* Authors' calculations from LifeLines Cohort Study, TwinsUK, and STR.
*Note:* Age forty-five for women, fifty-five for men, using all SNPs on score. PGS = polygenic score; NEB = number of children ever born, SNPs = single nucleotide polymorphisms, exponentiated coefficients. Standard errors in parentheses.
*$p < .05$; **$p < .01$; ***$p < .001$

**Table 2.** Within Families Regressions

| Regression coefficients | AFB OLS | AFB WF | NEB OLS | NEB WF |
|---|---|---|---|---|
| Beta (all SNPs) | 0.508*** | 0.317** | 0.0623*** | 0.0601* |
|  | (0.0450) | (0.115) | (0.00989) | (0.0256) |
| Constant | -0.00202 | -0.00367 | -0.00402 | -0.00401 |
|  | (0.0455) | (0.0371) | (0.0104) | (0.00907) |
| N | 11,613 | 11,613 | 14,206 | 14,206 |
| $R^2$ | 0.0118 | 0.00207 | 0.00280 | 0.00108 |
| $R^2$ within |  | 0.00207 |  | 0.00108 |
| $R^2$ between |  | 0.0131 |  | 0.00347 |
| N groups |  | 7,944 |  | 9,090 |

*Source:* Authors' calculations from TwinsUK and STR.
*Note:* AFB = Age at first birth; NEB = Number of children ever born, SNPs = single nucleotide polymorphisms; OLS = ordinary least-squares regression; WF= within-family.

for men in the pooled sample is twenty-eight and twenty-six for women. The hazard ratio of the PGS for AFB is 0.92 for women and 0.97 for men. This means that an increase of one standard deviation in the PGS is associated with a decrease of 8 percent in the probability of having a child at any age for women and 3 percent for men. Results for different cohorts and sex are presented in table 1.

### Childlessness

We used the score for NEB in an additional analysis to predict the probability of remaining childless at the end of the reproductive period. Despite its limited predictive power in the previous OLS model of NEB, our analysis shows that an increase of one SD of the polygenic score is associated with a decrease of around 9 percent in the probability to remain childless for women, and that no significant differences among men are discernable (see table 3). The results are consistent across cohorts.

To illustrate differences in childlessness by genetic predisposition, we estimated the proportion of individuals without children by polygenic score, comparing individuals with extreme polygenic scores. Figure 2 shows that men and women with a PGS lower than the 5th percentile are more likely to ever have had a child at any age compared to individuals in the 95th percentile. This underscores the relevance of our genetic measures for fertility research.

**Table 3.** Cox Regression Model, Age at First Birth on AFB Polygenic Score (all SNPs)

|  | Pooled Sample | | LifeLines | | STR | | TwinsUK |
| --- | --- | --- | --- | --- | --- | --- | --- |
|  | Women | Men | Women | Men | Women | Men | Women |
| PGS AFB (all SNPs) | 0.917*** | 0.968** | 0.944*** | 0.978 | 0.871*** | 0.960* | 0.938*** |
|  | (0.008) | (0.010) | (0.011) | (0.014) | (0.013) | (0.015) | (0.018) |
| N | 16,132 | 9,136 | 7,154 | 4,611 | 5,409 | 4,525 | 3,569 |

*Source:* Authors' calculations from LifeLines Cohort Study, TwinsUK, and STR.
*Note:* PGS = Polygenic Score; AFB = age at first birth, SNPs = single nucleotide polymorphisms. Exponentiated coefficients. Standard errors in parentheses.
*p < .05, **p < .01, ***p < .001

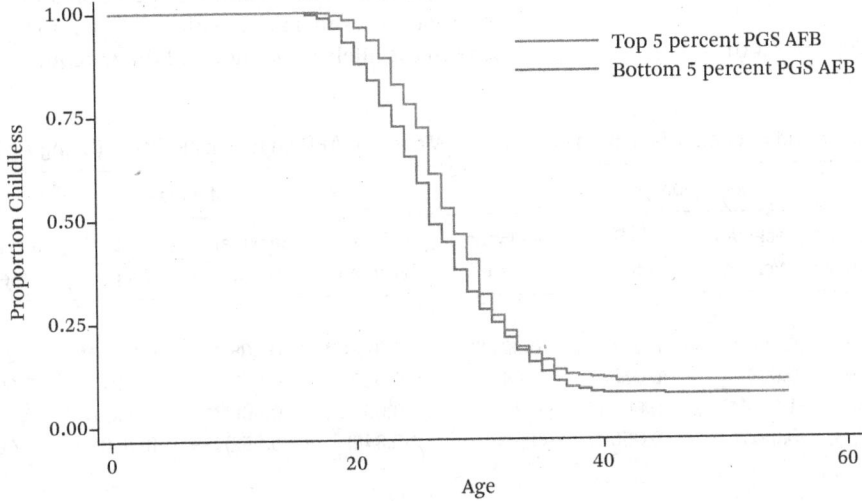

**Figure 2.** Kaplan-Meier Estimation of Childlessness by Age and by Polygenic Score

*Source:* Authors' calculations from LifeLines Cohort Study, TwinsUK, and STR.

## OTHER FERTILITY-RELATED TRAITS

We also wanted to know to what extent the linear PGS for AFB and NEB can predict related fertility traits, namely age at menarche and completed by age at menopause.

We used TwinsUK to model age at menarche. Age at menarche (AAM) has been assessed for 6,838 women using the following question: "How old were you when you had your first menstrual period?" The average age at AAM in the sample is thirteen (SD = 1.59 years). To examine menopause, we used the age at menopause measurement included in the Dutch Life-Lines cohort. Age at menopause is measured with the question: "At what age did you have your last menstrual period?" We excluded women from the sample who reported having had their last menstruation before age thirty or after age sixty. The median age at natural menopause (ANM) in the sample is forty-five.

Our results in table 4 indicate that those with a genetic propensity to have a later AFB also show a shift of the entire reproductive window, to both later onset of menarche and menopause. Table 4 shows that an increase of one standard deviation on the PGS of AFB is associated with an increase of 0.06 years, or just under one month (twenty-two days), on age at menarche. The PGS for AFB is likewise associated with a later ANM. Because a substantive proportion of the sample of women in Life-Lines is still in the pre-menopausal period, we

**Table 4.** Linear Prediction of Age at Menarche and Menopause Using AFB PGS Linear Score

|  | Age at Menarche OLS TwinsUK | Age at Menopause Cox Survival Model LifeLines |
|---|---|---|
| PGS AFB | 0.0560* | 0.971* |
|  | (0.028) | (0.012) |
| _cons | 13.00*** |  |
|  | (0.029) |  |
| N | 3,424 | 6,923 |
| $R^2$ | 0.00694 |  |

*Source:* Authors' calculations from LifeLines Cohort Study and TwinsUK.
*Note:* PGS = polygenic score. Standard errors in parentheses.
*$p < .05$; **$p < .01$; ***$p < .001$

estimated a proportional hazard model (Cox regression) in which we estimate ANM as a function of PGS for AFB. Our estimates indicate that having higher predisposition for AFB is associated with a later ANM. The hazard ratio estimate 0.97 indicates that an increase of one standard deviation of the PGS for AFB is associated with a decrease of the occurrence of menopause at any age of about 3 percent.

### SENSITIVITY TESTS

To test the robustness of our all-SNP polygenic scores, we estimated within family (WF) regressions of AFB and NEB on polygenic scores. These regressions control for possible bias due to population stratification. Population stratification refers to a systematic relationship between the allele frequency and the outcome of

**Table 5.** OLS Regressions and Heckman Two-Stage Regression Models of AFB on Polygenic Score (Using All SNPs)

|  | Pooled Sample | | | | LifeLines | | | |
|---|---|---|---|---|---|---|---|---|
|  | OLS Women | Heckman Women | OLS Men | Heckman Men | OLS Women | Heckman Women | OLS Men | Heckman Men |
| **Main** | | | | | | | | |
| PGS AFB | 0.483*** | 0.450*** | 0.331*** | 0.321*** | 0.392*** | 0.388*** | 0.267*** | 0.273*** |
|  | (0.037) | (0.036) | (0.050) | (0.049) | (0.050) | (0.049) | (0.065) | (0.065) |
| _cons | 0.0058 | -1.056*** | -0.00942 | -0.767*** | 0.00625 | -0.506*** | -0.00697 | -0.268*** |
|  | (0.037) | (0.042) | (0.050) | (0.053) | (0.048) | (0.052) | (0.064) | (0.065) |
| **Ever had children** | | | | | | | | |
| PGS NEB |  | 0.0368*** |  | 0.0355* |  | 0.0315 |  | 0.0627 |
|  |  | (0.010) |  | (0.016) |  | (0.020) |  | (0.033) |
| _cons |  | 1.126*** |  | 1.323*** |  | 1.454*** |  | 1.833*** |
|  |  | (0.013) |  | (0.019) |  | (0.022) |  | (0.036) |
| **Athrho** | | | | | | | | |
| _cons |  | 1.481*** |  | 1.412*** |  | 1.163*** |  | 1.211*** |
|  |  | (0.039) |  | (0.050) |  | (0.059) |  | (0.083) |
| **lnsigma** | | | | | | | | |
| _cons |  | 1.605*** |  | 1.611*** |  | 1.458*** |  | 1.500*** |
|  |  | -0.00839 |  | -0.0113 |  | (0.012) |  | (0.014) |
| N | 14,389 | 16,405 | 8,341 | 9,136 | 6,646 |  | 4,471 | 4,611 |
| $r^2$ | 0.012 |  | 0.006 |  | 0.010 |  | 0.004 |  |
| rho |  | 0.902 |  | 0.888 |  | 0.822 |  | 0.837 |

*Source:* Authors' calculations from LifeLines Cohort Study, TwinsUK, and STR.
*Note:* First stage selection models based on NEB polygenic scores (all SNPs). AFB = age at first birth; NEB = number of children ever born, SNPs = single nucleotide polymorphisms; OLS = ordinary least-squares regression; WF = within-family. Standard errors in parentheses.
*$p < .05$; **$p < .01$; ***$p < .001$

interest in different subgroups of the population. Genetic similarity is often correlated with geographical proximity because human genetic diversity is the result of the history of population migration, ethnic admixture, and residential segregation. In such studies, it is essential to clarify whether results are a true signal of similarities or merely attributable to the presence of two or more population subgroups having different genetic or allele frequencies that are a result of a coincidence of being correlated with different levels of a particular trait. A common example is the chopsticks gene finding. In this fictional scenario, a geneticist wanted to discover why some people eat with chopsticks and others do not and found a considerable correlation to account for about half of the variance. The finding, however, was attributed to the different genetic or allele frequencies in Asians and Caucasians, who use cutlery and chopsticks to different extents—that is, cultural rather than genetic reasons.

By examining differences in the polygenic scores between DZ twins, WF regressions cancel out possible confounders due to the population structure of the sample. Because DZ twins have the same family environment, results from a family fixed-effect regression model are net of any family-specific confounder, including ancestry. As we did in the standard model, we standardized NEB and AFB on birth year, birth year squared, birth year cubic and sex. Our regressions are based on 7,944 twin couples for AFB and 9,220 twin couples for NEB. Table 5 reports the results of standard OLS and WF statistical models.

|  | STR | | | | TwinsUK | |
|---|---|---|---|---|---|---|
| OLS Women | Heckman Women | OLS Men | Heckman Men | OLS Women | Heckman Women |
| 0.632*** | 0.458*** | 0.404*** | 0.342*** | 0.456*** | 0.467*** |
| (0.069) | (0.064) | (0.077) | (0.073) | (0.091) | (0.086) |
| 0.0269 | -1.179*** | -0.0126 | -1.359*** | -0.0217 | -2.100*** |
| (0.070) | (0.078) | (0.079) | (0.087) | (0.090) | (0.120) |
|  | 0.0459** |  | 0.0231 |  | 0.0293 |
|  | (0.015) |  | (0.018) |  | (0.019) |
|  | 1.111*** |  | 1.027*** |  | 0.733*** |
|  | (0.021) |  | (0.023) |  | (0.025) |
|  | 1.941*** |  | 1.617*** |  | 1.519*** |
|  | (0.110) |  | (0.070) |  | (0.072) |
|  | 1.679*** |  | 1.719*** |  | 1.749*** |
|  | (0.014) |  | (0.017) |  | (0.019) |
| 4,726 | 5,409 | 3,870 | 4,525 | 3,017 | 3,842 |
| 0.019 |  | 0.007 |  | 0.009 |  |
|  | 0.96 |  | 0.924 |  | 0.909 |

The regression analyses show that within family regression coefficients for both AFB and NEB are statistically different from zero when PGS are based on all SNPs. Both coefficients for AFB and NEB are larger than zero in within family analyses, confirming that the PGS uncover true polygenic signals. Overall, these results indicate a limited effect of population stratification and the existence of true polygenic signals.

A second potential problem is statistical selection; that is, individuals with a measurement of AFB may be genetically distinct from those who remain childless. If childless individuals are different from the general population, the association results on AFB may be biased by selection problems. To understand whether and how these issues would influence our results, we estimated bivariate Heckman selection models in which we estimate the probability of eligibility for AFB in a two-step procedure (Heckman 1974). Because we are interested in possible genetic differences among men and women who have had children rather than childless individuals, we used the PGS for NEB to model the probability of being at risk or eligible for AFB. The results from the Heckman selection models indicate slightly lower coefficients than OLS regression models but no substantial differences (for details, see table 5). We can therefore conclude that statistical selection due to genetic distinctiveness between those who have had a child (for which we have a measure for AFB) and those who have not does not influence our results.

## DISCUSSION AND CONCLUSION

The aim of this article is to demonstrate the power of polygenic scores of age at first birth and number of children in predicting the actual observed outcomes and related fertility traits and to ensure that these results were robust. Using an OLS regression model to estimate the overall variance explained or R-squared goodness-of-fit, we show that the predictive power of the AFB PGS was around 1 percent and of the NEB PGS was 0.2 percent. We also see that one SD increase in the AFB PGS is associated with an 8 percent reduction of the hazard ratio of having the first child for women and with a 3 percent reduction for men. The NEB PGS can also be used to study childlessness, a one SD increase in the PGS decreasing the probability of remaining childless by 9 percent in women. It is essential to distinguish clearly between, on the one hand, the predictive power or R-squared that looks at the proportion of variance explained with the OLS models and, on the other, our coefficients from the Cox regression models. We need to think of the interpretation of PGS as changes in one standard deviation of the PGS and how they are related to an increase or reduction in the hazard ratio of reproduction. It is likewise incorrect to state that a one SD of the PGS for AFB is associated with an 8 percent increase of AFB. Rather, our results are presented as relative risk ratios. One SD of the PGS for AFB is associated with an increase of 0.5 years in AFB (and 0.3 years with a fixed-effect model, table 2). We acknowledge that it remains awkward and not immediately intuitive to interpret PGS in terms of SD changes and survival models in terms of hazard and relative risk ratios. For the time being this remains the prominent manner to interpret these findings.

Our results also demonstrate a fascinating underlying genetic link with the shifting of the entire reproductive window for certain individuals. The AFB PGS is clearly linked to development and the reproductive window, those having a genetic propensity to later AFB also having a later genetic propensity for the onset of menarche and ANM. Detailed LD-Score regression analyses have indeed shown a strong genetic association between human development and AFB, including age at voice-breaking for boys and age at first sex (Bulik-Sullivan et al. 2015; Barban et al. 2016). A recent study also found that our AFB PGS is linked to longevity (Mostafavi et al. 2017).

Several conclusions are indicated. First, the predictive power of our polygenic scores when entered alone in the model remains considerably lower than previous research would indicate. Recall that the R-squared goodness-of-fit tests show a predictive power of the linear AFB PGS of around 1 percent and 0.2 percent for NEB. This is a fraction of what previous twin and family studies have found, which predicted these outcomes to be between 25 percent and 45 percent heritable (Mills and Tropf

2016). It is also much lower than recent SNP-based GREML whole-genome methods that predicted that 15 percent for AFB and 10 percent for NEB of the variance was attributed to genetic factors (Tropf, Stulp, et al. 2015). In other words, the ceiling of SNP heritability should likely be more in the range of 10 to 15 percent than 1 percent. Missing heritability can be explained several ways, including nonadditive genetic effects, epistatic effects, and inflated estimates from twin studies due to shared environmental factors (missing heritability, Manolio et al. 2009; nonadditive effects, Zhu et al. 2015; epistatic effects, Zuk et al. 2012; inflated estimates, Felson 2014). Empirical studies, however, find no evidence for any of these reasons.

Jian Yang and his colleagues argue that most genetic effects are too small to be reliably detected in GWAS of current sample sizes, which is why they propose the whole-genome restricted maximum likelihood estimation performed by GCTA software (Yang et al. 2010, 2011). Studies applying these whole-genome methods typically yield estimates with predictive power between twin studies and polygenic scores. A recent investigation also demonstrates that including rare genetic variants can strongly increase the predictive power of genes for body mass index (BMI) and height (Yang, Bakshi, Zhu, Hemani, Vinkhuyzen, Lee, et al. 2015). Similarly, the first meta-GWAS on educational attainment produced three significant hits with small effect size and a total predictive power based on all SNPs of 2 percent (Rietveld et al. 2013). Meanwhile, the most recent meta-GWAS, which finds seventy-four significant hits, explains around 3.2 percent of the observed variance (Okbay, Beauchamp, et al. 2016). This refers to the predictive power of SNPs, though not all SNPs, which is the same approach used in our study. The main differences between the studies are the increased sample size in the latter study as well as the inclusion of more genetic variants. Current predictions are that these differences will only continue to increase with the release of larger datasets such as the UKBiobank. We therefore anticipate that in future GWAS studies, as sample sizes grow and including more detailed genetic information becomes possible, these traits will be more in the range of 10 to 15 percent. Our PGS scores as they stand, however, still had a notable predictive power for the timing of first birth and childlessness.

Another explanation is possible. A recent study on fertility suggests that next to rare variants and insufficient sample size, GWAS discoveries might be limited by heterogeneity across cohorts and birth cohorts under study (Tropf et al. 2017). Heterogeneity can arise on the phenotypic level if the phenotypic measurement differs across cohorts and birth cohorts, on the genotypic level if linkage disequilibrium differs across populations under study, and by gene-environment interaction. They find that the predictive power of the whole-genome methods increases as much as fivefold when heterogeneity across cohorts and birth cohorts is taken into account. Investigations on height and BMI find barely evidence for genome-wide heterogeneity across countries and sexes (Yang, Bakshi, Zhu, Hemani, Vinkhuyzen, Nolte, et al. 2015). Fertility is in large part environmentally determined and modified (Mills et al. 2011). It is therefore highly likely that gene-environment interaction across the more than sixty cohorts, as well as across birth cohorts within cohorts, limited genetic discovery in the most recent GWAS and leads to comparably small predictive power of the polygenic scores.

It is also not surprising that genetic factors are not especially strong in predicting reproductive behavior. A large body of social science research has consistently demonstrated that socio-environmental conditions are key factors shaping human reproduction. We know that women's higher educational attainment and presence in the labor market has resulted in postponed entry into parenthood (Balbo, Billari, and Mills 2013). Another obvious point is that the models presented in this article are not multivariate models. When the gold standard social science variables that predict AFB and NEB such as age at entry into a union or marriage and educational attainment are entered alone in a model, they also have low predictive power (from 6 to 15 percent). It is therefore artificial and unusual within the social sciences to enter only one predictor in a model and to not consider confounders or interactions. The purpose of this article, however, is to introduce and demonstrate the polygenic scores in the hope that others will include and interrogate these further in multivariate models.

Genetics is likewise only one piece of the puzzle and in this study, we examine only one type of genetic variants (SNPs) and consider only one of the many possible biological and genetic ways in which individuals may vary. Other sources of molecular genetic variation remain to be discovered. We plan to examine our work further with denser genotyping platforms. Other GWAS studies for complex traits such as diseases have also consistently identified common variants with small effects, which explain only a small proportion of the trait of interest. This does not affect the biological importance of the findings, however, because many follow-up studies that have isolated particular genetic loci have the potential to substantially improve our understanding of human biology. In the context of human disease, for example, variants identified by GWAS for diabetes and cardiovascular diseases "tag" genes that encode well-known drug targets for the treatment of such diseases. This implies that a further understanding of the genes underlying the associations we identified for reproductive behavior may result in new reproductive strategies such as those for assisted reproductive technology treatment.

For social scientists who study reproductive behavior, we offer and provide an entirely new variable and way of theoretically thinking about and measuring human reproductive behavior. These polygenic scores for AFB and NEB will also be easily usable in publicly available datasets, which will allow researchers to include these predictors in their research. These PGS scores show that a genetic component underlies AFB and NEB and is related to other fertility traits such as childlessness, menarche, and menopause. This may force us to rethink existing behavioral theories that rarely included biology and genetics in their largely choice and preference-based theoretical models, such as the Theory of Planned Behavior, often used in social science fertility research (Ajzen 1991).

# REFERENCES

Ajzen, Icek. 1991. "The Theory of Planned Behavior." *Organizational Behavior and Human Decision Processes* 50(2): 179–211.

Balbo, Nicoletta, and Nicola Barban. 2014. "Does Fertility Behavior Spread Among Friends?" *American Sociological Review* 79(3): 412–31.

Balbo, Nicoletta, Francesco C. Billari, and Melinda C. Mills. 2013. "Fertility in Advanced Societies: A Review of Research." *European Journal of Population/Revue Européenne de Démographie* 29(1): 1–38.

Barban, Nicola, Rick Jansen, Ronald de Vlaming, Ahmad Vaez, et al. 2016. "Genome-Wide Analysis Identifies 12 Loci Influencing Human Reproductive Behavior." *Nature Genetics* 48(12): 1462–72.

Begall, Katia, and Melinda Mills. 2013. "The Influence of Educational Field, Occupation, and Occupational Sex Segregation on Fertility in the Netherlands." *European Sociological Review* 29(4): 720–42.

Bhrolcháin, Maire Ni, and Éva Beaujouan. 2012. "Fertility Postponement Is Largely Due to Rising Educational Enrolment." *Population Studies* 66(3): 311–27.

Boivin, Jacky, Laura Bunting, John A. Collins, and Karl G. Nygren. 2007. "International Estimates of Infertility Prevalence and Treatment-Seeking: Potential Need and Demand for Infertility Medical Care." *Human Reproduction* 22(6): 1506–12.

Brewster, Karin L., and Ronald R. Rindfuss. 2000. "Fertility and Women's Employment in Industrialized Nations." *Annual Review of Sociology* 26(1): 271–96.

Briley, Daniel A., Felix C. Tropf, and Melinda C. Mills. 2017. "What Explains the Heritability of Completed Fertility? Evidence from Two Large Twin Studies." *Behavior Genetics* 47(1): 36–51.

Bulik-Sullivan, Brendan K., Po-Ru Loh, Hilary K. Finucane, Stephan Ripke, et al. 2015. "LD Score Regression Distinguishes Confounding from Polygenicity in Genome-Wide Association Studies." *Nature Genetics* 47(3): 291–95. DOI: 10.1038/ng.3211.

Courtiol, Alexandre, Felix C. Tropf, and Melinda C. Mills. 2016. "When Genes and Environment Disagree: Making Sense of Trends in Recent Human Evolution." *Proceedings of the National Academy of Sciences* 113(28): 7693–95.

Cox, David R. 1972. "Regression Models and Life-

Tables." *Journal of the Royal Statistical Society. Series B (Methodological)* 34(2): 187–220.

Euesden, Jack, Cathryn M. Lewis, and Paul F. O'Reilly. 2014. "PRSice: Polygenic Risk Score Software." *Bioinformatics* 31(9): btu848–1468. Accessed August 21, 2017. http://bioinformatics.oxfordjournals.org/cgi/doi/10.1093/bioinformatics/btu848.

Felson, Jacob. 2014. "What Can We Learn from Twin Studies? A Comprehensive Evaluation of the Equal Environments Assumption." *Social Science Research* 43 (January): 184–99. Accessed May 11, 2017. http://www.sciencedirect.com/science/article/pii/S0049089X13001397.

Fisher, Ronald A. 1930. *The Genetical Theory of Natural Selection*. Oxford: Oxford University Press.

Heckman, James J. 1974. "Effects of Child-Care Programs on Women's Work Effort." *Journal of Political Economy* 82(2): 136–63.

Juster, F. Thomas, and Richard Suzman. 1995. "An Overview of the Health and Retirement Study." Special Issue, *Journal of Human Resources* 30: S7–56.

de Kaa, Dirk J. Van. 1987. "Europe's Second Demographic Transition." *Population Bulletin* 42(1): 1–59.

Klijs, Bart, Salome Scholtens, and Jornt J. Mandemakers. 2015. "Representativeness of the LifeLines Cohort Study." *PloS one* 10(9): e0137203.

Kohler, Hans-Peter, Joseph L. Rodgers, and Kaare Christensen. 1999. "Is Fertility Behavior in Our Genes? Findings from a Danish Twin Study." *Population and Development Review* 25(2): 253–88.

Leridon, Henri. 2008. "A New Estimate of Permanent Sterility by Age: Sterility Defined as the Inability to Conceive." *Population Studies* 62(1): 15–24.

Lichtenstein, Paul, Patrick F. Sullivan, Sven Cnattingius, Margaret Gatz, et al. 2006. "The Swedish Twin Registry in the Third Millennium: An Update." *Twin Research and Human Genetics* 9(6): 875–82.

Manolio, Teri A., Francis S. Collins, Nancy J. Cox, David B. Goldstein, et al. 2009. "Finding the Missing Heritability of Complex Diseases." *Nature* 461(7265): 747–53.

McDonald, Peter. 2002. "Gender Equity in Theories of Fertility Transition." *Population and Development Review* 26(3): 427–39.

Mills, Melinda C. 2011. *Introducing Survival and Event History Analysis*. Menlo Park, Calif.: Sage Publications.

Mills, Melinda C., Hans-Peter Blossfeld, and Erik Klijzing. 2005. "Becoming an Adult in Uncertain Times." In *Globalization, Uncertainty and Youth in Society*, edited by H. P. Blossfeld, Erik Klijzing, Melinda Mills, and Karin Kurz. London: Routledge.

Mills, Melinda C., Ronald R. Rindfuss, Peter McDonald, and Egbert te Velde. 2011. "Why Do People Postpone Parenthood? Reasons and Social Policy Incentives." *Human Reproduction Update* 17(6): 848–60.

Mills, Melinda C., and Felix C. Tropf. 2016. "The Biodemography of Fertility: A Review and Future Research Frontiers." Special Issue, *Kölner Zeitschrift für Soziologie und Sozialpsychologie* 55(Demography): 397–424.

Moayyeri, Alireza, Christopher J. Hammond, Anna M. Valdes, and Timothy D. Spector. 2013. "Cohort Profile: TwinsUK and Healthy Ageing Twin Study." *International Journal of Epidemiology* 42(1): 76–85.

Mostafavi, Hakhamanesh, Tomaz Berisa, Felix Day, John Perry, Molly Przeworski, and Joseph K. Pickrell. 2017. "Identifying Genetic Variants that Affect Viability in Large Cohorts." *PLoS Biology* 15(9): e2002458.

Murphy, Michael. 1993. "The Contraceptive Pill and Women's Employment as Factors in Fertility Change in Britain 1963–1980: A Challenge to the Conventional View." *Population Studies* 47(2): 221–43.

Okbay, Aysu, Bart M. L. Baselmans, Jan-Emmanuel De Neve, Patrick Turley, et al. 2016. "Genetic Variants Associated with Subjective Well-Being, Depressive Symptoms, and Neuroticism Identified through Genome-Wide Analyses." *Nature Genetics* 48(6): 624–33.

Okbay, Aysu, Jonathan P. Beauchamp, Mark A. Fontana, James J. Lee, et al. 2016. "Genome-Wide Association Study Identifies 74 Loci Associated with Educational Attainment." *Nature* 533(7604): 539–42.

Polderman, Tinca J. C., Beben Benyamin, Christiaan A. de Leeuw, Patrick F. Sullivan, Arjen van Bochoven, Peter M. Visscher, and Danielle Posthuma. 2015. "Meta-Analysis of the Heritability of Human Traits Based on Fifty Years of Twin Studies." *Nature Genetics* 47(7): 702–09.

Purcell, Shaun, Benjamin M. Neale, Kathe Todd-Brown, Lori Thomas, Manuel A. R. Ferreira, David Bender, Julian Maller, Paul I. W. de Bakker, Mark Daly, and Pak C. Sham. 2007. "PLINK: A Tool Set for Whole-Genome Association and Population-Based Linkage Analyses." *American Journal of Human Genetics* 81(3): 559–75.

Rietveld, Cornelius A., Sarah E. Medland, Jaime Derringer, Jian Yang, et al. 2013. "GWAS of 126,559 Individuals Identifies Genetic Variants Associated with Educational Attainment." *Science* 340(6139): 1467–71.

Rindfuss, Ronald R., S. Philip Morgan, and Kate Offutt. 1996. "Education and Changing Age Pattern of American Fertility: 1963–1989." *Demography* 33(3): 277–90.

Rodgers, Joseph Lee, Kimberly Hughes, Hans-Peter Kohler, Kaare Christensen, Debby Doughty, David C. Rowe, and Warren B. Miller. 2001. "Genetic Influence Helps Explain Variation in Human Fertility: Evidence from Recent Behavioral and Molecular Genetic Studies." *Current Directions in Psychological Science* 10(5): 184–88.

Tropf, Felix C., Nicola Barban, Melinda C. Mills, Harold Snieder, and Jornt J. Mandemakers. 2015. "Genetic Influence on Age at First Birth of Female Twins Born in the UK, 1919–68." *Population Studies* 69(2): 129–45.

Tropf, Felix C., and Jornt J. Mandemakers. 2017. "Is the Association Between Education and Fertility Postponement Causal? The Role of Family Background Factors." *Demography* 54(1): 71–91. Accessed May 11, 2017. http://link.springer.com/10.1007/s13524-016-0531-5.

Tropf, Felix C., Gert Stulp, Nicola Barban, Peter M. Visscher, Jian Yang, Harold Snieder, and Melinda C. Mills. 2015. "Human Fertility, Molecular Genetics, and Natural Selection in Modern Societies." *PloS One* 10(6): e0126821.

Tropf, Felix C., Renske M. Verweija, Peter J. van der Most, Gert Stulp, et al. 2017. "Hidden Heritability Due to Heterogeneity Across Seven Populations." *Nature Human Behavior* 1(10): 757–65.

Verweij, Renske M., Melinda C. Mills, Felix C. Tropf, René Veenstra, Anastasia Nyman, and Harold Snieder. 2017. "Sexual Dimorphism in the Genetic Influence on Human Childlessness." *European Journal of Human Genetics* 25 (9): 1067–74.

Yang, Jian, Andrew Bakshi, Zhihong Zhu, Gibran Hemani, et al. 2015. "Genome-Wide Genetic Homogeneity Between Sexes and Populations for Human Height and Body Mass Index." *Human Molecular Genetics* 24(25): 7445–49.

Yang, Jian, Beben Benyamin, Brian P. McEvoy, Scott Gordon, et al. 2010. "Common SNPs Explain a Large Proportion of the Heritability for Human Height." *Nature Genetics* 42(7): 565–69.

Yang, Jian, S. Hong Lee, Michael E. Goddard, and Peter M. Visscher. 2011. "GCTA: A Tool for Genome-Wide Complex Trait Analysis." *American Journal of Human Genetics* 88(1): 76–82.

Zhu, Zhihong, Andrew Bakshi, Anna A. E. Vinkhuyzen, Gibran Hemani, et al. 2015. "Dominance Genetic Variation Contributes Little to the Missing Heritability for Human Complex Traits." *American Journal of Human Genetics* 96(3): 377–85.

Zietsch, Brendan P., Ralf Kuja-Halkola, Hasse Walum, and Karin J. Verweij. 2014. "Perfect Genetic Correlation Between Number of Offspring and Grandoffspring in an Industrialized Human Population." *Proceedings of the National Academy of Sciences* 111(3): 1032–36.

Zuk, Or, Eliana Hechter, Shamil R. Sunyaev, and Eric S. Lander. 2012. "The Mystery of Missing Heritability: Genetic Interactions Create Phantom Heritability." *Proceedings of the National Academy of Sciences* 109(4): 1193–98.

# Geographic Clustering of Polygenic Scores at Different Stages of the Life Course

BENJAMIN W. DOMINGUE, DAVID H. REHKOPF, DALTON CONLEY, AND JASON D. BOARDMAN

*We interrogate state-level clustering of polygenic scores at different points in the life course and variation in the association of mean polygenic scores in a respondent's state of birth with corresponding phenotypes. The polygenic scores for height and smoking show the most state-level clustering (2 to 4 percent) with relatively little clustering observed for the other scores. However, even the small amounts of observed clustering are potentially meaningful. The state-mean polygenic score for educational attainment is strongly associated with an individual's educational attainment net of that person's polygenic score. The ecological clustering of polygenic scores may denote a new environmental factor in gene-environment research. We conclude by discussing possible mechanisms that underlie this association and the implications of our findings for social and genetic research.*

**Keywords:** polygenic scores, genetics, geography

The geographic clustering of specific genotypes could be an important biosocial pathway through which observed spatial correlations of morbidities and related health and social characteristics materialize (Kindig and Cheng 2013; Murray et al. 2006). Likewise, such potential clustering may complicate efforts to disentangle genetic from environmental influences with which they might covary. Early investigations into this issue did not find evidence for geographic clustering of genetic risk at the state level (Rehkopf, Domingue, and Cullen 2016). However, such studies focused only on genetic risks for physical health outcomes (coronary artery disease, diabetes, and ischemic stroke), quantified these genetic risks in a limited man-

**Benjamin W. Domingue** is assistant professor of education at Stanford University. **David H. Rehkopf** is assistant professor of medicine at the Stanford University School of Medicine. **Dalton Conley** is professor of sociology at Princeton University. **Jason D. Boardman** is professor in the Department of Sociology and director of the Health and Society Program in the Institute of Behavioral Science at the University of Colorado at Boulder.

© 2018 Russell Sage Foundation. Domingue, Benjamin W., David H. Rehkopf, Dalton Conley, and Jason D. Boardman. 2018. "Geographic Clustering of Polygenic Scores at Different Stages of the Life Course." *RSF: The Russell Sage Foundation Journal of the Social Sciences* 4(4): 137–49. DOI: 10.7758/RSF.2018.4.4.08. The Health and Retirement Study is sponsored by the National Institute on Aging (grant number NIA U01AG009740) and is conducted by the University of Michigan. Research supported in part by grants from the Eunice Kennedy Shriver National Institute of Child Health and Human Development (R24 HD066613: University of Colorado Population Center) and R21 HD078031 and the National Institute of Aging (K01AG047280). This research was facilitated by the Social Science Genetic Association Consortium. Direct correspondence to: Ben W. Domingue at bdomingue@stanford.edu, 520 Galvez Mall, Stanford, CA 94305; David H. Rehkopf at drehkopf@stanford.edu, 1070 Arastradero Rd., Room 305, Palo Alto, CA 94304; Dalton Conley at dconley@princeton.edu, 157 Wallace Hall, Princeton, NJ 08544; and Jason D. Boardman at boardman@colorado.edu, 1440 15th St., Boulder, CO 80309.

Open Access Policy: *RSF: The Russell Sage Foundation Journal of the Social Sciences* is an open access journal. This article is published under a Creative Commons Attribution-NonCommercial-NoDerivs 3.0 Unported License.

ner (using only genome-wide significant variants), and focused on the geographic concentration of genetic risk at birth. They thus did not allow for the potential dynamic of geographic mobility within a single generation, which may lead to an increase in the spatial patterning of genetic risk later in life. The test for such clustering at different stages of the life course adds an important new dimension to the health and aging literatures.

It has long been known that genotypes are not distributed randomly across environments (Plomin, DeFries, and Loehlin 1977). Within this literature, some models of gene-environment interplay have incorporated a life course perspective, but there is as of yet little empirical evidence about specific traits and periods of the life course in which genotypes will become increasingly or decreasingly clustered in particular environments (Shanahan and Boardman 2009). The active gene-environment correlation (rGE) hypothesis is especially salient here as it suggests that people actively select into environments as a function of their genotype. We can evaluate the salience of this active rGE hypothesis by examining genetic clustering at the state level at different points of the life course—that is, when individuals have low degrees of autonomy to sort themselves genetically (childhood) and when they do have the agency and freedom to change environments (adulthood). Thus, evaluating whether life course-related, inter-state mobility is associated with changes in geographic concentration in genetics would provide critical information about migration in the gene-environment interplay paradigm.

This observation motivates the first question in this study: is there any evidence for the geographic clustering of genotypes, as operationalized by polygenic scores, at different points in the life course (Belsky and Israel 2014; Dudbridge 2016)?

## GENETICS AND THE LIFE COURSE

Life course research begins with the observation that individual development is a constant exchange between the specific characteristics of individuals and their social, physical, and cultural environments (Elder 1998). A large body of work has examined the concordance and discordance of behavioral and personality traits among very young twin pairs to estimate the extent to which genes contribute to specific traits. Two main observations emerge from this work. First, nearly all traits of interest to behavioral and social scientists—such as health, physical size, communication skills, cognitive ability, and behavioral disinhibition—are moderately influenced by genetics in which genes account for roughly one-third to one-half of their overall variation (Turkheimer 2000; Polderman et al. 2015). Second, the relative contribution of genes to many behavioral traits can change considerably over the life course. A particularly striking example of the latter is known as the Wilson effect (Bouchard 2013), which suggests that the heritability of cognitive ability increases as individuals age. The gene-environment typology anticipates such variation as a consequence of shifting environmental exposures. However, shifting environmental exposures may themselves be related to genotype and such a possibility has important implications (Jaffee and Price 2007).

In the endeavor to understand the role of genetics in human behavior and well-being, a question of fundamental import is whether or not specific genetic polymorphisms affect complex traits similarly across different environments. Straightforward identification of gene-environment interactions (GxE) rests on the assumption that genes and environments are independent. Others have made clear that our ability to detect and understand GxE associations are seriously compromised in the face of rGE (Jaffee and Price 2007; Fletcher and Conley 2013). For example, early evidence suggested that sensitivity to stressful life events is conditioned by genotype. Individuals who have experienced the same stressful life event may have different mental health responses. Avshalom Caspi and colleagues suggest that some of this difference is due to the presence of the S' allele in the 5HTTLPR locus, which is linked to serotonergic production and maintenance (2003). However, evidence indicates that carriers of this short allele may be more likely than others to be exposed to increased levels of stress or different types of stress (Risch et al. 2009). In that event, the proposed GxE interaction may be better characterized as an rGE association (Culverhouse et al. 2017). Such complications may help explain the mixed replication history for this finding and for GxE findings in the candidate gene literature more generally (Duncan and Keller 2011). To avoid this concern, researchers have made efforts to use environmental exposures that are most likely to be independent of genotype (Schmitz and Conley 2016; Domingue, Liu, Okbay, and Belsky 2017).

Others have used state of residence for these purposes arguing that selection of state of residence is unlikely to be driven by genetic factors—for example, smokers choosing a state of residence based on its pro-smoking features (Boardman 2009). With longitudinal data, we have some capacity for evaluating this claim. Specifically, we present statistical estimates that characterize the extent to which specific genetic polymorphisms linked to important outcomes are clustered across U.S. states. We pay particular attention to differences in these estimates at different stages of the life course.

## MECHANISMS RELATED TO GENE-ENVIRONMENT CORRELATION

We consider several potential mechanisms (active, passive, evocative, and mortality selection) through which gene-environment correlations come to be and how they may be related to the specific phenotypes we investigate as well as different periods in the life course. Active gene-environment correlations exist when individuals select into specific environments because of genetic polymorphisms that are linked to particular phenotypes and endophenotypes. Consider, for example, individuals for whom a healthy lifestyle—including the avoidance of tobacco products—is, in part, genetically influenced. Over time, it is possible that such individuals may select to live in states that provide a greater access to outdoor activities and other cardiovascular health-enhancing behaviors.

In contrast to active rGE, passive rGE is a situation in which children inherit their genes and their environments from their parents. This may simply reflect a form of population stratification, along the lines of what has been shown on a comparable geographic scale (Novembre et al. 2008; Nelis et al. 2009; Han et al. 2017). We hypothesize that the effect of passive rGE will be most pronounced when state of residence is measured at birth. Relatedly, the evocative rGE mechanism occurs when specific genotypes evoke specific environments. The most common example is that genetically oriented behaviors in childhood such as hostility or irritability may evoke more harsh parenting and educational environments for certain children (Jaffee and Price 2007). This model generally focuses on younger children who have limited capacity to select into environments but who may evoke certain environmental responses, such as from parents or teachers. As in regard to active and passive rGE, we again suspect that the effect will be most pronounced when measured at state of birth (though the role of evocative rGE may be limited in this study given the nature of phenotypes we consider). Although the evocative rGE model may be relevant to elderly populations when considering housing selection toward the end of life, the likelihood that one's genetic characteristics would evoke selection into a specific state of residence seems implausible. We therefore focus on active and passive forms of rGE in our interpretation.

Finally, we consider a form of observed rGE that is rarely discussed in the rGE literature but that has special import given the nature of our sample of surviving older respondents (Zajacova and Burgard 2013). Our state-level estimates of average polygenic score (PGS) levels (and by extension, rGE and social genetic effects) are confounded by mortality selection in which the composition of those in the sample is increasingly the most healthy. Because the social and environmental characteristics of state or smaller places of residence may affect mortality, we could see greater state-level intraclass correlations (ICCs) later in the life course due to differential mortality associated with genotype (see Deaton and Lubotsky 2003).

## MECHANISMS RELATED TO ECOLOGICAL PENETRANCE

We consider the penetrance (association of genotype and phenotype) of the polygenic scores at both the individual and ecological (that is, state mean) level. Differences in penetrance between these two levels must be interpreted with care. We do not have the necessary data to make fine-grained distinctions about the mechanisms driving increased ecological penetrance and thus focus on asking about the operation of a single mechanism. Specifically, we ask whether penetrance has increased at the ecological level net of an individual's genetic endowment. This could suggest that the genetic load of an individual's within-state neighbors are predictive of an individual's response, that is, social genetic effects, thus leading to a larger ecological than individual-level penetrance (Domingue and Belsky 2017). This mechanism would be potentially observable via the predictive power of the mean level of a polygenic score in the state net of an individual's own polygenic score. However, a number of alternative mechanisms are also explanations for such a finding. The presence of direct environmental or GxE effects where the environmental influence is orthogonal to the effect of the mean polygenic score, attenuation due to measurement error, aggregation bias, and other nonlinearities could also drive increased ecological correlations. Uncertainty about the meaning of aggregate relationships would not be unique to this type of sociogenomic inquiry but may still provide insight into areas of GxE research that need proceed with caution (Mellor and Milyo 2001; Wilkinson 1996).

## DATA

We use data from the Health and Retirement Study (HRS). The HRS is a biennial survey of older Americans (age fifty and older), focusing on their health, family structure, and socioeconomic status. Due to the lack of comparability of genetic association results using the polygenic score approach across racial groups (Carlson et al. 2013; Martin et al. 2017), we focus on 8,629 respondents of European ancestry, as identified by their genetic data, born between 1905 and 1974 (mean = 1938, IQR = 1938–1946). We use behavioral, medical, and anthropometric measures.

### Measures

We describe the individual-level variables used in this study and provide their mean and standard deviation (SD) as operationalized here.

Alzheimer's disease (M = 0.06, SD = 0.23): whether a respondent reported ever having memory-problems (waves 1–9) or Alzheimer's (waves 10–11).

Body mass index (M = 29.7, SD = 6.0): maximum (Stokes and Preston 2016) over available waves.

Heart disease (M = 0.39, SD = 0.49): a binary indicator of whether a respondent ever reported heart disease.

Education (M = 13.2, SD = 2.5): total years of educational attainment.

Smoking (M = 0.57, SD = 0.50): an indicator of whether a respondent ever reported smoking.

Height (M = 1.7, SD = 0.1): maximum reported height.

Depression (M = 3.0, SD = 2.3): maximum number of Center for Epidemiological Studies-Depression (CESD) symptoms over all waves.

Arthritis (M = 0.75, SD = 0.43): an indicator of whether a respondent ever reports arthritis.

### States of Residence

Respondents' state of residence at each wave of data collection is recorded as well as the state of birth and schooling for the respondent. Use of these geographic measures is complicated by the sampling scheme of the HRS. HRS employs a multistage sampling design. The first stage of sampling is metropolitan statistical areas (MSAs) or non-MSA U.S. counties. Current residents of states that contain MSAs or counties sampled by HRS may be represented in the HRS sample independently of where they were born. At the first wave of HRS data collection in 1992, respondents were in thirty-seven states plus the District of Columbia. We have a minimum of two respondents in a state and a maximum of 377 (mean = 105, SD = 76, IQR = 59–135). HRS respondents had to live in one of the MSAs at the time of data collection to be eligible for HRS, but many residents of these MSAs would have come from elsewhere in the country. As a consequence, the HRS sample was born across all fifty states and the District of

Columbia. States have as few as one birth and as many as 646 (mean = 163, SD = 151, IQR = 40–240).

The sampling frame of U.S. MSAs and counties has two implications. First, people are sampled in a narrow geographic region in later life relative to where they were born. Thus, we anticipate more clustering later in life because of the geographic clustering induced by the sample design relative to at birth purely as a function of sample design. Furthermore, this restricts the generalizability of our findings in some respects since the HRS is not meant to be a representative sample at the state level. Second, not all states are represented in the baseline HRS survey, although HRS did sample from the most populous states, minimizing the negative implications for generalizability. To examine the degree to which our findings may fail to generalize due to the sampling scheme, we compared those who left their birth state at some point in the HRS to those who did not. The movers were heavier, had less education, and were more likely to have smoked. Thus, findings may be somewhat specific to the sample analyzed here.

## Genetic Data

Genetic data for the HRS is based on single nucleotide polymorphisms (SNPs) collected via two methods. The first phase was collected via buccal swabs in 2006 using the Quiagen Autopure method. The second phase used saliva samples collected in 2008 and extracted with Oragene. Genotype calls were then made based on a clustering of both data sets using the Illumina HumanOmni2.5–4v1 array (for a detailed report on the HRS genetic data, see Weir 2012). SNPs are removed if they are missing in more than 5 percent of cases, have low minor allele frequency (0.01), and are not in Hardy-Weinberg equilibrium ($p < .001$). We retain approximately 1.7 million SNPs after removing those that did not pass the quality control filters. We focus on non-Hispanic whites for several reasons. First, allele frequency differences make direct comparisons of the distributions of polygenic scores across populations impossible. Second, due to differences in patterns of linkage, Genome-Wide Association Study (GWAS) results discovered in European samples may not replicate in non-European samples (Carlson et al. 2013) and scores constructed from such results will perform differently out of sample (Martin et al. 2017). Third, the nonwhite sample of genotyped HRS respondents shows substantial selection relative to the non-Hispanic white sample (Domingue, Belsky, Harrati, Conley, Weir, and Boardman 2017).

## POLYGENIC SCORE CONSTRUCTION

We constructed polygenic scores (PGS) using published GWAS results. We computed scores for Alzheimer's (Lambert et al. 2013), BMI (Locke et al. 2015), educational attainment (Okbay et al. 2016), cardiovascular disease (Schunkert et al. 2011), smoking (Tobacco and Genetics Consortium 2010), height (Wood et al. 2014), major depressive disorder (Ripke et al. 2013), and rheumatoid arthritis (Okada et al. 2014). These were selected to cover a range of health, anthropometric, and behavioral outcomes. Briefly, polygenic scoring was done with the PLINK software (Chang et al. 2015) using a previously discussed pipeline (Conley et al. 2016). SNPs in the HRS genetic database were matched to SNPs with reported results in a GWAS. For each SNP, a loading was calculated as the number of phenotype-associated alleles multiplied by the effect-size estimated in the original GWAS. Loadings were summed across SNPs to calculate the polygenic score. Scores were first residualized on the top ten PCs computed only among the non-Hispanic white respondents of HRS and then standardized to have a mean of zero and standard deviation of one for analysis for ease of interpretation.

## MODELING OF GENOTYPE AND PHENOTYPE CLUSTERING

Our analytic strategy for the detection of genetic clustering involves models of the form

$$G_{is} = \alpha + u_s + e_{is}, \quad (1)$$

where $G_{is}$ is the polygenic score for individual in the $s$-th state. Most importantly, $e_{is}$ captures the individual-level error term and $u_s$ is a state-specific random intercept (capturing either state of birth or state of current residence). We assume that $u_s \sim \text{Normal}(0, \sigma_u^2)$ and then consider

$$ICC = \frac{\sigma_u^2}{\sigma_u^2 + \sigma_e^2}. \quad (2)$$

This quantity, the state-level ICC coefficient, is our key index of genetic concentration. That is, the contribution of $\sigma_u^2$ to overall variation in polygenic risk ($\sigma_u^2 + \sigma_e^2$) is summarized as a ratio that simply describes the proportion of genetic variance nested within states.

## MODELS FOR PENETRANCE

To further evaluate the extent to which states matter for the clustering of specific phenotypes and their corresponding PGS values, we first compare individual-level correlations between each trait and the PGS for that trait with ecological correlations (for example, average state-level education with average state-level PGS) focusing on *state at birth*. Instances in which the ecological correlation exceeds what we would expect based on the individual-level correlation provide further support for importance of gene-environment interplay. We then present results in which we model the individual and ecological contributions of PGS to individual phenotype. For outcome $y_{is}$ (where individual $i$ is born in state $s$), we consider

$$y_{is} = \alpha + b_1 g_{is} + b_2 \bar{g}_s + u_s + \text{controls} + \varepsilon_{is}. \quad (3)$$

We consider both individual-level PGS ($g_{is}$) and state-average PGS value ($\bar{g}_s$) to evaluate contributions of average genotype to state-level variation in each phenotype net of individual genetic endowments. Standard errors are corrected for state-level clustering (Zeileis 2004). We include demographic covariates (sex and birth year) as controls.

We also consider two sensitivity analyses related to equation (3). First, we estimate equation (3) in decennial birth cohorts to ensure that mortality selection and the changing salience of educational attainment are not driving our findings. Second, we further explore mortality selection via the use of weights previously discussed (Domingue, Belsky, Harrati, Conley, Weir, and Boardman 2017). These weights predict mortality prior to the genotyping window in HRS based on year of birth and a number of health conditions as well as educational attainment. We then use them as inverse probability weights to consider the sensitivity of key findings to the fact that the HRS genetic data does not contain information on respondents who died prior to 2006 (Cole and Hernán 2008).

## STATE-LEVEL CLUSTERING OF PHENOTYPES

We first consider the state-level clustering of the phenotypes to establish benchmarks for interpreting the state-level genetic concentrations. The left panel of figure 1 summarizes state-level clustering for each trait at birth and then in later life. As described, these estimates characterize the proportion of variation for each trait that is due to clustering at the state level. An ICC of zero would indicate identical average education scores across all states (that is, all the variation occurs within states) and an ICC of one would indicate that there was no individual variation within states. In our analysis, the overall contribution of state of residence and state of birth are relatively small for all of the traits that we examine (for example, ICCs < 5 percent) but the magnitude of these ICCs are in line with other work in this area (Mehta and Chang 2009).

Education is a clear outlier in having state-level ICC values that are considerably higher than the other traits at all points of the life course. Differences are clear in resources (such as tax levels to support education), structures (such as city, county, and state differences in the governance and support of districts), and opportunities (such as labor demands for different levels of skills) that would translate to observable differences across states. Education is also the only trait that shows a substantial increase in state clustering across the latter part of the life course. We note two potential explanations. First, it may indicate that states with higher average levels of education also have lower mortality rates, and the composition of those with more education becomes more pronounced in certain states as a result. This is particularly important given the increasing levels of morbidity and mortality among middle-aged white adults in the United States (Case and Deaton 2015). Second, it could be due to migration associated with retirement. Both of these processes could in fact be acting in tandem to drive this increase.

**Figure 1.** State-Level Clustering and Their Corresponding Polygenic Scores Across the Life Course

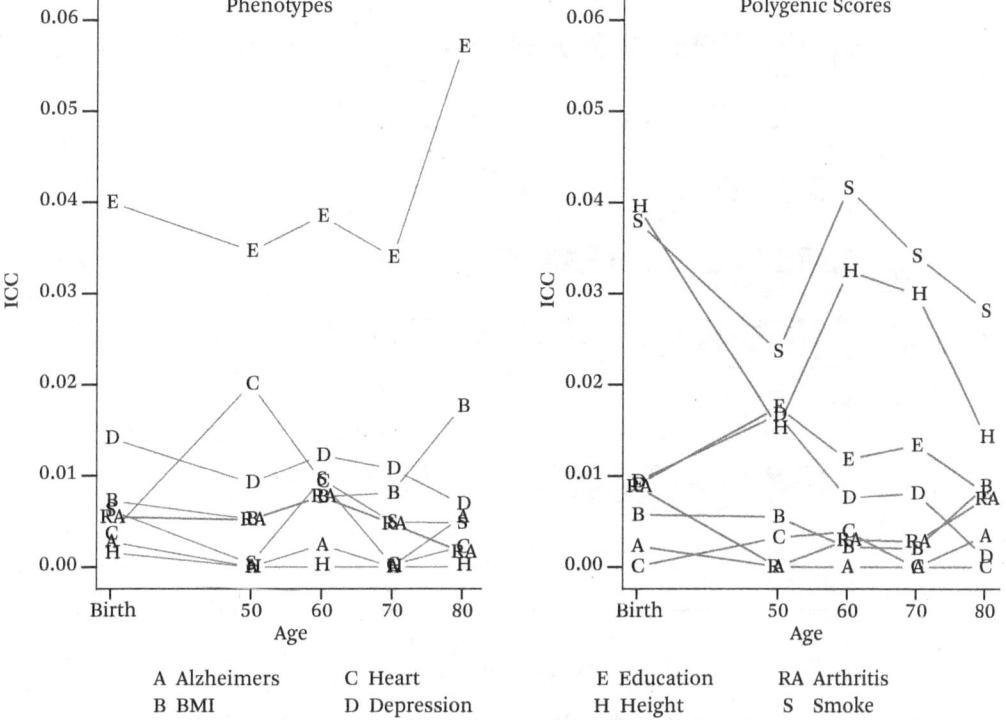

*Source:* Author's calculations based on HRS Rand files and genetic data (Weir 2012).

## STATE-LEVEL CLUSTERING OF POLYGENIC SCORES (rGE)

We now consider one of the primary goals of this paper: to evaluate the degree of PGS clustering at the state level. The right side of figure 1 characterizes these magnitudes and how they change as a function of when in the life course state of residence is measured. We observe the largest clustering for the height and smoking polygenic scores. For these scores, observed clustering is higher than for any phenotype other than education. For education, we observe between 1 and 2 percent of the overall variation in the score to be clustered within state at any point in the life course. Next we explore the potential relevance of this clustering.

## ECOLOGICAL VERSUS INDIVIDUAL PENETRANCE

We now turn to considerations of penetrance at the individual and ecological level *based on state of birth*. By comparing the individual and ecological correlations, we can provide indirect evidence for potential environmental enhancement of rGE through mechanisms that are generally, and perhaps incorrectly, characterized as GxE associations. In figure 2, the light gray bars focus on the correlation of individual phenotypes and PGSs. At the individual level, the largest observed association is (r = .26) is for BMI followed by education (r = .23) and height (r = .22). The darker bars in this figure depict state-level ecological correlations. Consider first height. The individual and ecological correlations are roughly comparable, suggesting a situation in which the translation of height-related genetics to physical stature is an individual-level phenomenon. This is perhaps intuitive given our understanding of physical growth as a largely within-person phenomenon.

But the story is quite different for depression, smoking, and education. In these cases, ecological correlations are larger than the individual correlations. This suggests the possi-

**Figure 2.** Correlations Between Polygenic Risk Scores and Their Corresponding Traits at Individual and Ecological Levels

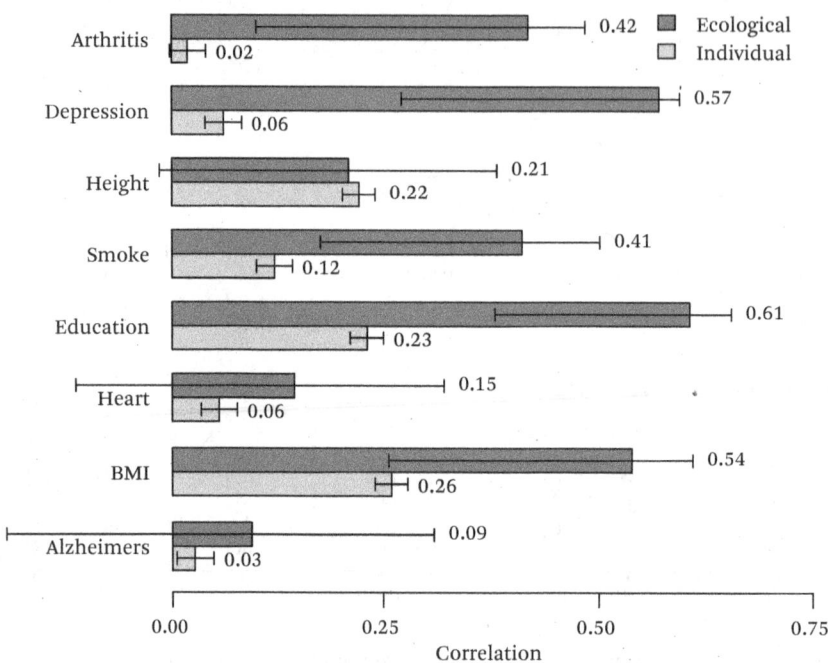

*Source:* Author's calculations based on HRS Rand files and genetic data (Weir 2012).

ble existence of higher-order process through which environmental differences (such as the mean genetic endowment within a state) are moderating the genotype-phenotype association when considered at higher levels (other explanations are also possible, we return to these in discussion). Consider the ecological correlation between the state mean education and the associated PGS ($r = 0.61$). This is 2.7 times the individual-level correlation and provides clear evidence that there is something additional of interest occurring in the context of states. To further interrogate this possibility, we examine analyses in which we predict individual phenotype using both individual and state-level genotype.

In figure 3, we consider estimates from equation (3). Returning to height, as expected, the state-level PGS did not offer any predictive power net of individual PGS. We observe similar results for smoking, heart disease and BMI, suggesting that, for these phenotypes, little residual information is left in the state-mean polygenic score. However, we observe markedly different findings for depression and educational attainment. For these phenotypes, the state-mean PGS predicts net of one's polygenic score. We conducted two additional sensitivity analyses. First, we adjusted results for mortality selection prior to genotyping. Results were comparable; after weighting, the coefficient for state-level PGS mean was 0.08 (se = 0.012) for educational attainment and 0.08 (se = 0.012) for depression in their respective analyses. Second, we considered analyses for education restricted to the birth cohorts of the 1930s and 1940s to determine how sensitive results were to the changing salience of education over the years represented in the HRS birth cohorts. Again, findings were largely consistent. For 1930–1939 births, we estimated a coefficient of 0.06 (se = 0.020) for the mean educational attainment PGS. For 1940 to 1949 births, the respective estimate was 0.10 (se = 0.021). This allows for the possibility of a crucial role being played by the environment in determining how quantities of human capital develop; that is, these phenomena may have important between-person mechanisms.

**Figure 3.** Standardized Multilevel Regression Estimates for the Effect of Each PGS

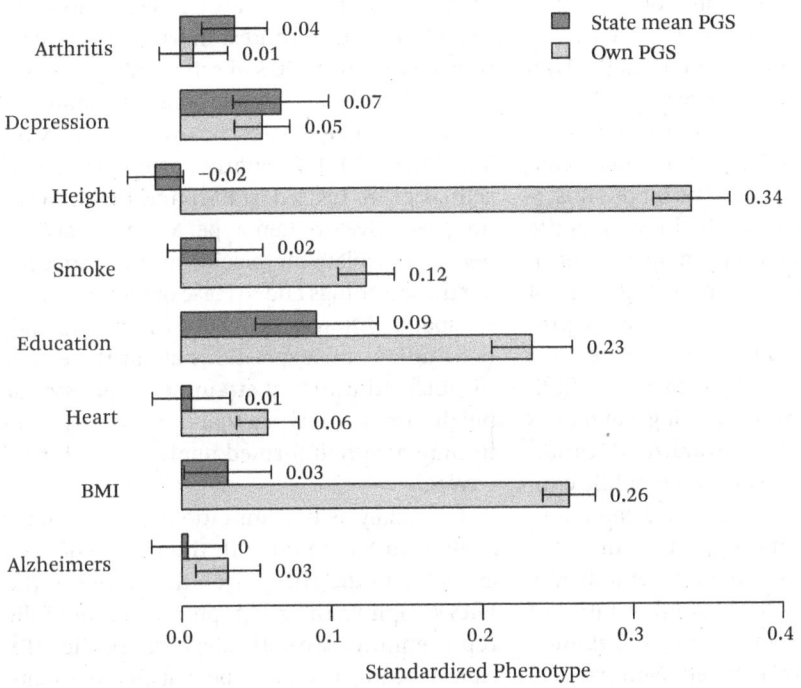

*Source:* Author's calculations based on HRS Rand files and genetic data (Weir 2012).

## DISCUSSION

This study focuses on the potential for geographic clustering and moderation of genetic effects across a number of outcomes important for both mental and physical health. Polygenic scores demonstrate different magnitudes of clustering with most scores showing relatively little clustering. These results are important for research in gene-environment interaction research because the environment is often believed to be independent of genotype. Earlier work relied on the assumption that the state of residence was unlikely to be associated with specific genetic polymorphisms associated with specific genetic polymorphism. Thus, states were ideal candidates for the study of GxE given their relative exogeneity (Boardman 2009). This work noted the potential implications of rGE between specific polymorphisms and state of residence, but was unable to test this assumption given the lack of appropriate molecular data at that time.

Here, we are able to provide estimates about the likelihood of this type of selection bias.

This clustering is indeed small, but also similar to the observed phenotypic clustering in many cases. Genes related to smoking were among the most concentrated. It is unclear whether this selection affects the previously reported GxE results at the state level (Boardman 2009). Even the small amounts of genetic clustering observed in figure 1 may be substantively important depending on the genetic penetrance for that phenotype (for example, weak genetic concentration for a highly penetrant phenotype might be of interest).

Indeed, there do seem to be occasions in our data in which relatively weak geographic PGS concentrations lead to provocative associations. In particular, we observe cases where ecological correlations are substantially larger than individual correlations. Moreover, for depression and education, we have evidence to suggest that the state-level mean polygenic score for these traits is predictive of the trait net of an individual's own genetic endowment. This might be so for a number of reasons. One set of explanations is mechanical. For example, misspecification at the individual level (such as nonlinearity in the penetrance of the PGS or measurement error) or even the nonrepresentative geographic sampling scheme of the HRS may lead to the inflated ecological correlations

An alternative explanation has to do with the nature of the phenotype. Although we cannot rule out mechanical reasons for our observations in figure 3, one key distinction merits attention. Educational attainment is a social phenotype. The very act of accruing years of education is a process that is typically provided by society and co-occurs with one's age peers. These facts may help explain our findings in a number of ways. Having neighbors more inclined themselves toward education may bolster the effects of existing public education infrastructure because of greater support, via increased funding, for example, of educational programs. Such a mechanism is potentially related to the dual inheritance of genes and culture (Cavalli-Sforza and Feldman 1981). To the extent that the educational PGS merely reflects subtle genetic stratification that itself is correlated with cultural (or other environmental) conditions associated with educational attainment, what we report here could be confounded. Previous work uses sibling models to show the robustness of the PGS within families (after breaking any ancestry-PGS confounding) so at least some evidence suggests that the influence of confounding should be relatively limited (Domingue et al. 2015; Conley et al. 2015; Rietveld et al. 2014). That said, confidence in a lack of confounding at the individual level may not easily translate to the aggregate level. Social mechanisms also have a role in the etiology of depression, but research on the extent to which the results from that GWAS are susceptible to confounding is scant (Thoits 1995).

Findings related to the educational attainment polygenic score are consistent with the existence of "social genetic effects" but not dispositive (Domingue and Belsky 2017; Baud et al. 2017; Rauscher, Conley, and Siegal 2015). Identification of compositional effects is challenging (Angrist 2014). As in earlier work, we rely on cross-phenotype comparisons to guide interpretation (Cohen-Cole and Fletcher 2008). In particular, we note a clear distinction between educational attainment and height-BMI. Findings observed here are similar to those observed in another context in which the educational attainment PGS of schoolmates is associated with educational attainment (Domingue, Belsky, Fletcher, Conley, Boardman, and Mullan Harris 2017). In contrast, the genetics of school peers related to BMI and height were not predictive of phenotype. More research is needed to isolate the specific mechanism driving these findings and to tease out implications for spatial differences in education. This said, our findings raise questions about the extent to which educational attainment and BMI or height are phenotypes that are exchangeable in biologically informed analyses, such as a GWAS.

Our analysis has limitations. The primary limitation has to do with the nature of data available in the HRS. Given the nature of the HRS sampling, the geographic data is not fully representative. Specifically, because the HRS samples counties, it may be that all the respondents from a state are drawn from a relatively urban county that does not reflect the diversity of residential experiences within the state. This limits our ability to understand anything about levels for a particular state, and whether differential migration or other mechanisms of selection occur more strongly at finer levels of geography. U.S. metropolitan areas are a natural candidate for examination given the recent interest in smaller area mortality rates (Chetty et al. 2016). Finally, the phenotypes considered here are not clinical phenotypes and presumably contain measurement error.

**REFERENCES**

Angrist, Joshua D. 2014. "The Perils of Peer Effects." *Labour Economics* 30 (October): 98–108.

Baud, Amelie, Megan K. Mulligan, Francesco P. Casale, Jesse F. Ingels, et al. 2017. "Genetic Variation in the Social Environment Contributes to Health and Disease." *PLoS Genetics*. Accessed August 24, 2017. DOI: 10.1371/journal.pgen.1006498.

Belsky, Daniel W., and Salomon Israel. 2014. "Integrating Genetics and Social Science: Genetic Risk Scores." *Biodemography and Social Biology* 60(2): 137–55.

Boardman, Jason D. 2009. "State-Level Moderation of Genetic Tendencies to Smoke." *American Journal of Public Health* 99(3): 480–86.

Bouchard, Thomas J. 2013. "The Wilson Effect: The Increase in Heritability of IQ with Age." *Twin Research and Human Genetics* 16(5): 923–30.

Carlson, Christopher S., Tara C. Matise, Kari E. North, Christopher A. Haiman, et al. 2013. "Generalization and Dilution of Association Results from European GWAS in Populations of Non-European Ancestry: The PAGE Study." *PLoS Biology* 11(9): e1001661.

Case, Anne, and Angus Deaton. 2015. "Rising Morbidity and Mortality in Midlife Among White Non-Hispanic Americans in the 21st Century." *Proceedings of the National Academy of Sciences* 112(49): 15078–83.

Caspi, Avshalom, Karen Sugden, Terrie E. Moffitt, Alan Taylor, Ian W. Craig, HonaLee Harrington, Joseph McClay, Jonathan Mill, Judy Martin, Antony Braithwaite, and Richie Poulton 2003. "Influence of Life Stress on Depression: Moderation by a Polymorphism in the 5-HTT Gene." *Science* 301(5631): 386–89. DOI: 10.1126/science.1083968.

Cavalli-Sforza, Luigi Luca, and Marcus W. Feldman. 1981. *Cultural Transmission and Evolution: A Quantitative Approach*. Princeton, N.J.: Princeton University Press.

Chang, Christopher C., Carson C. Chow, Laurent C. A. M. Tellier, Shashaank Vattikuti, Shaun M. Purcell, and James J. Lee. 2015. "Second-Generation PLINK: Rising to the Challenge of Larger and Richer Datasets." *GigaScience* 4 (February). DOI:10.1186/s13742-015-0047-8.

Chetty, Raj, Michael Stepner, Sarah Abraham, Shelby Lin, Benjamin Scuderi, Nicholas Turner, Augustin Bergeron, and David Cutler. 2016. "The Association between Income and Life Expectancy in the United States, 2001–2014." *Journal of the American Medical Assocation* 315(16): 1750–66.

Cohen-Cole, Ethan, and Jason M. Fletcher. 2008. "Detecting Implausible Social Network Effects in Acne, Height, and Headaches: Longitudinal Analysis." *British Medical Journal* 337: a2533.

Cole, Stephen R., and Miguel A. Hernán. 2008. "Constructing Inverse Probability Weights for Marginal Structural Models." *American Journal of Epidemiology* 168(6): 656–64. DOI:10.1093/aje/kwn164.

Conley, Dalton, Benjamin Domingue, David Cesarini, Christopher Dawes, Cornelius Rietveld, and Jason Boardman. 2015. "Is the Effect of Parental Education on Offspring Biased or Moderated by Genotype?" *Sociological Science* 2(6): 82–105. DOI:10.15195/v2.a6.

Conley, Dalton, Thomas M. Laidley, Jason D. Boardman, and Benjamin W. Domingue. 2016. "Changing Polygenic Penetrance on Phenotypes in the 20th Century Among Adults in the U.S. Population." *Scientific Reports* 6: 30348.

Culverhouse, Robert C., Nancy L. Saccone, Amy C. Horton, Yinjiao Ma, et al. 2017. "Collaborative Meta-Analysis Finds No Evidence of a Strong Interaction Between Stress and 5-HTTLPR Genotype Contributing to the Development of Depression." *Molecular Psychiatry*. DOI: 10.1038/mp.2017.44.

Deaton, Angus, and Darren Lubotsky. 2003. "Mortality, Inequality and Race in American Cities and States." *Social Science & Medicine* 56(6): 1139–53.

Domingue, Benjamin W., and Daniel W. Belsky. 2017. "The Social Genome: Current Findings and Implications for the Study of Human Genetics." *PLoS Genetics* 13(3): e1006615.

Domingue, Benjamin W., Daniel W. Belsky, Dalton Conley, Kathleen Mullan Harris, and Jason D. Boardman. 2015. "Polygenic Influence on Educational Attainment." *AERA Open* 1(3): 2332858415599972.

Domingue, Benjamin, Daniel W. Belsky, Jason Fletcher, Dalton Conley, Jason D. Boardman, and Kathleen Mullan Harris. 2017. "The Social Genome of Friends and Schoolmates in the National Longitudinal Study of Adolescent to Adult Health (Add Health)." *bioRxiv* 107045. DOI: 10.1101/107045.

Domingue, Benjamin W., Daniel W. Belsky, Amal Harrati, Dalton Conley, David Weir, and Jason D. Boardman. 2017. "Mortality Selection in a Genetic Sample and Implications for Association Studies." *International Journal of Epidemiology* 46(4): 1285–94. DOI: 10.1093/ije/dyx041.

Domingue, Benjamin W., Hexuan Liu, Aysu Okbay, and Daniel W. Belsky. 2017. "Genetic Heterogeneity in Depressive Symptoms Following the Death of a Spouse: Polygenic Score Analysis of the U.S. Health and Retirement Study." *American Journal of Psychiatry* 174(10): 963–70. DOI: 10.1176/appi.ajp.2017.1611120.

Dudbridge, Frank. 2016. "Polygenic Epidemiology." *Genetic Epidemiology* 40(4): 268–72. DOI:10.1002/gepi.21966.

Duncan, Laramie E., and Matthew C. Keller. 2011. "A Critical Review of the First 10 Years of Candidate Gene-by-Environment Interaction Research in Psychiatry." *American Journal of Psychiatry* 168(10): 1041–49. DOI:10.1176/appi.ajp.2011.11020191.

Elder, Glen H., Jr. 1998. "The Life Course as Developmental Theory." *Child Development* 69(1): 1–12.

Fletcher, Jason M., and Dalton Conley. 2013. "The Challenge of Causal Inference in Gene-Environment Interaction Research: Leveraging Research Designs from the Social Sciences." *American Journal of Public Health* 103(S1): S42–S45.

Han, Eunjung, Peter Carbonetto, Ross E. Curtis, Yong Wang, et al. 2017. "Clustering of 770,000 Genomes Reveals Post-Colonial Population Structure of North America." *Nature Communications* 8: 14328. DOI:10.1038/ncomms14238.

Jaffee, Sara R., and Thomas S. Price. 2007. "Gene-Environment Correlations: A Review of the Evidence and Implications for Prevention of Mental Illness." *Molecular Psychiatry* 12(5): 432–42.

Kindig, David A., and Erika R. Cheng. 2013. "Even as Mortality Fell in Most U.S. Counties, Female Mortality Nonetheless Rose in 42.8 Percent of Counties from 1992 to 2006." *Health Affairs* 32(3): 451–58.

Lambert, Jean-Charles, Carla A. Ibrahim-Verbaas, Denise Harold, Adam C. Naj, et al. 2013. "Meta-Analysis of 74,046 Individuals Identifies 11 New Susceptibility Loci for Alzheimer's Disease." *Nature Genetics* 45(12): 1452–58.

Locke, Adam E., Bratati Kahali, Sonja I. Berndt, Anne E. Justice, et al. 2015. "Genetic Studies of Body Mass Index Yield New Insights for Obesity Biology." *Nature* 518(7538): 197–206. DOI:10.1038/nature14177.

Martin, Alicia R., Christopher R. Gignoux, Raymond K. Walters, Genevieve L. Wojcik, Benjamin M. Neale, Simon Gravel, Mark J. Daly, Carlos D. Bustamante, and Eimear E. Kenny. 2017. "Human Demographic History Impacts Genetic Risk Prediction across Diverse Populations." *American Journal of Human Genetics* 100(4): 635–49.

Mehta, Neil K., and Virginia W. Chang. 2009. "Mortality Attributable to Obesity among Middle-Aged Adults in the United States." *Demography* 46(4): 851–72.

Mellor, Jennifer M., and Jeffrey D. Milyo. 2001. "Income Inequality and Health." *Journal of Policy Analysis and Management* 20(1): 151–55.

Murray, Christopher J. L., Sandeep C Kulkarni, Catherine Michaud, Niels Tomijima, Maria T. Bulzacchelli, Terrell J. Iandiorio, and Majid Ezzati. 2006. "Eight Americas: Investigating Mortality Disparities Across Races, Counties, and Race-Counties in the United States." *PLoS Med* 3(9): e260.

Nelis, Mari, Tõnu Esko, Reedik Mägi, Fritz Zimprich, et al. 2009. "Genetic Structure of Europeans: A View from the North-East." *PLoS One* 4(5): e5472.

Novembre, John, Toby Johnson, Katarzyna Bryc, Zoltán Kutalik, et al. 2008. "Genes Mirror Geography within Europe." *Nature* 456(7218): 98–101. DOI:10.1038/nature07331.

Okada, Yukinori, Di Wu, Gosia Trynka, Towfique Raj, et al. 2014. "Genetics of Rheumatoid Arthritis Contributes to Biology and Drug Discovery." *Nature* 506(7488): 376–81. DOI:10.1038/nature12873.

Okbay, Aysu, Jonathan P. Beauchamp, Mark Alan Fontana, James J. Lee, et al. 2016. "Genome-Wide Association Study Identifies 74 Loci Associated with Educational Attainment." *Nature* 533(7604): 539–42.

Plomin, Robert, John C. DeFries, and John C. Loehlin. 1977. "Genotype-Environment Interaction and Correlation in the Analysis of Human Behavior." *Psychological Bulletin* 84(2): 309.

Polderman, Tinca J. C., Beben Benyamin, Christiaan A. De Leeuw, Patrick F. Sullivan, Arjen Van Bochoven, Peter M. Visscher, and Danielle Posthuma. 2015. "Meta-Analysis of the Heritability of Human Traits Based on Fifty Years of Twin Studies." *Nature Genetics* 47(7): 702–09.

Rauscher, Emily, Dalton Conley, and Mark L. Siegal. 2015. "Sibling Genes as Environment: Sibling Dopamine Genotypes and Adolescent Health Support Frequency Dependent Selection." *Social Science Research* 54 (November): 209–20.

Rehkopf, David, Benjamin W. Domingue, and Mark R. Cullen. 2016. "Gene-Environment Correlation: The Geographic Distribution of Genetic Risk for Chronic Disease in the United States." *Biodemography and Social Biology* 62(1): 126–42.

Rietveld, Cornelius A., Dalton Conley, Nicholas Eriksson, Tõnu Esko, et al. 2014. "Replicability and Robustness of Genome-Wide-Association Studies for Behavioral Traits." *Psychological Science* 25(11): 1975–86.

Ripke, Stephan, Naomi R. Wray, Cathryn M. Lewis, Steven P. Hamilton, et al. 2013. "A Mega-Analysis of Genome-Wide Association Studies for Major Depressive Disorder." *Molecular Psychiatry* 18(4): 497–511.

Risch, Neil, Richard Herrell, Thomas Lehner, Kung-Yee Liang, Lindon Eaves, Josephine Hoh, Andrea Griem, Maria Kovacs, Jurg Ott, and Kathleen Ries Merikangas. 2009. "Interaction between the Serotonin Transporter Gene (5-HTTLPR), Stressful Life Events, and Risk of Depression: A Meta-Analysis." *Jama* 301(23): 2462–71.

Schmitz, Lauren, and Dalton Conley. 2016. "The Long-Term Consequences of Vietnam-Era Conscription and Genotype on Smoking Behavior and Health." *Behavior Genetics* 46(1): 43–58.

Schunkert, Heribert, Inke R. König, Sekar Kathiresan, Muredach P. Reilly, et al. 2011. "Large-Scale Association Analysis Identifies 13 New Susceptibility Loci for Coronary Artery Disease." *Nature Genetics* 43(4): 333–38.

Shanahan, Michael J., and Jason D. Boardman. 2009. "Genetics and Behavior in the Life Course: A Promising Frontier." In *The Craft of Life Course Research*, edited by Glen H. Elder Jr. and Janet A. Giele. New York: Guildford Press.

Stokes, Andrew, and Samuel H. Preston. 2016. "Revealing the Burden of Obesity Using Weight Histories." *Proceedings of the National Academy of Sciences* 113(3): 572–77.

Thoits, Peggy A. 1995. "Stress, Coping, and Social Support Processes: Where Are We? What Next?" *Journal of Health and Social Behavior* 36 (Suppl.): 53–79.

Tobacco and Genetics Consortium. 2010. "Genome-Wide Meta-Analyses Identify Multiple Loci Associated with Smoking Behavior." *Nature Genetics* 42(5): 441–47. DOI:10.1038/ng.571.

Turkheimer, Eric. 2000. "Three Laws of Behavior Genetics and What They Mean." *Current Directions in Psychological Science* 9(5): 160–64.

Weir, David R. 2012. "Quality Control Report for Genotypic Data." University of Washington. Accessed August 24, 2017. http://hrsonline.isr.umich.edu/sitedocs/genetics/HRS_QC_REPORT_MAR2012.pdf.

Wilkinson, Richard G. 1996. *Unhealthy Societies: The Afflictions of Inequality*. London: Routledge.

Wood, Andrew R., Tonu Esko, Jian Yang, Sailaja Vedantam, et al. 2014. "Defining the Role of Common Variation in the Genomic and Biological Architecture of Adult Human Height." *Nature Genetics* 46(11): 1173–86. DOI:10.1038/ng.3097.

Zajacova, Anna, and Sarah A. Burgard. 2013. "Healthier, Wealthier, and Wiser: A Demonstration of Compositional Changes in Aging Cohorts Due to Selective Mortality." *Population Research and Policy Review* 32(3): 311–24.

Zeileis, Achim. 2004. "Econometric Computing with HC and HAC Covariance Matrix Estimators." *Journal of Statistical Software* 11(10): 1–17.